Reading Austen
in America

Reading Austen in America

Juliette Wells

Bloomsbury Academic
An imprint of Bloomsbury Publishing Plc

B L O O M S B U R Y
LONDON · OXFORD · NEW YORK · NEW DELHI · SYDNEY

Bloomsbury Academic
An imprint of Bloomsbury Publishing Plc

50 Bedford Square	1385 Broadway
London	New York
WC1B 3DP	NY 10018
UK	USA

www.bloomsbury.com

BLOOMSBURY and the Diana logo are trademarks of Bloomsbury Publishing Plc

First published 2017

British Library Cataloguing-in-Publication Data
A catalogue record for this book is available from the British Library.

ISBN:	HB:	978-1-3500-1205-9
	PB:	978-1-3500-1204-2
	ePDF:	978-1-3500-1207-3
	eBook:	978-1-3500-1206-6

Library of Congress Cataloging-in-Publication Data
Name: Wells, Juliette, 1977– author.
Title: Reading Austen in America / Juliette Wells.
Description: New York : Bloomsbury Academic, 2017. | Includes bibliographical
references.
Identifiers: LCCN 2017005670 | ISBN 9781350012059 (hardback) |
ISBN 9781350012042 (pb)
Subject: LCSH: Austen, Jane, 1775–1817—Influence. | Austen, Jane, 1775–1817—
Appreciation. | Austen, Jane, 1775–1817—Books and reading. | Authors and
readers—United States. | Reader-response criticism—United States. | BISAC:
LITERARY CRITICISM / Women Authors. | LITERARY CRITICISM / Gothic &
Romance. | LITERARY CRITICISM / Books & Reading.
Classification: LCC PR4037 .W46 2017 | DDC 823/.7—dc23 LC record
available at https://lccn.loc.gov/2017005670

Cover design by Eleanor Rose
Cover image: *An Interesting Story (Miss Ray)* by William Wood (British, 1769–1810),
miniature painted onto ivory, 1806 © The Moses Lazarus Collection / The Met
Museum, New York

Typeset by RefineCatch Limited, Bungay, Suffolk

To find out more about our authors and books visit www.bloomsbury.com. Here
you will find extracts, author interviews, details of forthcoming events and the
option to sign up for our newsletters.

For Rodney, Lucy, and Eric

CONTENTS

Illustrations   ix
Abbreviations   x

Introduction   1

Part One   The 1816 Philadelphia *Emma* and its Readers

1   The Origins of the First Austen Novel Printed in America   13
What did it mean to "reprint" *Emma*?   14
Who was "M. Carey," and why did he choose *Emma*?   17
When in 1816 was Carey's *Emma* published, and how many copies were issued?   23
How did the Philadelphia *Emma* compare to the London edition, and why have so few copies of the American edition survived?   26
How did readers first become aware of Carey's *Emma*?   30
How did Americans first learn of Austen's authorship?   35

2   Tales of Three Copies: Books, Owners, and Readers   49
Lovers of books, if not of Austen: the du Pont sisters of Delaware   50
A careful and curious reader: Jeremiah Smith of New Hampshire   63

Unimpressed by *Emma*: subscribers to a Rhode Island
circulating library   73

3   An Accomplished Scotswoman Reads Austen
Abroad: Christian, Countess of Dalhousie in
British North America   87

Plants, drawing, reading, riddles: girlhood education   91
A literary marriage   96
Encounters with Austen's novels during a "transatlantic
life"   102
Reading tastes and book acquisition   114

Part Two   Transatlantic Austen Conversations

4   Enthusiasts Connected Through the "Electric
Telegraph of Genius": The Quincy Sisters of
Boston and the Francis W. Austen Family of
Portsmouth   137

Recommended reading and fertile imaginations   140
Admirers, rewarded with a relic, envision a society of
devotees   143
Two families meet during Anna's literary pilgrimage   152
Americans contribute to Austen's international fame   161

5   Collectors and Bibliographers: Alberta H. Burke
of Baltimore and David J. Gilson of Oxford   185

Unusual approaches to collecting Austen   188
Balancing erudition with enthusiasm   195

*Appendix: Census of Surviving Copies of the 1816
Philadelphia* Emma   209
Bibliography   213
Index   225

ILLUSTRATIONS

1.1 Title page of Murray's London edition of *Emma* and of Carey's Philadelphia edition of *Emma*   16

1.2 Mathew Carey, portrait by John Neagle (1825)   18

1.3 First page of Murray's London edition of *Emma* and of Carey's Philadelphia edition of *Emma*   28

1.4 *Monthly Literary Advertiser*, January 1817   32

2.1 E. I. du Pont's copy of *Emma*   51

2.2 Victorine du Pont Bauduy (Mme Ferdinand Bauduy), portrait by Rembrandt Peale (1813)   54

2.3 "The Pleasures of Society," drawing by Sophie M. du Pont (1827)   57

2.4 Jeremiah Smith, portrait by Francis Alexander (1835)   64

2.5 Exterior of Jeremiah Smith's copy of *Emma*   65

2.6 Endpapers of volume 1 of Jeremiah Smith's copy of *Emma*, showing his notes on the purchase and on Austen's life, as well as repair stitches   66

2.7 Pages preceding the title page of volume 1 of Jeremiah Smith's copy of *Emma*, showing his further notes on Austen's life and his signature   67

2.8 James Hammond's Circulating Library copy of *Emma*   74

3.1 "Christian Broun, 1786–1839. Wife of the 9th Earl of Dalhousie," by Sir John Watson Gordon [1829]   89

3.2 Page from Christian Broun's commonplace book, with interleaved plant specimen   92

3.3 Portion of page from Lady Dalhousie's June 1818 diary, showing her reading of *Persuasion*   105

3.4 Portion of page from Lady Dalhousie's June 1820 diary, showing her reading of *Pride and Prejudice* and *Mansfield Park*   108

3.5 Watercolor by Countess of Dalhousie [1819]   110

3.6 Watercolor by Countess of Dalhousie [1819]   111

ABBREVIATIONS

Databases

AHN   *America's Historical Newspapers*

EAI   *Early American Imprints*

Individuals

FWA   Admiral Sir Francis W. Austen

AHB   Alberta H. Burke

DJG   David J. Gilson

JEAL   James Edward Austen-Leigh

ESQ   Eliza Susan Quincy

ACLW   Anna Cabot Lowell [Quincy] Waterston

Introduction

This book began when my curiosity was sparked by the obscure origins of a very rare book owned by Goucher College, where I now teach: the 1816 Philadelphia printing of Jane Austen's *Emma*, the sole Austen novel published in the United States during the author's lifetime. Only four copies of this American *Emma* had survived, according to the eminent Austen bibliographer David Gilson, and how it had come to be we would never know, since publisher's records could not be found.[1] As the bicentennial of this *Emma*'s publication approached in 2016, I was keen to see what more, if anything, could be discovered about this first edition of an Austen novel for American readers.

I hoped too that the remaining copies of the 1816 Philadelphia *Emma* might hold clues about Austen's earliest transatlantic readers, who, I had come to realize, represented a missing piece in literary history. Several chapters of my previous book, *Everybody's Jane: Austen in the Popular Imagination*, examine what Austen's readers in America did with—and to—her novels in the twentieth and early twenty-first centuries, from collecting, to writing hybrid fiction, to founding the Jane Austen Society of North America (JASNA).[2] But how did Americans initially encounter and respond to Austen's writings? A prequel of sorts to *Everybody's Jane* was needed, I felt, with an exclusive focus on Austen's overlooked American readers.

Just a few tantalizing glimpses of these readers and their attitudes appear in B. C. Southam's invaluable reference *Jane Austen: A Critical Heritage*. Remarking that the "earliest American response is something we know very little about," Southam notes that James Fenimore Cooper's first novel, *Precaution* (1820), was modeled on Austen's *Persuasion*. Southam tells, too, the anecdote of US Supreme Court Chief Justice John Marshall standing up in a Phi Beta Kappa meeting at Harvard in 1826 to tell the speaker, Joseph Story, whose topic was English women novelists, that he should have included the works of Miss Austen.[3] Mary A. Favret's essay "Free and Happy: Jane Austen in America," in Deidre Lynch's edited collection *Janeites: Austen's Disciples and Devotees*, contributes a study of transatlantic Austen-mania at the turn of the twentieth century.[4] Katie Halsey's *Jane Austen and Her Readers, 1786–1945*, the fullest consideration to date of Austen's British reception, looks across the Atlantic only very briefly, to consider Mark Twain's notoriously disparaging remarks about Austen's novels in his private writings.[5] Americans are equally absent from all but a handful of pages in Claudia L. Johnson's monograph *Jane Austen's Cults and Cultures* and Claire Harman's internationally successful popular book *Jane's Fame: How Jane Austen Conquered the World*, both of which track the growth of Austen's reputation and fandom.[6]

For such a thoroughly studied author as Austen, it is always surprising and exciting to happen upon an area where much remains to be discovered. I believe that British scholars have neglected American reception of Austen chiefly because they, with the significant exception of Gilson, have considered the subject to be less inherently important than British reception. (The case would doubtless have been different had Austen, like such successors as Dickens and Wilde, personally traveled to America or been closely involved with her American publications.) What's more, because Gilson's bibliographical research on Austen was overall so exhaustive, Austen scholars everywhere have trusted that he discovered everything possible about early American editions of her works. That many potentially relevant research sources are located in America, of course, likely deterred British scholars from further investigation. For their part, American literary historians have been primarily concerned with the development of a distinct literary tradition in the new nation. Even with the recent rise in transatlantic studies, the influence of British authors on American readers has not proved a compelling interest— aside from Shakespeare, who has been well studied.[7]

My investigation of Austen's early American publications and readers integrates approaches from several scholarly areas. Book history contributes a focus on books as unique objects, whose physical materials and traces of owners' use convey individual stories.[8] The history of the book trade helps explain how editions came to be: who—i.e., publishers, printers, and binders—created the actual books and how they were advertised and distributed to readers by booksellers and libraries.[9] The intersecting fields of reception studies and the history of reading justify attention to the responses and behaviors of readers beyond professional critics and provide frameworks for investigating these phenomena—the traces of which, in Austen's case, had previously been considered mere curiosities or "Janeana."[10] My home area of literary criticism too has recently begun to pay attention to readers' engagement with books, albeit typically from a perspective as much theoretical as historical.[11] (In a different vein, recent historically-inflected Austen scholarship has asserted the great importance of places, people, and objects to Austen's life and works.[12]) Unlike art history, to which studies of collecting and curatorship have long been central, literary collecting and literary editing are just beginning to be studied seriously.[13] Fan studies, so crucial to *Everybody's Jane*, is less directly pertinent here, with the exception of recent work on nineteenth-century enthusiasts as precursors of today's fans.[14]

Reading Austen in America recovers Americans' involvement with Austen's writings in capacities including publisher, book buyer, reader, devotee, literary tourist, collector, and bibliographer. In each of these roles, Americans contributed to the gradual rise of Austen's renown: from the modest recognition she received during her lifetime, to the international fame that resulted from the publication in 1870 of the first full-length biography of her (J. E. Austen-Leigh's *A Memoir of Jane Austen*), to the divergence in the twentieth century of scholarly and fan approaches to her writings. These vignettes of book production, reading, and literary enthusiasm comprise the first distinctively American history of Austen's readers and devotees.

As in *Everybody's Jane*, I have attempted what many consider to be impossible: to write for both academic and nonacademic readers, those two halves of the world that truly "cannot understand the pleasures of the other," to quote Emma Woodhouse.[15] Towards this goal, I have chosen to feature primary sources and images that bring to life readers and the circumstances of their engagement with Austen's writings. Data, which is so central to a great deal of book history, I keep to a minimum. Historical context, too, I include only as necessary to illuminate specific encounters between readers and books. I hope that scholarly readers will understand the adjustments

I have made to increase accessibility, and I encourage everyone else to ignore the endnotes and read for what interests you.

My first chapter centers on the production of the 1816 Philadelphia *Emma*, concerning which, contrary to Gilson's assumption, many records have indeed survived. I show how the entrepreneurial American publisher Mathew Carey (whose portrait I include) took a risk on an author whose name he did not know, but who had begun to receive significant critical praise in Britain, notably from a review written by Walter Scott. While no bestseller, Carey's American printing of *Emma* did bring the title to the notice of American booksellers and readers. In addition to advertisements for *Emma* itself, one of which I reproduce in facsimile, English obituaries for Austen were reprinted in American newspapers and periodicals later in 1817: further contributions to her early transatlantic renown. Additional photographs highlight differences and similarities in presentation and format between the first London and first Philadelphia editions of *Emma*.

I turn next to the surviving copies of the 1816 Philadelphia *Emma*, of which I have discovered two more, for a total of six. These have much to tell us about American readers' responses to *Emma*, and to Austen more generally, before her fame was widespread. In Chapter 2, I examine the copies originally owned by the cultured E. I. du Pont family of Delaware; by Jeremiah Smith, a New Hampshire chief justice; and by a Rhode Island circulating library. I place the du Pont copy in the context of the family's reading tastes and attitudes, as reconstructed from their private papers. Smith's much-annotated *Emma* is a gold mine of references to articles about Austen from the 1810s to 1830s and establishes him as the first identifiable Austen enthusiast in America. By contrast, early evidence of American readers' strong dislike for Austen emerges from the circulating library volumes, which are annotated with personal responses—many quite negative—to *Emma*. Photographs of these three copies, portraits, and a charming scene of domestic reading drawn by a du Pont sister illustrate this chapter.

How reading Austen's novels in America fit into the life of an adventurous, and non-American, woman is the subject of my third chapter. The Countess of Dalhousie, a Scotswoman best remembered for her botanical collecting, lived in Halifax and Quebec in the late 1810s and early 1820s, thanks to her husband's leadership positions in the British colonial government. Lady Dalhousie's personal writings, which have never before been published, reveal her to have been a witty, highly literary woman, whose experiences offer thought-provoking parallels with those of Austen and her characters. My extended portrait of Lady Dalhousie is the most substantial, multi-dimensional treatment to date of one of Austen's contemporary readers of any nationality. I accompany it with images of the countess herself, of her diary pages, and two of her delightfully satiric watercolors of Halifax society.

Chapter 4 examines a turning point in Austen's American reception, when a new complete edition of her novels printed in Philadelphia brought her writings to a much larger audience in the US. Among these readers was a family of fervent enthusiasts, the Quincys of Boston, who, over several decades, recorded in both private and published writings their passionate devotion to Austen's novels—and their equally strong attachment to Austen's brother Admiral Sir Francis W. Austen, whom one Quincy sister met in person in 1856. The acquaintance between the Quincy and Austen families was both deeper and much better documented than scholars have recognized. Moreover, this transatlantic friendship held important implications for Austen's reputation not only in America but also around the world. Mentions of the Quincys in Austen family writings from J. E. Austen-Leigh's *Memoir* through R. A. Austen-Leigh's 1942 publication *Austen Papers 1704–1856* demonstrate the value that the Austen family placed on the evidence of the Quincys' regard.

As a twentieth-century counterpart to the transatlantic conversation between the Quincys and Austens, Chapter 5 presents the lively, learned correspondence enjoyed by two readers who supported each other's committed interests in Austen bibliography and collecting, to the eventual benefit of Austen scholars and fans alike. In *Everybody's Jane*, I introduced Alberta H. Burke of Baltimore as an "Austen omnivore" and forerunner of today's Austen fans. Here, I consider Mrs. Burke from a different angle: as an expert on Austen publishing history who, through her friendship with and encouragement of the bibliographer David Gilson, made a significant contribution to Austen studies. Their acquaintance began with mutual interest in the copy of the 1816 Philadelphia *Emma* that Mrs. Burke acquired in the 1940s, which eventually became part of her legacy to Goucher.

I am grateful for opportunities to share elements of this research in progress with a range of audiences. For invitations to give public lectures, my thanks go to Elizabeth Frengel at the Beinecke Rare Book and Manuscript Library, Yale University; Debra Roush and Linda Slothouber of JASNA; Alexander McCall Smith and the Institute for Advanced Study in the Humanities (IASH) at the University of Edinburgh; Nicholas Mason and Valerie Hegstrom at Brigham Young University; the Hamilton Street Club of Baltimore; the Mount Vernon Club of Baltimore; the Baltimore Bibliophiles; Gary Richards at the University of Mary Washington; Carolyn Berman at the New School; Gillian Dow at Chawton House Library; Paul Savidge of JASNA–Eastern Pennsylvania; and Annette LeClair at Union College. I have benefited from responses of scholarly colleagues at conferences of the Society for the History of Authorship, Reading, and Publishing; the American Society for Eighteenth-Century Studies (ASECS) and East-Central ASECS; the Reception Study Society; and Chawton House Library's "Pride and Prejudices: Women's Writing of the Long Eighteenth Century." I gratefully acknowledge research support from the Isabel Dalhousie Fellowship, IASH; the Hagley Museum and Library; and the Provost's Office of Goucher College. My work would not have been possible without James N. Green's course on early American publishing history, offered through Rare Book School, and his subsequent generous mentorship.

For research assistance and permissions, I am thankful to the staff members of the American Antiquarian Society, Dartmouth College Library, Hagley Museum and Library, Hampshire Record Office, Historical Society of Pennsylvania, Library Company of Philadelphia, Massachusetts Historical Society, Morgan Library and Museum, National Register of Archives of Scotland, New York Society Library, Nova Scotia Museum, Scottish National Gallery, and Winterthur Library and Museum. My dedicated colleagues at Goucher College Library deserve special mention. For access to and permission to quote from Lady Dalhousie's papers, I am grateful to the private owner of the Broun-Lindsay papers.

Portions of chapters one and two appeared as "The 1816 Philadelphia *Emma*: A Forgotten Edition and Its Readers," in *Persuasions: The Jane Austen Journal* 38 (2016), and are reprinted by permission.

At Bloomsbury, my thanks go to David Avital, who has encouraged this project from its earliest days; to Lucy Brown,

Paul King and Merv Honeywood; and to the anonymous readers who gave valuable feedback.

To my family, who came with me to Scotland, and who have heard a very great deal about the 1816 Philadelphia *Emma*, thank you, and much love—in particular to Rodney Yoder, whose thoughtful reading and warm support were crucial as ever.

Notes

1 David Gilson, "Jane Austen's 'Emma' in America: Notes on the Text of the First and Second American Editions," *The Review of English Studies* n.s. 53: 212 (2002): 517. By contrast, Austen's publication in Britain has been well studied: see Gilson's highly respected *A Bibliography of Jane Austen*, new edn (New Castle, DE: Oak Knoll Press, 1997), and also Jan Fergus, *Jane Austen: A Literary Life* (New York: St. Martin's, 1991) and Anthony Mandal, *Jane Austen and the Popular Novel: The Determined Author* (Houndmills, Basingstoke: Palgrave Macmillan, 2007). On Austen's publication history in Europe, see Anthony Mandal and Brian Southam, eds, *The Reception of Jane Austen in Europe* (London: Continuum, 2007).

2 Juliette Wells, *Everybody's Jane: Austen in the Popular Imagination* (New York: Bloomsbury Academic, 2011). Devoney Looser's *The Making of Jane Austen* (Baltimore: Johns Hopkins University Press, forthcoming 2017) promises to add more chapters to the story of American reinterpretations of Austen.

3 B. C. Southam, ed., *Jane Austen: The Critical Heritage* (London: Routledge & Kegan Paul, 1968), 26–7; Southam mistakenly gives "John" as Story's first name. Southam also includes in his introduction and in the anthology proper excerpts from Longfellow's 1839 journal; Emerson's 1861 journal; an 1834 reference book, *Female Biography*; an 1849 American textbook titled *Outlines of General Literature*; and an 1853 essay from the *North American Review*. Much of Southam's American material he borrowed from an earlier article, Charles Beecher Hogan's "Jane Austen and Her Early Public," *The Review of English Studies* n.s. 1 (1950): 39–54. For a more recent anthology demonstrating the rise in Austen's literary reputation, see Joan Klingel Ray, ed., *Jane Austen's Popular and Critical Reception: A Documentary Volume* (Detroit: Gale, 2012).

4 Mary A. Favret, "Free and Happy: Jane Austen in America," in *Janeites: Austen's Disciples and Devotees*, ed. Deidre Lynch, 166–87 (Princeton: Princeton University Press, 2000).

5 Katie Halsey, *Jane Austen and Her Readers, 1786–1945* (London: Anthem, 2012), 184–7.

6 Claire Harman, *Jane's Fame: How Jane Austen Conquered the World* (Edinburgh: Canongate, 2009); Claudia L. Johnson, *Jane Austen's Cults and Cultures* (Chicago: University of Chicago Press, 2012). A variety of twentieth- and twenty-first-century American writers are quoted in Susannah Carson, ed., *A Truth Universally Acknowledged: 33 Great Writers on Why We Read Jane Austen* (New York: Random House, 2009).

7 On Shakespeare, see Alden T. Vaughan and Virginia Mason Vaughan, *Shakespeare in America* (Oxford: Oxford University Press, 2012); James Shapiro, ed., *Shakespeare in America: An Anthology from the Revolution till Now* (New York: Library of America, 2014); and Katherine West Scheil, *She Hath Been Reading: Women and Shakespeare Clubs in America* (Ithaca: Cornell University Press, 2012). Among historical studies of American readers that do emphasize British titles are Nina Baym, *Novels, Readers, and Reviewers: Responses to Fiction in Antebellum America* (Ithaca: Cornell University Press, 1984) and Cathy N. Davidson, *Revolution and the Word: The Rise of the Novel in America* (Oxford: Oxford University Press, 1986).

8 Of the many excellent recent treatments of book history for audiences beyond specialists, I have found especially helpful David Pearson's *Books as History*, rev. edn (London and New Castle, DE: The British Library and Oak Knoll Press, 2012).

9 Most pertinent to my study is Robert A. Gross and Mary Kelley, eds, *A History of the Book in America Vol. 2: An Extensive Republic: Print, Culture, and Society in the New Nation, 1790–1840* (Chapel Hill: American Antiquarian Society/University of North Carolina Press, 2010). My third chapter, which addresses a reader in what is now Canada, also draws on Patricia Lockhart Fleming, Gilles Gallichan, and Yvan Lamonde, eds, *History of the Book in Canada Vol. 1: Beginnings to 1840* (Toronto: University of Toronto Press, 2004).

10 See in particular Shafquat Towheed and W. R. Owens, eds, *The History of Reading, Volume 1: International Perspectives, c. 1500–1900* (New York: Palgrave Macmillan, 2011); Katie Halsey and W. R. Owens, eds, *The History of Reading, Volume 2: Evidence from the British Isles, c. 1750–1950* (New York: Palgrave Macmillan, 2011); and Rosalind Crone and Shafquat Towheed, eds, *The History of Reading, Volume 3: Methods, Strategies, Tactics* (New York: Palgrave Macmillan, 2011). Representative of earlier generations' approach to

reception material is M. A. de Wolfe Howe, "A Jane Austen Letter, with other 'Janeana' from an old book of autographs," *The Yale Review* 15 (Jan. 1926): 319–35. On nineteenth-century American readers in particular, see Gillian Silverman, *Bodies and Books: Reading and the Fantasy of Communion in Nineteenth-Century America* (Philadelphia: University of Pennsylvania Press, 2012). On American reception study, see Philip Goldstein, *Modern American Reading Practices: Between Aesthetics and History* (New York: Palgrave Macmillan, 2009) and Philip Goldstein and James L. Machor, eds, *New Directions in American Reception Study* (Oxford: Oxford University Press, 2008).

11 See especially Deidre Shauna Lynch, *Loving Literature: A Cultural History* (Chicago: University of Chicago Press, 2015).

12 Key among historically-focused recent works on Austen are Paula Byrne, *The Real Jane Austen: A Life in Small Things* (New York: Harper, 2012); Janine Barchas, *Matters of Fact in Jane Austen: History, Location, and Celebrity* (Baltimore: Johns Hopkins University Press, 2012); and Margaret Doody, *Jane Austen's Names: Riddles, Persons, Places* (Chicago: University of Chicago Press, 2015).

13 On American literary collectors, I have found most helpful Heidi Ardizzone, *An Illuminated Life: Belle da Costa Greene's Journey from Prejudice to Privilege* (New York: W. W. Norton, 2007), a study of the remarkable self-taught librarian to J. P. Morgan; and Stephen H. Grant, *Collecting Shakespeare: The Story of Henry and Emily Folger* (Baltimore: Johns Hopkins University Press, 2014). On the impulse to collect and create a private institution for one's holdings, valuable too is Anne Higgonet, *A Museum of One's Own: Private Collecting, Public Gift* (Pittsburgh: Periscope, 2009). The role of Austen's editors, especially R. W. Chapman, has been well established by Kathryn Sutherland in *Jane Austen's Textual Lives: From Aeschylus to Bollywood* (Oxford: Oxford University Press, 2005).

14 For example, Daniel Cavicki, "Fandom before 'Fan': Shaping the History of Enthusiastic Audiences," in *Reception: Texts, Readers, Audiences, History* 6 (2014): 52–72.

15 "That is the case with us all, papa. One half of the world cannot understand the pleasures of the other," says Emma Woodhouse to her father, apropos of the lively games that her brother-in-law plays with his children. Jane Austen, *Emma*, ed. Richard Cronin and Dorothy McMillan (Cambridge: Cambridge University Press, 2005), 87.

PART ONE

The 1816 Philadelphia *Emma* and its Readers

1

The Origins of the First Austen Novel Printed in America

Known today chiefly to book historians and serious literary collectors, the 1816 Philadelphia *Emma* was the first work by Jane Austen published in America and the only one printed in the United States during her lifetime (1775–1817). This earliest American edition of an Austen novel was not a great success. It did not sell briskly enough either to warrant reprinting or to spur publishers to issue American editions of other Austen novels. Indeed, more than a decade and a half elapsed before an Austen novel was again printed in the US, again in Philadelphia, by the firm of Carey & Lea.[1]

So little impression did this earliest American publication of Austen make that its very existence failed to be remembered. Geoffrey Keynes's *Jane Austen: A Bibliography* (1929), the first catalogue of historic editions of Austen's novels, included no mention of the 1816 Philadelphia *Emma*. In 1939, a copy of this forgotten edition turned up at auction, reminding the rueful Keynes, and collectors around the world, that Carey & Lea's 1832–1833 American editions of Austen had a predecessor. David Gilson's *A Bibliography of Jane Austen* (1982) restored the 1816 Philadelphia *Emma* to the historical record, together with descriptions of the very few copies—just four, by the time of Gilson's 2002 article "Jane Austen's 'Emma' in America"—known to survive. In that article, Gilson compared in some detail the text of the first London and Philadelphia editions. Yet he left unanswered many crucial questions about the latter's origins and reception, including the exact date of publication of Carey's *Emma* and its print run.

I have identified two copies of the 1816 Philadelphia *Emma* in addition to those catalogued by Gilson, bringing the total of confirmed copies to six. (For a descriptive list—what book historians call a census—see the Appendix.) Five copies are held in American college, university, research, or private membership libraries: at Goucher College, Yale University, the New York Society Library, Dartmouth College, and Winterthur Library. One is in England, at King's College, University of Cambridge. In numerical terms, this first American edition of *Emma* is significantly more rare than either Shakespeare's First Folio, of which there are 235 known copies and counting, or the Bay Psalm Book, the first book printed in the American colonies, of which eleven copies remain.[2] Notably, the 1816 Philadelphia *Emma* is *not* in the collections of the most distinguished libraries in the English-speaking world, including the Library of Congress and Oxford's Bodleian.

Unbeknownst to Gilson, a considerable amount of information about the printing and promotion of the 1816 Philadelphia *Emma* does indeed survive, in publishers' records and newspaper advertisements. Most of these sources have never been published, and few have been digitized.[3] From them, I have reconstructed the production of Carey's *Emma* from the publisher's first encounter with the novel, through the drawn-out process of reprinting it, to the hasty binding that had long-term consequences for the copies' survival, to the ways in which Carey, his bookselling partners, and libraries presented this novel to potential readers. While the 1816 Philadelphia *Emma* elicited no American reviews, advertisements for it did bring Austen to the notice of readers throughout the US, as we will see. Moreover, mentions of Austen continued to appear in American periodicals throughout the 1820s, indicating that interest in Austen's writings and authorship was beginning to grow.

What did it mean to "reprint" *Emma*?

The story of the 1816 Philadelphia *Emma* begins with the choices made by John Murray, with Austen's approval, for his London edition. (London, then as now, was the center of the English book publishing business.) As Thomas Egerton, Austen's prior publisher, had done with *Sense and Sensibility* (1811), *Pride and Prejudice* (1813), and *Mansfield Park* (1814), Murray issued *Emma* in the spacious, luxurious three-volume format that was conventional for novels at the time. In both size and price, however, Murray's edition of *Emma* reflected his greater prestige and ambition as a publisher: the very qualities that attracted Austen to him. He had 2,000 copies of *Emma* printed, while scholars estimate that Egerton published 750 copies of *Sense and Sensibility* and 1,250 copies each of *Pride and Prejudice* and *Mansfield Park*. And Murray's *Emma* cost a guinea (a pound plus a shilling, or twenty-one shillings), significantly more than the fifteen- to eighteen-shilling prices of Egerton's editions.[4] So costly were printed books at this time that Austen herself was able to afford to buy very few; she borrowed most of what she read, either from friends or from libraries.[5] In my introduction to *Emma* for Penguin Classics, I propose the very rough equivalence of $100 for the guinea price of Murray's *Emma*.[6]

Austen negotiated financial terms confidently with Murray, in person, and kept a careful eye on the edition's printing. Indeed, her close involvement with the production of *Emma*—the last of her novels she was able to see through the press—remains crucial evidence of her sense of herself as a professional author. So too does her lively correspondence with James Stanier Clarke about the Prince Regent's "invitation" to dedicate the novel to him.[7] Unfortunately for Austen, the royal dedication resulted in neither a sellout edition nor, apparently, any great increase in her readership or fame.

As figure 1.1 makes clear, Austen's name did not appear on the title page of Murray's edition, which identified her only as "THE AUTHOR OF 'PRIDE AND PREJUDICE', &C. &C." The designation "BY A LADY" had appeared on the title page of *Sense and Sensibility*, Austen's first novel to be printed, thereby making known her gender and suggesting her social class as a gentlewoman; subsequently, each title page referred to one or more of her previous novels. Austen's identity as author was made publicly known only after her death, first through obituaries and then through the "Biographical Notice" included with Murray's December 1817 publication of *Northanger Abbey* and *Persuasion* (dated 1818 on its title page). While an explanation of Austen's decision to veil her name has not survived, her doing so was certainly in keeping with ideas of the time regarding published authorship for women, especially unmarried women.[8]

So far, all is well known to those steeped in Austen. We enter less familiar territory with the title page of the first American edition of *Emma*—which, like Murray's, conveys important information about the book's origins. Indeed, what is not present is as significant as what is. No mention appears here of John Murray or of London. Only one element hints that this edition is not an original publication: the phrase "three volumes in two," which contemporary American bookbuyers would have understood to mean that this book had been reprinted, most likely from a London publication.

Reprinting might seem to us today to be piracy. In the early nineteenth century, however, reprinting an English publication in America, on the Continent, or in Ireland without the author's or publisher's permission was legal, since British copyright law banned re-publication only within England and Scotland. According to one historian of copyright, "American publishers were perfectly free to

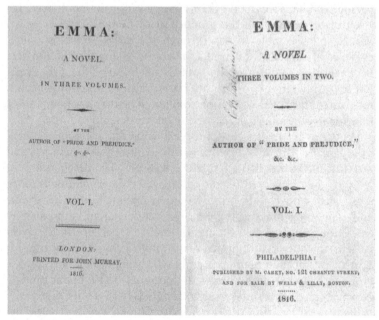

FIGURE 1.1 *Title page of Murray's London edition of* Emma *(left) and of Carey's Philadelphia edition (right). Courtesy of Goucher College Special Collections and Archives.*

reprint British copyright works, and did so."[9] To the dismay of American authors, their titles too were reprinted without authorization in Britain.[10] International copyright laws came into existence later in the nineteenth century, as a result in part of forceful advocacy by such internationally famous authors as Charles Dickens.

Austen's lifetime came at the end of what is known as the "hand-press period," when books were still, in the words of the book historian David Pearson, "unique handcrafted objects" created using much the same artisan techniques as in the era of Gutenberg.[11] By the early nineteenth century, when American-authored literature was still nascent, all the materials involved in bookmaking were produced within the US. In the young nation, so recently and proudly independent from British laws and taxation policies, producing and consuming American-made goods was considered decidedly patriotic. Buyers of an American reprint supported not only local booksellers, publishers, printers, and binders but also paper-makers, type-casters, ink-makers, and leather-tanners—all while paying a price significantly cheaper than an English import.[12]

With no permission required for legal reprinting in the US, an author and publisher in England may well never have known that a transatlantic reprint existed. No evidence indicates that either Austen or John Murray was aware of the 1816 Philadelphia *Emma*. Certainly neither of them profited from it.

Would Austen have cared that her novel was published in the United States? I believe that she would have. Austen seems, as Patricia M. Ard has persuasively argued, to have given very little thought to America in general.[13] Yet she certainly concerned herself with the "Profits of [her] Novels," as she headed the scrap of paper on which she kept track of some of her earnings. The list she compiled of "Opinions of *Emma*" makes clear her desire, too, to know what her readers thought of her writings.[14] It seems reasonable to guess that she would also have been interested in her international reception.

Who was "M. Carey," and why did he choose *Emma*?

Fittingly, the man who brought out the 1816 Philadelphia *Emma* was the foremost publisher in the United States at the time, although his name is not well known today.[15] Mathew Carey was born in Dublin in 1760, where he learned the printing trade, as well as the business of unauthorized but legal reprinting. After emigrating to the US in 1784, Carey quickly established himself as an ambitious, well-connected businessman, as well as a civically engaged man and a noted political writer.[16] Carey's keen intelligence and certainty of purpose can be descried in John Neagle's 1825 life portrait of him (see figure 1.2), which hangs at the Library Company of Philadelphia.

FIGURE 1.2 *Mathew Carey, portrait by John Neagle (1825). Courtesy of the Library Company of Philadelphia.*

(Founded in 1731 by Benjamin Franklin, the Library Company is now a research institution; it holds almost every title printed by Carey, except his 1816 *Emma*.) In the early nineteenth century, Philadelphia was the center of American publishing, having only recently—in 1800—been replaced by Washington as capital of the nation.[17]

Book historians identify Carey, who died in 1839, as one of the first printers and booksellers in the United States to become a publisher as we understand that term today: an entrepreneur who selected books to publish, supplied capital for their production, and coordinated their sales and marketing. Such work was financially risky—especially during the economic downturn brought about by the War of 1812, which caused many publishing businesses to fail[18]—and thus personally stressful. In autobiographical writings published in his later years, Carey expressed a hope that his life story "can hardly fail to have a beneficial tendency, by a display of the overwhelming difficulties and dangers, with which I have had to struggle for a full third part of my life, when I was almost daily on the verge of bankruptcy—dangers which I could not have overcome but by the most unshrinking perseverance and industry." For his eventual success, he also credited his wife for being "industrious, prudent, and economical, and well calculated to save whatever I made": essential qualities indeed for a family raising seven children (two more died in infancy).[19]

Highlights of Carey's extensive publishing record include the first Catholic Bible printed in America, in 1790, and the first American atlases, a few years later, which were a landmark in printing technique and quality in the US.[20] The steady production of King James Bibles in a variety of formats kept Carey's publishing business (relatively) solvent for decades. As was typical at the time, Carey sold books in his own bookshop as well as by mail, both to individual purchasers and to booksellers in other cities.

His son, Henry C. Carey (1793–1879), worked with him increasingly in the late 1810s before becoming his full partner in January 1817, a change reflected in the firm's new imprint "M. CAREY AND SON." Henry took over the business entirely in 1824, when Mathew retired in order to devote himself more fully to his political writings.[21] (Henry was the "Carey" of Carey & Lea, the firm that published the first complete American edition of Austen's novels; "Lea" was Isaac Lea, Mathew's son-in-law.) Henry too struggled for years to make a profit from the publishing business, much to his own and his father's dismay. "I have carried on business for a great many years—have had as much care & anxiety as any man I know, & yet at 37 I find that I cannot indulge in the luxury of keeping a horse," Henry wrote poignantly to his father in 1830.[22] Henry's fortunes improved later in his life, when he became an influential economist.[23]

Both personally and professionally, Mathew Carey took a keen interest in novels, a popular genre that had existed in English only since the early 1700s.[24] In his autobiography, he recalled how much he had loved reading such works in his youth, in Dublin, and the lengths to which he had gone to feed his enthusiasm:

> I had been a great, indeed a voracious reader before I was bound apprentice—and had clandestinely subscribed to a circulating library, contrary to the wishes, and indeed with out the knowledge, of my parents, who were opposed to the kind of books which, alone, I was desirous of reading. I used to be dissatisfied that I could not exchange books oftener than once a day. I used to sit up till twelve and one o'clock, reading novels and romances.[25]

Carey's diaries make clear that his "voracious" reading of novels continued into adulthood, albeit tempered by then with critical judgment. "During this day, read two volumes & a half of Opie's Tales of the Heart," he recorded on 24 September 1820. "Hardly second rate." "Finished Kenilworth," he noted on 7 March 1821, referring to the newest novel by the "author of Waverley," i.e., Walter Scott. (While Scott published his fiction anonymously, his identity was widely guessed.) Again, Carey's review was uncompromising: "Story marked by great impossibilities like all the rest of his writing." Like all of Scott's novels, however, Kenilworth sold very well in America, as it had in Britain. "Published Kenilworth. Sold by retail nearly 50 copies," Carey recorded on 10 March 1821, and on the next day: "Determined to print 1000 more of Kenilworth."[26]

Throughout Carey's publishing career, novels featured prominently among the titles he reprinted from English originals. Catalogues of his firm's offerings highlighted such works in the category of "Novels & Romances," in which authors' names make clear the substantial proportion of women novelists published by Carey.[27] (Many novelists published anonymously at this time.) Most significantly, Carey published the first edition of what is now considered to be the first American novel: Susanna Rowson's *Charlotte* (1794), later known as *Charlotte Temple*.[28]

Carey's reprinting of English novels accelerated in 1816, following the tripling of customs duty on books imported from England from 5 percent to 15 percent.[29] In his *Autobiography*, Carey downplayed the business effects of this increase (and recalled a slightly higher percentage): "By the importation of books I had never experienced the least inconvenience. I was wont to import as many books as probably any other bookseller in the United States, and the amount never formed a sixth of my sales, which were chiefly confined to books of American manufacture. The duty on those imported, 16½ per cent. was ample protection."[30]

Developing a market for novels in the United States represented a challenge, however, when all books—even reprints—were expensive, and only very cultured and privileged Americans owned more than Bibles, schoolbooks, and practical reference works.[31] In the US as in the UK, subscribing to circulating libraries was much more affordable than buying novels individually.[32]

Thus Carey's decision to publish *Emma*, while it fit in well with his own predilection for novels and his firm's emphasis on reprinting English fiction for American bookbuyers, represented a definite financial risk. Unfortunately, since Carey did not keep a diary during 1816 and 1817, no record remains either of his response to first reading *Emma* or of his decision to publish it.[33] This circumstance is the first of three significant gaps in the archival history related to his edition of *Emma*.

The bibliographer David Gilson guessed that Carey was influenced by the long, laudatory review of *Emma* that appeared, with no byline, in the March 1816 issue of John Murray's periodical the *Quarterly Review*. As Gilson noted, Carey quoted a key portion of this appraisal in his advertising for his edition of *Emma*.[34] Gilson knew of Carey's *Catalogue of an Extensive Collection* and of the twenty-four-page catalogues included with his new publications. As I will address more fully later in this chapter, quotations from the *Quarterly Review* also accompanied listings for *Emma* in other advertisements by Carey, including *The Monthly Literary Advertiser* reproduced in figure 1.4.

The *Quarterly Review* piece on *Emma* represented the first serious critical appraisal that Austen had received. It was written by Walter Scott, by invitation from their mutual publisher John

Murray.[35] Carey's use of the *Quarterly Review* quotation could indicate that he shared the critic's admiration of *Emma*. Or perhaps Carey simply hoped to improve sales of a novel by an author whom he knew, and could identify, only as "the author of 'Sense and Sensibility,' 'Pride and Prejudice,' &c."[36]

Whatever Carey's motivations, the praise he quoted made a strong case for the appeal of *Emma*. In particular, the reviewer's use of the first-person plural that was conventional among book reviewers at the time has the effect, when presented to American audiences, of asserting that the interest of this new novel transcends national boundaries. With emphasis added, that portion of Carey's quotation reads: "Keeping close to common incidents, and to such characters as occupy the ordinary walks of life, she has produced sketches of such spirit and originality, that *we* never miss the excitation which depends upon a narrative of uncommon events, arising from the consideration of minds, manners, and sentiments, greatly above *our* own." The reviewer's declaration, in the preceding sentence, that "[t]he work before us proclaims a knowledge of the human heart" likewise implies broad interest. In contrast, critics today generally view *Emma* as the most explicitly English of Austen's novels.[37]

Evidence indicates, however, that Carey first came across *Emma* independently of the *Quarterly Review*. Packing lists from a London bookseller who regularly supplied Carey with new English publications show that Carey received not one but two copies of *Emma*, in quick succession, in April 1816, each time as part of a large shipment.[38] James N. Green, who located the second invoice, has conjectured that this apparently accidental duplication drew *Emma* to Carey's attention.[39] Furthermore, it seems likely that both shipments of *Emma* resulted not from a particular request of Carey's but instead from a standing order for new releases. Given transatlantic shipping times, it would have been impossible for Carey to have received and read the March *Quarterly Review*, then sent an order to London for *Emma*, and have already received the book by mid-April.

It appears, then, that Carey initially noticed *Emma* essentially by chance. Yet his decision to reprint *Emma* must have been intentional, Green believes.[40] A savvy businessman like Carey would have invested in reprinting a novel by an unknown author only if he thought that the work had merit and would sell. Thus, while no thoughts of Carey's about reading *Emma* are known to have survived, the very existence of his reprint edition can be taken as proof of his esteem for it.

It may still be true, as Gilson hypothesized, that Carey was influenced in part by the *Quarterly Review*. Carey's correspondence shows that he initiated the printing of *Emma* in August 1816, a full four months after receiving the duplicate copies. So the *Quarterly Review* could well have contributed to Carey's decision to reprint *Emma*, even though the periodical was not responsible for first bringing the novel to his notice.

When in 1816 was Carey's *Emma* published, and how many copies were issued?

That Carey published, rather than printed, *Emma* is discernible from the title page, which identified the volumes as having been "PUBLISHED BY M. CAREY" (see figure 1.1). (John Murray conveyed the same meaning on his edition's title page using different words: "PRINTED FOR JOHN MURRAY.") The names of Carey's printers appeared on the last page of the second volume: "Justice & Cox" of Trenton, New Jersey.[41] Located a relatively short distance away from Philadelphia via the Delaware River, Trenton was a manufacturing city rather than a cultural center.

The short-lived printing firm of Justice & Cox consisted of an experienced printer, Joseph Justice (1785–1864) and a much younger associate, Horatio Cox (1801–1883), whose age suggests that he may have been an apprentice.[42] During their brief partnership, which lasted from June 1816 till March 1818, Justice & Cox printed several titles for Carey.[43]

No record remains of Carey's commission of Justice & Cox to print *Emma*. In the second important gap in the archives relating to Carey's *Emma*, his firm's letterbook covering the spring and summer of 1816 is missing. (Letterbooks preserved handwritten copies of outgoing mail.) Letters from Joseph Justice to the Carey firm do survive, however, which make clear that the printing of *Emma* started off promisingly. On 12 August 1816, Justice wrote to Henry C. Carey, Mathew's son and business partner, to estimate the total length of a book that we can deduce must be *Emma*, though Justice did not mention the work by name: "it will make as nigh as we can calculate from 260 to 270 pages per Volume."[44] Justice's estimate was quite accurate: each volume eventually contained 264 pages. In the same letter, Justice noted that he included a sample printed page for the Careys to review: "The page we send you does not look very well—we did not lock it—only [tie]d it and took a proof—however it gives you the size and number of ms," meaning the increment by which printing costs were calculated. In this era, when type was set by hand, the type compositor's calculation of the work's eventual length served two purposes: to reckon the total cost of the printing work and to allow the proper quantity of paper to be ordered—itself a considerable expense, given that all paper was handmade by skilled artisans. Indeed, in American and English publishing alike, the cost of paper was the single greatest contributor to the price of a book.[45]

As summer 1816 gave way to autumn, Justice's letters reveal that Carey did not provide enough paper at the outset to complete the job, presumably because of supply problems with his network of paper manufacturers. Pleas for more paper came again and again from Trenton, while on Carey's end, impatience evidently grew. "We are doing nothing for want of paper send some if you possibly can," Justice entreated in August; "we are now idle for want of paper," he repeated in October.[46] Carey began asking "when will Emma be finished [?]" on 30 September, and on 4 November 1816, he complained, "On Saturday Week I sent you Six Bundles of paper for Emma which I presumed you had rec'd early last Week. It would be well to make some arrangement with the Shippers so as to prevent the Trouble & Disappointment that so frequently occur in our intercourse. There are more miscarriages in my parcels to Trenton than any other direction."[47] Since copies of outgoing correspondence in the Carey firm's letterbook are not signed, and are in a clerk's handwriting, the original author of this letter—Mathew or Henry—cannot be determined absolutely. The irate tone, however, strongly suggests Mathew. Justice addressed his letters alternately to Mathew and Henry; as I noted earlier, Henry became a full partner in the firm of "M. Carey and Son" beginning in January 1817. This letter evidently crossed one from Justice & Cox, also dated 4 November, which assured Carey that "[w]e have received the paper you had the goodness to send us, and will proceed immediately, and have the work out without delay."[48]

Almost, but not quite. "When will Emma be done?" Carey pressed on 30 November.[49] "You wish to know when Emma will be done," replied Justice; "we shall finish it in 2 weeks from this day, if nothing happens to delay us—we shall want 1 bundle of paper more to finish the work."[50]

An element of suspense then entered the correspondence, as winter weather threatened the delivery of *Emma*, by water, from Trenton to Philadelphia. (In the US at this time, shipping by water was faster, more reliable, and less expensive than shipping over land.[51]) On 11 December, Justice requested "one more bundle" of paper so that "we can send it down before the river closes [that is, freezes]—it shall be less expense." He promised that the job will be finished by "Wednesday or Thursday next."[52] "It is of importance to me that the Book should be published before our River closes; you will therefore oblige me by using your utmost exertions to finish it," Carey exhorted on 13 December.[53]

On 17 December, Justice wrote again with an elaborate apology:

we was in hopes that we should be able to send Emma this day— but we was disappointed owing to the packet [vessel] being crowded full so that we could not get it on board. We could not get it ready until she was ready to start—and Capt. Ashmore declared to me that he could not take another article. He said he was sorry, and wished we had come earlier—but it was entirely out of our power, we did our best. ——If the river does not close before tomorrow, another packet starts—and Mr. Cox will come down with her and have all Emma along.[54]

Carey's account books show that he paid Justice & Cox on 20 December, so presumably young Horatio Cox did travel down from Trenton on the 18th with "all Emma along."[55] It's remarkable that this date is almost a year to the day after Murray's London edition was completed, according to his firm's ledger dated 19 December 1815.[56]

The protracted, halting process of printing *Emma* establishes that there was no urgency at all to bring to the market this work by an unnamed, little known English novelist. In contrast, reprints of bestselling works by Scott and, later, Dickens were rushed into production to gratify eager American readers—and to enrich entrepreneurial publishers.[57] Nor did Carey consider his reprinting of *Emma* to be momentous in any way. In a letter dated 30 December 1816, he lamented, "This year has not produced much fruit___ It has not been gainful to me[.] but I live in hopes that the next will make amends___."[58]

The financial risk Carey took in funding the production of *Emma* is underscored by the modest size of his edition. Justice twice asked "what number is to be printed on Emma," which suggests that Carey may not have made a final decision about the print run in advance.[59] A record of Carey's payment to Justice and Cox for "press work" on *Emma*, when decoded, reveals the edition's print run: 500 copies.[60] In the United States as in England, it made better business sense to print a small edition and, if a title sold briskly, to commission more copies, rather than to sink capital into a large print run that might not sell out—as, unfortunately for Austen, was the case with Murray's 2,000 copy edition of *Emma*.[61] Evidently, Carey's edition of *Emma* did not sell well enough to merit a second printing.

Carey's investment in *Emma* was not complete when he paid Justice & Cox for the presswork. What he received from them were large printed sheets, which required binding—a skilled process, also done by hand in this period—to transform them into sellable books. According to Carey's financial records, on 26 December 1816, just a week after he received "all Emma" from Trenton, the bindery of Wakeling & Allen billed him for binding 400 copies of *Emma* in boards and fifty "full bound," leaving the final fifty to be bound at a later date.[62] In the next section, I will explain the importance of the difference between "boards" and "full bound" and address the consequences of this very speedy binding work.

Nowadays, publishing companies establish book release dates months in advance. When exactly we consider the Philadelphia *Emma* to have been "published," however, depends on what we take that term to mean: available for sale? advertised? actually bought? The date when bound copies were ready to be sold at Carey's shop, 26 December 1816, seems a reasonable choice.

How did the Philadelphia *Emma* compare to the London edition, and why have so few copies of the American edition survived?

I have referred to the 1816 Philadelphia *Emma* several times as an "American edition" of Austen. Yet this term is misleading, if it suggests a re-publication for American readers with changed spellings and rewordings, such as is customary today when an English writer's work is issued in the United States. In early American printing, practices varied: some American reprints in the late eighteenth and early nineteenth centuries boldly changed the text of the originals, while others aimed to be identical in content to the English editions.[63]

Justice & Cox's effort to create as close a copy of Murray's *Emma* as possible is evident beginning on their title page (see figure 1.1). Although their type fonts were not exactly the same as those used by Murray's printers, Justice & Cox closely imitated the formatting and text ornaments of the English title page. Justice & Cox also replicated the identification of the novelist as "THE AUTHOR OF 'PRIDE AND PREJUDICE'"—which would have meant little to American readers, since *Pride and Prejudice* was available in the US only as an imported book. But, in this case, to reprint meant, literally, to reprint.

Likewise, Justice & Cox made no concerted effort to "Americanize" Austen's text. In contrast, as Gilson has shown, the 1832–1833 first complete American edition of Austen's novels published by Carey & Lea bowdlerized her prose, including changes to all instances in which a character takes God's name in vain.[64] As Gilson has documented, many typographical errors are present in Justice and Cox's printing of *Emma*, some very noticeable indeed, such as two chapters headed "CHAPTR" and consecutive pages numbered 202 and 103.[65] Some changes are unintentionally entertaining: to take an example not noted by Gilson, rather than exclaiming "Insufferable woman!" in reference to Mrs. Elton, Emma Woodhouse, in the Philadelphia edition, exclaims "Insufferable women!" (Imagine if there were more than one Mrs. Elton!) Such oversights are perhaps not surprising, given Horatio Cox's young age of fifteen, and given too the charmingly ungrammatical way in which Joseph Justice expressed himself in his letters. Carey did employ proofreaders for some of his titles, but evidently he did not consider *Emma* to be worth that effort and cost. We will see in Chapter 2 how one reader of the 1816 Philadelphia *Emma*, Jeremiah Smith, reacted to its many misprints.

The most significant difference between the 1816 London and Philadelphia *Emma*s lies in formatting. To use less paper and thus save a considerable amount of money, Carey compressed the text of the novel into two volumes from the three of Murray's English

E M M A.

————

CHAP. I.

Emma Woodhouse, handsome, clever,
and rich, with a comfortable home and
happy disposition, seemed to unite
some of the best blessings of existence;
and had lived nearly twenty-one years
in the world with very little to distress
or vex her.

She was the youngest of the two
daughters of a most affectionate, indulgent father, and had, in consequence
of her sister's marriage, been mistress
of his house from a very early period.
Her mother had died too long ago for
her to have more than an indistinct remembrance of her caresses, and her
place had been supplied by an excellent woman as governess, who had

VOL. I.   B   fallen

E M M A.

—◦◎◦◦—

CHAP. I.

Emma Woodhouse, handsome, clever, and rich,
with a comfortable home and happy disposition,
seemed to unite some of the best blessings of existence; and had lived nearly twenty-one years in the
world with very little to distress or vex her.

She was the youngest of the two daughters of a
most affectionate, indulgent father, and had, in consequence of her sister's marriage, been mistress of
his house from a very early period. Her mother
had died too long ago for her to have more than an
indistinct remembrance of her caresses; and her
place had been supplied by an excellent woman as
governess, who had fallen little short of a mother in
affection.

Sixteen years had Miss Taylor been in Mr.
Woodhouse's family, less as a governess than a
friend, very fond of both daughters, but particularly
of Emma. Between them it was more the intimacy
of sisters. Even before Miss Taylor had ceased to
hold the nominal office of governess, the mildness
of her temper had hardly allowed her to impose any
restraint; and the shadow of authority being now
long passed away, they had been living together as
friend and friend very mutually attached, and Em-
A-2

FIGURE 1.3 *First page of Murray's London edition of* Emma *(left) and of Carey's Philadelphia edition (right). Courtesy of Goucher College Special Collections and Archives.*

edition. The effects of this compression are evident on the pages of Carey's edition, which are more tightly printed, with narrower margins, than those of Murray's edition, making the Philadelphia edition less relaxing to read (see figure 1.3).

Another cost-saving strategy of Carey's was to choose a less expensive grade of paper than Murray had used. This decision made good business sense for Carey, since, as I have noted, he could not be sure how well an anonymously authored English novel would sell in the American market. The number of ripped, damaged, and altogether missing pages in the surviving copies of the 1816 Philadelphia *Emma*, however, attest to the poor quality of much of the paper on which Carey's edition was printed.

The binding executed for Carey by Wakeling & Allen was likewise economical rather than durable. The hastiness of the binders' work at folding, cutting, and sewing is evident in the many askew pages that appear in surviving copies, as well as the bulging spines of some. What's more, binding "in boards," as was done for 400 of the 500 copies of Carey's *Emma*, meant issuing the volumes in flimsy covers with thin leather adorning only the spines and corners. At significant additional cost, a purchaser could choose to have such a copy rebound with better-quality leather and more care in construction.[66] Without such an investment, the volumes would remain fragile and vulnerable. Few first editions of any book survive in boards; those that do are prized by collectors and fetch high prices.

Of course, it made sense for Carey to cut costs wherever possible. He was a businessman trying to sell books to American purchasers for whom these items were expensive, though much less so than imported English volumes. A comprehensive catalogue of Carey's holdings dated 1818 makes the price differential apparent. His own Philadelphia edition of *Emma* is listed at two price points, $2 and $2.50, with the cheaper version identified as "bds," i.e., in boards, while the London three-volume edition of *Emma* is listed at $4.[67]

The combination of shoddy paper and cheap binding is likely responsible for how few copies of the 1816 Philadelphia *Emma* survive, as well as the damaged condition of several. Green offers a further explanation based on readers' esteem for Austen's writing: "the decision to bind so much of the edition in boards might help explain the rarity of the book today. Boarded books couldn't survive repeated readings and *Emma* was a novel that was reread."[68] The truth of Green's statement will become fully apparent in Chapter 2, when I examine the most dilapidated of the surviving copies of the 1816 Philadelphia *Emma*, which was formerly owned by a circulating library.

Might additional copies have survived? It's certainly possible that out of the 500 copies that Carey had printed, more than six copies remain. Most likely, a further copy would be found in a family collection or a small institutional library that hasn't fully catalogued its holdings. (Every time I visit a house museum that has early nineteenth-century books on display, I always take a good look and ask if the contents have been catalogued.) It's also possible, however, that the six copies that we know about are indeed the only survivors. Given the (understandably) low production values of Carey's reprinted *Emma*, volumes would likely have disintegrated unless an owner cared enough to invest in having them rebound well.

How did readers first become aware of Carey's *Emma*?

Purchasers of Carey's *Emma* would have understood from its title page—"PUBLISHED BY M. CAREY, NO. 121 CHESNUT STREET, AND FOR SALE BY WELLS & LILLY, BOSTON"—that this novel was jointly distributed by its Philadelphia publisher and a Boston bookseller. Partnering with a bookseller in another geographical region, or with several booksellers in a range of cities, was a typical business practice in American publishing at the time. By doing so, a publisher could both ensure wide distribution of new titles and, in the event of reader demand, forestall competing reprints in those markets.[69]

The careful negotiations required to establish and maintain reciprocal publishing partnerships are evident in the Carey firm's correspondence. In December 1815, Carey consented to the following terms for his firm's partnership with Wells & Lilly: "to send none of my books to New England, and you to send none to Philadelphia or South of it . . . . In all the books published, your name will be inserted with mine as publisher, and I presume you will do the same."[70] Business partners monitored each other's compliance closely. "Have you advertised our edition of Comick Drama?" Wells & Lilly inquired in August 1817. "We have not observed it advertised in any of the Philadelphia papers. We are very particular in advertising all your books as extensively as we do our own."[71] Apprising each other of books in press was an equally crucial part of the agreement. Yet Carey's letters to Wells & Lilly while the printing of *Emma* was underway contain no mentions of this novel. Apparently, he did not consider it important enough to discuss.

Correspondence and surviving advertisements make clear that Carey distributed copies of *Emma* not only to Wells & Lilly but also to several firms in New York and beyond. On 27 December 1816, just a day after receiving bound copies of *Emma* from Wakeling & Allen, Carey sent parcels with accompanying invoices and brief cover letters, via Swiftsure Stage stagecoach, to four booksellers in New York—W. B. Gilley, D. Longworth, Thos. Kirk, and Van Winkle & Wiley—as well as to W. T. Williams of Savannah.[72] Carey sent Wells & Lilly's package on 2 January 1817. On only one of his cover letters did he single out the new title: to Thos. Kirk, Carey mentioned sending "50 Emma."

The Carey firm's own advertising featured *Emma* prominently. As figure 1.4 shows, *Emma* was the first novel described in the January 1817 issue of *The Monthly Literary Advertiser*, the firm's catalogue for the bookselling trade, and the only title that appeared on the pamphlet's first page.[73] After the sales details (*"In 2 vols. 12mo. Price 2 dollars, in boards"*) came three quotations of critical praise, beginning with the *Quarterly Review* excerpt that I discussed earlier. Next came an assessment from the July 1816 *Monthly Review*, which is familiar to Austen scholars thanks to B. C. Southam's inclusion of it in his compilation *Jane Austen: The Critical Heritage*.[74] The final, unattributed excerpt, however, is much less well known, having not been collected by Southam. This sentence comes from the opening of a review of *Emma* in the May 1816 issue of the *Augustan Review*, which praises the novel on the whole, though with a concluding encouragement to Austen to broaden her scope.[75] To rediscover an English review of Austen through research on her American publication and reception is certainly a bonus.

Carey's identification of Austen here as "the author of 'Sense and Sensibility,' 'Pride and Prejudice,' etc." draws on descriptions from both the *Quarterly Review* and the *Augustan Review* (neither of which mentioned her most recent novel, *Mansfield Park*). Evidently, Carey considered it worthwhile to make clear that the creator of *Emma* was an experienced novelist, even if very few prospective bookbuyers could be expected to recognize the titles of her prior publications.

It is possible that Carey also advertised *Emma* on its own. Justice & Cox, his printers, wrote in January 1817 to request that he send them "1 copy Emma" and also "show bills for Emma": that is, advertising posters.[76] If indeed Carey did produce such show bills for *Emma*, none has survived.

Carey continued to advertise *Emma* in the twenty-four-page catalogues of current titles that he included with new publications, as well as in separate sales catalogues for the firm. An abridged form of the critical praise from the *Quarterly Review* appeared in all these venues, accompanied in some instances by the *Monthly Review* comments; the *Augustan Review* sentence Carey did not use again. Most significantly, a portion of the *Quarterly Review*

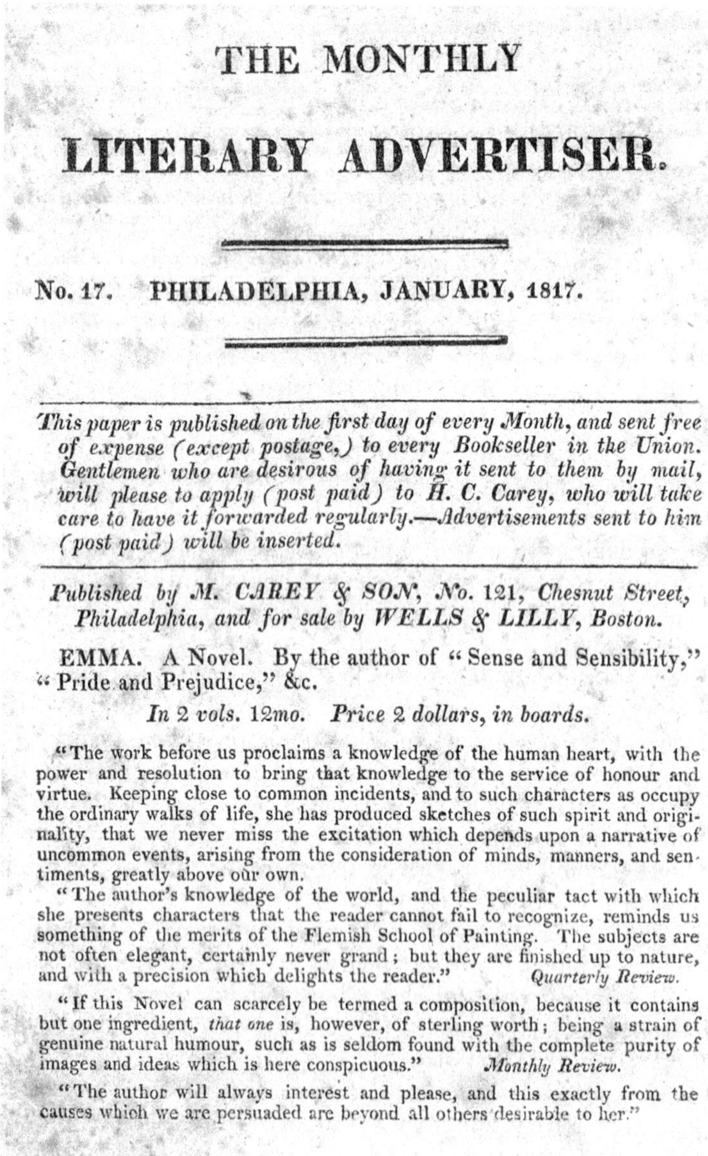

THE MONTHLY
LITERARY ADVERTISER.

No. 17.   PHILADELPHIA, JANUARY, 1817.

*This paper is published on the first day of every Month, and sent free
of expense (except postage,) to every Bookseller in the Union.
Gentlemen who are desirous of having it sent to them by mail,
will please to apply (post paid) to H. C. Carey, who will take
care to have it forwarded regularly.—Advertisements sent to him
(post paid) will be inserted.*

Published by *M. CAREY & SON*, *No.* 121, *Chesnut Street*,
Philadelphia, and for sale by WELLS & LILLY, Boston.

EMMA. A Novel. By the author of " Sense and Sensibility,"
" Pride and Prejudice," &c.

In 2 vols. 12mo.   Price 2 dollars, in boards.

"The work before us proclaims a knowledge of the human heart, with the
power and resolution to bring that knowledge to the service of honour and
virtue. Keeping close to common incidents, and to such characters as occupy
the ordinary walks of life, she has produced sketches of such spirit and originality, that we never miss the excitation which depends upon a narrative of
uncommon events, arising from the consideration of minds, manners, and sentiments, greatly above our own.

"The author's knowledge of the world, and the peculiar tact with which
she presents characters that the reader cannot fail to recognize, reminds us
something of the merits of the Flemish School of Painting. The subjects are
not often elegant, certainly never grand; but they are finished up to nature,
and with a precision which delights the reader."   *Quarterly Review.*

"If this Novel can scarcely be termed a composition, because it contains
but one ingredient, *that one* is, however, of sterling worth; being a strain of
genuine natural humour, such as is seldom found with the complete purity of
images and ideas which is here conspicuous."   *Monthly Review.*

"The author will always interest and please, and this exactly from the
causes which we are persuaded are beyond all others desirable to her."

FIGURE 1.4 Monthly Literary Advertiser, *January 1817, page 1.*
Courtesy of the American Antiquarian Society.

quotation appeared in two M. Carey and Son catalogues in which few other titles were blurbed: an undated broadside (single sheet publication) headed "Catalogue of Novels and Romances" and a comprehensive, 4,055–item catalogue of books in every genre, and from every place of publication, for sale by M. Carey and Son that was published in 1818.[77]

Apparently by accident, the twenty-four-page catalogues that Carey sent directly to bookbuyers included no prices for *Emma*. His catalogues for fellow members of the book trade, however, did specify prices. The 1818 catalogue is especially valuable for conveying the three price points at which Carey sold *Emma*:

1649 Emma. A Novel. By the author of "Sense and Sensibility," "Pride and Prejudice," &c. 2 vols. $2 50   *Philad.* 1816
1650 Same work, bds. $2   ibid.
1651 Same work, 3 vols. $4   *Lond.* 1816[78]

In the absence of the abbreviation "bds." (boards), the price given refers to a bound copy. The third listing shows that Carey, having completed his reprint of *Emma*, was ready to sell off at least one of the London copies that he had received in April 1816 from Longman & Co. Whether any American buyer chose to pay such a premium for the English edition we do not know.

Carey's bookselling partners worked quickly to place newspaper advertisements for *Emma*, in accordance with their reciprocal business agreements. First, on 30 December 1816, came the following in the New York *Evening Post*: "EMMA, a novel, by the auth[o]r of "Pride and Prejudice," 2 vols price $2. Just published and for sale at the Literary Rooms by Dec 30 JAMES EASTBURN & CO." In the next day's issue of the *New-York Courier* appeared: "EMMA : a novel, three vols. in two, by the author of 'Pride and Prejudice," &c.—price $2, just received and for sale at No. 3 Wall street, by VAN WINKLE & WILEY." On 10 January 1817, the same newspaper, the *New-York Courier*, carried an advertisement from a second bookseller, Th. Longworth, Jr., in which *Emma* headed a list of new publications in a variety of genres: "EMMA, a new novel; Guy Mannering 2d edition; Sir Matthew Hale's advice to his Grand Children; the Maid of Moscow, Mrs. Hoffland's last work; Moore's Irish Melodies and Sacred Songs; Lord Byron's works complete; Hobhouse's Letters from France." A third bookseller, W. B. Gilley, placed recurring ads for *Emma* in the *New-York Courier* beginning on 20 January 1817 and in the *Commercial Advertiser* (another New York paper) beginning 21 January 1817. Wells & Lilly, the partners named on the title page of Carey's *Emma*, took out ads in two Boston papers, the *Columbian Centinel* and the *New-England Palladium*.[79] None of these advertisements specified *Emma*'s place of publication or revealed anything further about its author.

By February 1817, *Emma* was available from booksellers in cities beyond New York and Boston, including two separate bookshops in Providence, Rhode Island: those of Miller & Hutchens and J. Johnson. By April, buyers in Georgetown, near the nation's capital, had access to *Emma* at the premises of Geo. Richards. In distant Hallowell, Massachusetts (now Maine, following the establishment of that state in 1820) the *Hallowell Gazette* carried an ad for *Emma* placed by E. Goodale in April 1817 and another in November announcing the novel's sale at the Kennebec Book-Store.[80] *Emma* remained in stock at Eastburn & Co., the New York sellers who were first to advertise it, into 1818, and at W. B. Gilley into 1819, according to published catalogues of these sellers' respective holdings.[81]

As advertisements for *Emma* as a "new" book became less frequent, announcements began to appear of this novel's availability in circulating library collections. In May 1817, the Union Circulating Library in Georgetown initiated a long series of advertisements for recent additions to its catalogue, among them "Emma, a Novel : three volumes in two. By the author of 'Pride and Prejudice,' &c. &c." Mentions of *Emma* in a repeatedly published "Supplement to the Catalogue of the Union C. Library" continued into February 1819.[82] Three Massachusetts libraries added Carey's *Emma* between 1817 and 1819: the Washington Circulating Library in Boston, the Essex Circulating Library in Salem, and the Charlestown Circulating Library in Charlestown.[83]

Even as late as January 1821, *Emma* was still being touted as a new addition to libraries. In a striking coincidence, an announcement by "H Thayer" of Keene, New Hampshire concerning books "added for circulation at his Library" listed *Emma* immediately before *Precaution*, the Austen-inspired novel published anonymously in 1820 by James Fenimore Cooper.[84] Just a few months earlier, in November 1820, Ladd & Morrill of Belfast, Maine advertised *Emma* among many other titles on a list headed "BOOKS—

Cheap!!"[85] Apparently, *Emma* was available by then as a secondhand book.

Apart from this valuable evidence of the geographical spread of copies of Carey's *Emma*, it is not easy to trace the overall sales of the edition, because of a final gap in the archival record: no cost book survives that lists copies on hand and those sold. In contrast, John Murray's account book with records of his firm's sales of Austen's novels does exist, as does the cost book of Carey & Lea, the successor firm that published the first full American edition of Austen.[86]

Some tracking of the sales of *Emma* is possible through Carey's correspondence and financial records in 1817–1819. Wells & Lilly received eighty copies of *Emma* in January 1817, of which fifty-eight were still in stock by the end of that month.[87] Wells & Lilly sent thirty-three copies of *Emma* back to Carey, on his request, in August plus six more in September; fourteen remained on hand in 1818, of which thirteen were returned to Carey on 13 July 1819.[88] In August 1817, W. B. Gilley in New York requested "12 Emma" as part of a larger shipment.[89] Further research into the Carey archives and into the catalogues and borrowing records of circulating libraries may reveal more about the circulation of the 1816 Philadelphia *Emma*.

How did Americans first learn of Austen's authorship?

In England, Austen's name and authorship were first made public in the obituaries—eleven in total, according to Gilson—that were published after her death on 18 July 1817.[90] In America too, I have discovered, the name of the author of *Emma* was first brought forward in obituaries, reprinted from English originals, which appeared in newspapers in Boston and Providence as well as in one Boston monthly periodical. (Additional reprinted obituaries may yet be found.)

The earliest announcement in America of Austen's death and of her authorship was printed in the *Columbian Centinel*, a Boston newspaper, on 17 September 1817, under the heading "Obituary Notices of Eminent Europeans." The notice read as follows:

> In England, July 18, Miss JANE AUSTEN—authoress of "*Emma,*" "*Mansfield Park,*" "*Pride of* [*sic*] *Prejudice,*" and "*Sense and Sensibility.*" She was daughter to the Rev. George Austen, Rector of Steventon.—Her manners were gentle; her affections ardent; and she lived and died as became a humble Christian.[91]

This text is adapted from the obituary first published on 22 July 1817 in the *Courier,* which was subsequently reprinted in several other English newspapers.[92] Directly afterwards, the *Columbian Centinel* printed a much longer obituary for Madame de Staël, whose death, the paper noted, "is the subject of numerous eulogies in the European papers." This juxtaposition, together with the heading "Eminent Europeans," conveyed a decided sense of Austen's importance as a novelist.[93]

That the editors of the *Columbian Centinel* opted to include Austen in this obituary roundup suggests strongly that they expected their readers to be aware of the recently published *Emma.* The same newspaper had advertised *Emma* less than eight months before, on 1 February 1817, on behalf of Wells & Lilly. And *Emma* was still for sale in Boston in September 1817, judging from Wells & Lilly's ability to send copies back to Carey on his requests in August and September.

In Providence, likewise, one of the newspapers that had previously advertised *Emma* ran an obituary for its author. The 26 September 1817 issue of the *Rhode-Island American* reprinted the *Columbian Centinel*'s death notice word for word, including the misprint in the title of *Pride and Prejudice.* Here too the company Austen kept is noteworthy. Preceding her are several Americans; following her is

> Professor C. D. Ebeling of Hamburg, aged 78—celebrated for the extent and accuracy of his geographical works. He began his correspondence in America with the excellent Dr. Belknap of Boston, and did not refuse to condescend to correspond with Editors of publick papers. With a Rev. Editor in Salem, it is said he continued in constant communication until near his death. He was one of the most learned and indefatigable Scholars of that region of learning and application, Germany. He has received the merited honors of many of the literary societies of America.[94]

Though Austen had neither received such honors nor engaged in such correspondences, by implied comparison, her writings are also to be understood as worthy of notice by American readers.

Of course, the very presence of these obituaries in the US press helped cultivate interest in Austen and awareness of her works. The title *Mansfield Park* in particular was new to American eyes, since that novel received no reviews in British periodicals and (as a result) was not mentioned in Carey's advertising for *Emma*.

A different English obituary for Austen, that of the August 1817 *Gentleman's Magazine*, was reprinted in the second volume of *The Atheneum; Or, Spirit of the English Magazines*, a compilation of excerpts published in Boston by Munroe and Francis. According to a blurb on its title page, this new periodical aimed to preserve "a multitude of useful hints, observations, and facts, which otherwise might have disappeared," and thereby to serve as a "means of diffusing a general habit of reading throughout the nation."[95] In the midst of a multi-page "Necrology" (list of death notices) covering all of Europe can be found a brief notice, under the heading "AUTHOR OF 'EMMA,' &C.": "at Winchester, Miss Jane Austen, youngest daughter of Rev George Austen, Rector of Steventon, Hants, authoress of 'Emma,' 'Mansfield Park,' 'Pride and Prejudice,' and 'Sense and Sensibility.'"[96] The editors' choice to identify Austen as the "AUTHOR OF 'EMMA,' &C." indicates their awareness of how Americans would best know her.

The same firm, Munroe and Francis, subsequently identified *Emma* as "a Novel, by Miss Austin" in a catalogue they printed for the Boston Library Society.[97] As I will show in Chapter 2, the *Atheneum*'s reprinted obituary was also noticed by Jeremiah Smith, an owner of the 1816 Philadelphia *Emma*, who transcribed excerpts from this obituary into his copy of *Sense and Sensibility*. The notes on Austen's life and authorship that Smith placed in the Austen novels he owned bring to light further mentions of Austen in the US press in the years between the publication of Carey's *Emma* and Carey & Lea's first full edition of Austen.

In addition to the obituaries, the initial advertising of *Emma* in American newspapers had one more apparent outgrowth, several years later. In June 1826, the *Hallowell Gazette*—the Maine newspaper that had printed several advertisements for *Emma* in 1817, back when Hallowell was still part of Massachusetts—published a short commentary on a review of the new novel *Granby* (authored by Thomas Henry Lister) that had recently appeared in the *United States Literary Gazette*. "We protest," wrote the *Hallowell Gazette*, "against classing the novels of any period together. Nothing can be more absurd, in speaking of the peculiar and distinctive characteristics of a book, as he is speaking of *Granby*; unless he is prepared to connect Scott and miss Edgeworth, or lady Morgan and miss Austen, or Mackenzie and Godwin, in the same line, as he has already placed Mrs. Roche and miss Burney!"[98] That Austen's name arose in a critical discussion of *Granby* was no coincidence: in one chapter epigraph, a *Granby* character speaks dismissively of the works of both Edgeworth and Austen.[99] Given the prior availability of *Emma* in Hallowell, however, it seems likely that the writer of this commentary was indeed familiar with the writings of "miss Austen," and could reasonably expect some of the *Hallowell Gazette*'s readers to be so, too.

Advertisements, catalogues, obituaries, and commentaries brought *Emma* and Austen to the notice of the American public. But who actually bought Carey's reprinted edition? Did the owners of this *Emma* read it, and if so, what did they think of it? For answers to these intriguing questions, we must turn to the surviving copies of the edition and to the personal papers of their owners.

Notes

1   On the 1832–1833 Philadelphia edition printed by Carey & Lea and the relation of those volumes to the 1816 Philadelphia and London editions of *Emma*, see David Gilson, "Jane Austen's 'Emma' in America: Notes on the Text of the First and Second American Editions," *The Review of English Studies* n.s. 53: 212 (2002): 517–25; and Gilson, "The Early American Editions of Jane Austen," *Book Collector* 18 (1969): 340–52, reprinted in Gilson, *Jane Austen: Collected Articles and Introductions*, 23–37 (privately printed, 1998). 2016 also marked the bicentennial of the first publication of *Emma* in French translation: see Gillian Dow, "Translations," in *The Cambridge Companion to* Emma, ed. Peter Sabor, 166–85 (Cambridge: Cambridge University Press, 2015).

2   On the non-rarity of the First Folio and its status as a totem for moneyed collectors, see Emma Smith, *Shakespeare's First Folio: Four Centuries of an Iconic Book* (Oxford: Oxford University Press, 2016); on the Bay Psalm Book, see "Census of Copies of the Bay Psalm Book,

with Provenance, Sale, and Other Relevant Histories," *Sotheby's*, http://www.sothebys.com/en/auctions/2013/the-bay-psalm-book-sale-n09039/The-Bay-Psalm-Book/2013/10/census-of-copies-of-.html.

3   In contrast, digitized documents relating to the first English editions of Austen's novels are available and searchable on *British Fiction, 1800–1829: A Database of Production, Circulation & Reception* at http://www.british-fiction.cf.ac.uk/, a site created by Peter Garside, Jacqueline Belanger, and Sharon Ragaz.

4   Jan Fergus, *Jane Austen: A Literary Life* (New York: St. Martin's, 1991), 131, 145, 191–2, 159. See too Anthony Mandal's contextual study of Austen's publishing, *Jane Austen and the Popular Novel: The Determined Author* (Houndmills, Basingstoke: Palgrave Macmillan, 2007). For general background on the literary marketplace in which Austen published, see William St Clair, *The Reading Nation in the Romantic Period* (Cambridge: Cambridge University Press, 2004).

5   Katie Halsey, *Jane Austen and Her Readers, 1786–1945* (London: Anthem, 2012), 17. On books owned by Austen, see also Olivia Murphy, *Jane Austen the Reader: The Artist as Critic* (London: Palgrave Macmillan, 2013), 177–82 and David Gilson, "Jane Austen's Books," *Book Collector* 23 (1974): 547–50, reprinted in Gilson, *Jane Austen: Collected Articles and Introductions*, 73–89.

6   Juliette Wells, introduction to *Emma*, by Jane Austen, xiii–xxix (New York: Penguin Classics, 2015).

7   On the significance of Austen's involvement with the London publication of *Emma* and her correspondence with Stanier Clarke, see Wells, introduction to *Emma*.

8   See for example Catherine Gallagher, *Nobody's Story: The Vanishing Acts of Women Writers in the Marketplace, 1670–1820* (Berkeley: University of California Press, 1994).

9   Catherine Seville, *The Internationalisation of Copyright Law: Books, Buccaneers, and the Black Flag in the Nineteenth Century* (Cambridge: Cambridge University Press, 2006), 156. See also Robert A. Gross, "Introduction: An Extensive Republic," in *A History of the Book in America Vol. 2: An Extensive Republic: Print, Culture, and Society in the New Nation, 1790–1840*, ed. Robert A. Gross and Mary Kelley (Chapel Hill: American Antiquarian Society/University of North Carolina Press, 2010), 21–2; and Meredith L. McGill, *American Literature and the Culture of Reprinting, 1834–1853* (Philadelphia: University of Pennsylvania Press, 2003).

10 See Cathy N. Davidson, *Revolution and the Word: The Rise of the Novel in America* (New York: Oxford University Press, 1986), 17 and Joseph Rezek, *London and the Making of Provincial Literature: Aesthetics and the Transatlantic Book Trade* (Philadelphia: University of Pennsylvania Press, 2015), chapter one.

11 David Pearson, *Books as History*, rev. edn (London and New Castle, DE: The British Library and Oak Knoll Press, 2012), 22.

12 James N. Green, "The Rise of Book Publishing," in *A History of the Book in America Vol. 2*, ed. Gross and Kelley, 79. On early Americans' appetite for British-authored fiction, see Nina Baym, *Novels, Readers, and Reviewers: Responses to Fiction in Antebellum America* (Ithaca: Cornell University Press, 1984), chapters one and two.

13 Patricia M. Ard, "Betrayal: Jane Austen's Imaginative Use of America," *Persuasions On-Line* 33.1 (Winter 2012).

14 Jane Austen, "Opinions of *Emma*," in *Later Manuscripts*, ed. Janet Todd and Linda Bree, 235–9 (Cambridge: Cambridge University Press, 2008); "Profits of my Novels," in *Jane Austen's Fiction Manuscripts: A Digital Edition*, ed. Kathryn Sutherland (2010). See too Gilson's consideration of Austen's interest in her reception in "The Early American Editions."

15 Cathy Matson and James N. Green, "Ireland, America, and Mathew Carey: Special Issue Introduction," *Early American Studies* 11:3 (2013): 395. The articles in this special issue address the extent of Carey's contributions to business and to political and cultural life.

16 Green, "Rise," 84–5. For Carey's account of his own training in printing, of the incendiary political publications that led first to exile from Ireland and then to his emigration, and of the publication of which he was most proud—his own book *The Olive Branch*, first printed in 1814—see Mathew Carey, *Autobiography* (New York: Schwaab, 1942), 4–8, 118–22.

17 On the rise of Philadelphia as a publishing city, see Davidson, *Revolution and the Word*, 21–2.

18 Green, "Rise," 97.

19 Carey, *Autobiography*, 1, 24, 25.

20 James N. Green, *Mathew Carey: Publisher and Patriot* (Philadelphia: The Library Company of Philadelphia, 1985), 9–10, 17–20.

21 Green, *Mathew Carey*, 30.

22 [Henry C. Carey to Mathew Carey], n.d., Henry Carey Letterbook, 1815–1835, Manuscripts Division, William L. Clements Library, University of Michigan. The year that Henry wrote this particular letter can be deduced from his reference to his own age. All

transcriptions from manuscript sources reproduce the spelling, punctuation, capitalization, and formatting of the originals as exactly as possible.

23 See Rodney J. Morrison, "Henry C. Carey and American Economic Development," *Transactions of the American Philosophical Society* 76.3 (1986): 1–91.

24 Green, *Mathew Carey*, 20–4.

25 Carey, *Autobiography*, 3. On the importance of the category of "romance" to early American fiction, see Baym, *Novels, Readers, and Reviewers*, 225–35.

26 Mathew Carey, Diary, 1791–1821, Edward Carey Gardiner collection, Historical Society of Pennsylvania (hereafter HSP), Philadelphia, Pennsylvania, 227A/5c/26. On the contemporary rage for Scott's novels, see Annika Bautz, *The Reception of Jane Austen and Walter Scott: A Comparative Longitudinal Study* (London: Continuum, 2007) and Rezek, *London and the Making of Provincial Literature*, chapter two.

27 See for instance *Catalogue of Novels and Romances, Being Part of an Extensive Collection for Sale by M. Carey and Son* (n.p., n.d.), *EAI*; *Catalogue of an Extensive Collection of Books in Every Department of Ancient and Modern Literature, for Sale by M. Carey and Son* (Philadelphia: Thomas H. Palmer, 1818), *GoogleBooks*. I am grateful to David J. Black for stressing Mathew Carey's importance in promoting English women authors and intellectual women ("bluestockings") in Philadelphia. Personal conversation with author, 29 June 2016.

28 Green, "Rise," 103. See also Davidson, *Revolution and the Word*, 17.

29 Green, *Mathew Carey*, 22.

30 Carey, *Autobiography*, 101–2.

31 Green, *Mathew Carey*, 10.

32 See Kenneth E. Carpenter, "Libraries," in *A History of the Book in America Vol. 2*, ed. Gross and Kelley, 273–86.

33 Surviving volumes of Carey's diary cover overlapping spans of years, but none treats the crucial—for us—period of the publication of *Emma*. Only a few entries are present dated 1815 and none in 1816 or 1817 in Mathew Carey, Diary, 1810–1819, Edward Carey Gardiner collection, HSP, 227A/5c/27.

34 Gilson, "Jane Austen's 'Emma,'" 517. The issue of the *Quarterly Review* was misdated October 1815.

35 Fergus, *A Literary Life*, 158.

36 *Catalogue of Novels and Romances.*

37 See for instance Brian Southam, "*Emma*: England, Peace, and
    Patriotism," 2000, reprinted in *Jane Austen's Emma: A Casebook*, ed.
    Fiona J. Stafford, 269–91 (Oxford: Oxford University Press, 2007).

38 Accounts vol. 29, box 21, Mathew Carey Papers, 1785–1859,
    American Antiquarian Society, Worcester, Massachusetts (hereafter
    AAS). The AAS has recently made available a searchable database of
    the Mathew Carey papers: see http://www.americanantiquarian.org/
    careydatabase. On the significance of Longman & Co. in the British
    book trade, see Asa Briggs, "The Longmans and the Book Trade,
    c1730–1830," in *The Cambridge History of the Book in Britain,
    vol. 5: 1695–1830*, ed. Michael F. Suarez, S. J., and Michael L. Turner,
    397–412 (Cambridge: Cambridge University Press, 2007).

39 James N. Green, "Introduction to *Emma* Exhibit," lecture, Jane
    Austen Society of North America, Eastern Pennsylvania Region at the
    Library Company of Philadelphia, 19 September 2015. Green
    explained in this lecture that he had long presumed that Carey chose
    Emma because the English edition of that novel, alone among
    Austen's works, was then owned by the Library Company of
    Philadelphia, a membership organization to which Carey belonged
    and from which he often borrowed books in order to reprint them.

40 Green, "Introduction to *Emma* Exhibit."

41 A full digital facsimile of the 1816 Philadelphia *Emma* is available on
    Goucher College's open-access website "*Emma* in America": www.
    emmainamerica.org.

42 "Printers' File," compiled by Avis Clarke, AAS, n.d., MS. In a letter
    to Carey dated 15 April 1816 and addressed "My respected
    employer," Justice explained that after many years in Philadelphia,
    where he had worked for Carey, he had returned to Trenton, his
    home. In spite of being so "afflicted with the rumatic pains that I can
    scarcely walk," he apprised Carey, "Mr Cox and I are going to open a
    book store and printing office the first of May, and have taken an
    excellent stand by the Market house in Trenton." Joseph Justice to
    Mathew Carey, 15 April 1816, Lea & Febiger records 1785–1982,
    HSP, 227B/99. After the dissolution of Justice & Cox, Justice
    subsequently formed other partnerships in Trenton, while Horatio
    Cox moved to Ohio and became a lawyer ("Printers' File").

43 Prior to *Emma*, Justice & Cox printed *Paris Chit-Chat*, a translation
    from the French. Less than two weeks after the delivery of *Emma*,
    Carey commissioned Justice & Cox to print 500 copies of Northcote's
    Life of Sir Joshua Reynolds. [M. Carey] to Justice & Cox, 4
    November 1816, Mathew Carey letterbook, Lea & Febiger records,
    HSP, 227B/v. 30. For a list of printers employed by Carey in 1816, see

Karen Nipps, *Lydia Bailey: A Checklist of Her Imprints* (Philadelphia: Pennsylvania State University Press, 2013), 40, n. 72.

44 Justice & Cox to Henry C. Carey, 12 August 1816, Lea & Febiger records, HSP, 227B/99. (While all letters from Justice & Cox are in Justice's handwriting, he alternated between signing his own name and that of his firm.)

45 James Mosley, "The Technologies of Print," in *The Book: A Global History*, ed. Michael F. Suarez, S. J. and H. R. Wooudhuysen (Oxford: Oxford University Press, 2014), 139. A compositor who was setting type from manuscript also performed many of the tasks we now identify as editing, including regularizing spelling, usage, and paragraphing. On the role of the compositors of the first London editions of Austen's novels in producing what is now thought of as her style, see Kathryn Sutherland, *Jane Austen's Textual Lives: From Aeschylus to Bollywood* (Oxford: Oxford University Press, 2005), 157.

46 Justice & Cox to Henry C. Carey, [21?] August 1816; Justice & Cox to M. Carey, 19 October 1816, Lea & Febiger records, HSP, 227B/99. (While the day of the month is missing in Justice's salutation on the first of these letters, a note in a clerk's hand marked the letter as received on 22 August.) Wells & Lilly's correspondence with Carey in the autumn of 1816 also mentioned delays caused by "want of paper." Wells & Lilly to [M. Carey], 29 November 1816, Lea & Febiger records, HSP, 227B/102.

47 [M. Carey] to Justice & Cox, 30 September 1816; [M. Carey] to Justice & Cox, 4 November 1816, Mathew Carey letterbook, Lea & Febiger records, HSP, 227B/v. 20.

48 Justice & Cox to Henry C. Carey, 4 November 1816, Lea & Febiger records, HSP, 227B/99.

49 [M. Carey] to Justice & Cox, 30 November 1816, Mathew Carey letterbook, Lea & Febiger records, HSP, 227B/v. 230.

50 Justice & Cox to Henry C. Carey, 3 December 1816, Lea & Febiger records, HSP, 227B/99.

51 On the cost of shipping books, see Davidson, *Revolution and the Word*, 21.

52 Justice & Cox to Henry C. Carey, 11 December 1816, Lea & Febiger records, HSP, 227B/99.

53 [M. Carey] to Justice & Cox, 13 December 1816, Mathew Carey letterbook, Lea & Febiger records, HSP, 227B/v. 30.

54 Justice & Cox to Henry C. Carey, 17 December 1816, Lea & Febiger records, HSP, 227B/99.

55 Accounts vol. 30, box 21, Mathew Carey papers, AAS.

56 Gilson, *Collected Articles*, 13.

57 Rezek, *London and the Making of Provincial Literature*, 40–61.

58 [M. Carey] to Mason L. Weems, 30 December 1816, Mathew Carey letterbook, Lea & Febiger records, HSP, 227B/v. 30.

59 Justice & Cox to Henry C. Carey, 15 August 1816; [Justice & Cox] to Mathew Carey, 26 August 1816, Lea & Febiger records, HSP, 227B/99.

60 Accounts vol. 30, box 21, Mathew Carey papers, AAS. I am grateful to Mitch Fraas, Curator of Special Collections at the Kislak Center at the University of Pennsylvania, for first locating this record and to James N. Green for decoding it. To Wells & Lilly, Carey explained in September 1815, when the two firms were establishing the terms of their partnership, that his "Editions are uniformly small (most commonly 500)." [Mathew Carey] to Wells & Lilly, 21 September 1815, Mathew Carey letterbook, Lea & Febiger records, HSP, 227B/v. 29.

61 Fergus, *A Literary Life*, 159.

62 Accounts vol. 30, box 21, Mathew Carey papers, AAS. A 30 July 1817 bill from Wakeling & Allen included the binding of "25 Emma 2 Vols boards." Accounts vol. 30, box 22, Mathew Carey papers, AAS.

63 Gross, "Introduction," 28–9.

64 Gilson, "Jane Austen's 'Emma,'" 520.

65 Gilson, *Bibliography*, 99, "Jane Austen's 'Emma,'" 521–4.

66 A purchaser who wished to commission finer binding would seek a copy in boards, which were easily removed and replaced with better materials. "A Gentleman who wishes a copy of Ramsay's M. S. in better bind[in]g than those sent me has requested a copy in bds," that is, in boards, wrote W. B. Gilley to M. Carey, 17 March 1817, Lea & Febiger records, HSP, 227B/104.

67 *Catalogue of an Extensive Collection*, 115.

68 James N. Green, email to author, 7 January 2016.

69 Green addresses cooperation and competition among early American publishers in "Rise," 91–9.

70 [Mathew Carey] to Wells & Lilly, 26 December 1815, Mathew Carey letterbook, Lea & Febiger records, HSP, 227B/v. 29.

71 Wells & Lilly to M. Carey and Son, 23 August 1817, Lea & Febiger records, HSP, 227B/108.

72 [Mathew Carey] to W. B. Gilley, December 1816; [Mathew Carey] to D. Longworth, 27 December 1816; [Mathew Carey] to Thos. Kirk,

27 December 1816; [Mathew Carey] to Van Winkle & Wiley, 27 December 1816; [Mathew Carey] to W. T. Williams, 24 [miscopy for 27] December 1816, Lea & Febiger records, HSP, 227B/v. 30. Some of these publishers were engaged in their own entrepreneurial reprinting of English titles. As Seville notes, "[i]n 1817 Thomas Kirk, a New York publisher, offered a third of his net profits to John Murray, for early sheets of British works. Kirk had previously published British works without payment." Seville, *Internationalisation of Copyright Law*, 156–7.

73 *The Monthly Literary Advertiser*, no. 17 (Philadelphia: January 1817), 1, EBSCO*host*.

74 "Unsigned Notice, *Monthly Review*," July 1816, reprinted in B. C. Southam, ed., *Jane Austen: The Critical Heritage* (London: Routledge & Kegan Paul, 1968), 70.

75 Because the *Augustan Review*'s consideration of *Emma* has not been reprinted, I will quote it at some length. It begins, "[t]here is a remarkable sameness in the productions of this author. The Emma and Knightley of the work before us, are exactly the Elizabeth and Davey [*sic*] of 'Pride and Prejudice;' the prototypes of which were the hero and heroine in 'Sense and Sensibility.' Nor is there more variety in the subordinate characters, or the incidents; both are of a description that occurs every day in the rank of life to which they are allotted. Yet the author will always interest and please, and this exactly from the causes which we are persuaded are beyond all others desirable to her. From a certain elegance of mind, and acquaintance with the usages of polite society, from a just sense of duty which makes her show the performance of it, in all its bearings, to be its own reward, and from that rational view of happiness which enables her to teach her readers to look for it where it is certain to be found. 'In the mild majesty of private life,' in the culture of intellectual endowments, and in the exercise of the social affections, we find nothing ridiculed that ought not be ridiculed; no undue consequence annexed to things which have not consequence in themselves; and every person has his place, and his influence assigned him in the scale of society, with the propriety and good sense which the author is fond of exhibiting as the characteristics of her heroines." In conclusion, the reviewer notes, "our author shews so much skill in agreeably entangling the slender materials which she brings before us to excite conjecture, that we cannot but think that a greater variety of incidents would, in such hands as hers, well supply the place of some of that colloquial familiarity and minuteness to which she has hitherto perhaps too much confined herself." "*Emma*: a Novel," *Augustan Review* No. XIII Vol. II (May 1816): 484–6, *GoogleBooks*. *Emma*

appeared in a list of "Works recently published" in the previous issue
of the *Augustan Review*, No. XII Vol. II (April 1816).

76 Justice & Cox to M. Carey and Son, 17 January 1817, Lea & Febiger
records, HSP, 227B/105.

77 *Catalogue of Novels and Romances*; *Catalogue of an Extensive
Collection*, 115.

78 *Catalogue of an Extensive Collection*, 115.

79 James Eastburn, *Evening Post* [New York] 30 December 1816: [3]; Van
Winkle & Wiley, *New-York Courier* 31 December 1816: [3];
Longworth, *New-York Courier* 10 January 1817: [3]; W. B. Gilley,
New-York Courier 3 January 1817: [3]; W. B. Gilley, *Commercial
Advertiser* [New York] 30 January 1817: [4]; Wells & Lilly, *Columbian
Centinel* [Boston] 1 February 1817: [3]; Wells & Lilly, *New-England
Palladium* [Boston] 7 February 1817: [4]. All sources from *AHN*.

80 Miller & Hutchens, *Providence Patriot* 8 February 1817: [3]; J.
Johnson, *Rhode-Island American* 14 February 1817: [1]; Geo.
Richards, *Daily National Intelligencer* 5 April 1817: [1]; E. Goodale,
Hallowell Gazette [Massachusetts] 30 April 1817: [1]; Kennebec
Book-Store, *Hallowell Gazette* [Massachusetts] 12 November 1817:
[1]. All sources from *AHN*.

81 *A Catalogue of Books for 1818; Including Many Rare and Valuable
Articles in Ancient and Modern Literature, Now on Sale by James
Eastburn & Co. at the Literary Rooms, Broadway, Corner of Pine-
Street, New-York at the Prices Affixed* (New York: Printed by Abraham
Paul, May 1818), GoogleBooks; *Catalogue of Recent Publications, for
sale by W. B. Gilley* (New York: J. [S]eymour, 1819), *EAI, Series 2*.

82 Union C. Library, *Daily National Intelligencer* [Washington] 1 May
1817: [1]; "Supplement to the Catalogue of the Union C. Library,"
National Messenger [Georgetown] 17 February 1819: [1]. Both
sources from *AHN*.

83 *Catalogue of the Washington Circulating Library* (Boston: T. G. Bangs,
1817), 33; *Essex Circulating Library Catalogue of Books, for sale or
circulation by Cushing & Appleton* (Salem: Thomas C. Cushing, 1818),
38; *Catalogue of the Charlestown Circulating Library* (Boston: True &
Weston for T. M. Baker, 1819), 15. All sources from *EAI, Series 2*.

84 On *Precaution*, see Barbara Alice Mann, *The Cooper Connection: The
Influence of Jane Austen on James Fenimore Cooper* (New York:
AMS Press, 2014).

85 H. Thayer, *New Hampshire Sentinel* 27 January 1821: [4]; Ladd &
Morrill, *Hancock Gazette* [Belfast, Maine] 16 November 1820: [4].
Both sources from *AHN*.

86 Murray's account book, among other records of his firm's dealings with Austen and with her family, is held in the John Murray Archives at the National Library of Scotland in Edinburgh. See David Kaser, ed., *The Cost Book of Carey & Lea, 1825–1838* (Philadelphia: University of Pennsylvania Press, 1963).

87 Accounts, vol. 31, box 23, Mathew Carey papers, AAS.

88 Wells & Lilly to M. Carey & Son, 14 August 1817; Wells & Lilly to M. Carey & Son, 8 September 1817, Lea & Febiger records, HSP, 227B/108; Accounts, vol. 31, box 23 and vol. 39, box 24, Mathew Carey papers, AAS.

89 W. B. Gilley to M. Carey & Son, 2 August 1817, Lea & Febiger records, HSP, 227B/104.

90 Gilson, *Bibliography*, 470–1; Gilson, "Obituaries," in *The Jane Austen Companion*, ed. J. David Grey (New York: Macmillan, 1986), 320–21. The "Biographical Notice" appended to Murray's December 1817 publication of *Northanger Abbey* and *Persuasion* apprised a wider audience of Austen's authorship and supplied further details about her life.

91 "Obituary Notices of Eminent Europeans," *Columbian Centinel*, 17 September 1817: [4], *AHN*.

92 Gilson, *Bibliography*, 470, which catalogues the *Courier* obituary as M5 iii and hypothesizes that its text was written by Austen's surviving siblings. The full text of this obituary ran as follows: "DIED. On the 18th inst. at Winchester, Miss Jane Austen, youngest daughter of the late Rev. George Austen, Rector of Steventon, in Hampshire, and the Authoress of Emma, Mansfield Park, Pride and Prejudice, and Sense and Sensibility. Her manners were most gentle; her affections ardent; her candor was not to be surpassed, and she lived and died as became a humble Christian." Gilson, *Bibliography*, 470. Omitted for the American publication were the city of Austen's death (Winchester); the identification of her as the "youngest" Austen daughter; the description of her father as "the late Rev."; the specification of Steventon's location in the county of Hampshire; the modification "most gentle" in the description of Austen's manners, and a fourth phrase of personal description: "her candor was not to be surpassed."

93 On Austen and Staël, see Chris Viveash, "Jane Austen and Madame de Staël," *Persuasions* 13 (1991): 39–40.

94 [Untitled death notice], *Rhode-Island American* 26 September 1817: [3], *AHN*.

95 *The Atheneum; Or, Spirit of the English Magazines*, vol. II (October 1817 to April 1818): i. As Andie Tucker points out, in this era, "most

of the productions that rejoiced in the title 'magazine' were not
repositories of a vigorous new American literature but rather pale
imitations of (or unabashed lootings from) the British reviews."
"Newspapers and Periodicals," in *A History of the Book in America
Vol. 2*, ed. Gross and Kelley, 397. *The Atheneum* is not to be confused
with the British periodical *The Athenaeum*, which in 1831 printed an
article on Austen: see David Gilson, "Jane Austen and the *Athenaeum*
Again," *Persuasions* 19 (1997): 20–2.

96 *The Atheneum*, 488.

97 *Catalogue of Books in the Boston Library, June 1824* (Boston:
Munroe and Francis, 1824), 23, *GoogleBooks*.

98 "'Granby,'" *Hallowell Gazette* [Maine] 21 June 1826: [3], *AHN*.

99 On *Granby*'s mention of and relationship to Austen, see Edward
Copeland, *The Silver Fork Novel: Fashionable Fiction in the Age of
Reform* (Cambridge: Cambridge University Press, 2012), 44.

2

Tales of Three Copies:

Books, Owners, and Readers

Each of the six surviving copies of the 1816 Philadelphia *Emma* is a unique artifact, thanks to choices made by its owners and readers. Some purchasers selected, and paid extra for, special styles of binding. Some added their signatures or bookplates, thus helping to establish the volumes' history of ownership or, to use the book-historical term, their "provenance." Some readers wrote in—annotated—the volumes.[1]

In addition to the evidence of ownership and reading visible in the volumes themselves, valuable information about reading practices emerges from additional sources left by the books' owners, such as letters, diaries, and account books. (A summary of the physical attributes of the six copies and relevant contextual sources concerning their original owners appears in the Appendix.) Just two of the surviving copies—those now held at King's College Library, Cambridge University and at the Beinecke Library, Yale University—bear owners' signatures that cannot be traced. The other four copies all yield stories of the individuals, families, and historical circumstances in which the 1816 Philadelphia *Emma* was first bought and read. Among those four are the two I rediscovered: those now at Winterthur Library and Dartmouth College.

Biographies of books, as investigations like these are known, are typically created for publications of great historical importance: Copernicus' *De revolutionibus*, for example, or Shakespeare's First Folio.[2] As a humble, unremarkable American reprint, the 1816

Philadelphia *Emma* is an unusual candidate for such an exploration. To recover the missing history of Austen's earliest American readers, however, there is no better way than to pursue the traces they left in the books they read.

The owners and readers of the 1816 Philadelphia *Emma* included both prominent people—the E. I. du Pont family of Delaware; Jeremiah Smith, chief justice of New Hampshire; Christian, Countess of Dalhousie, wife of the governor-in-chief of British North America—and ordinary ones: Rhode Island circulating-library patrons who wrote in the volumes they borrowed. Wide-ranging, too, is the evidence of reading left by those who interacted with the 1816 Philadelphia *Emma*. The du Pont sisters' personal writings reveal them to have been avid readers, who, typically for their time, were more interested in the bestselling novels of Walter Scott and in the poetry of the scandalous Lord Byron than in the anonymously published *Emma*. In contrast, Jeremiah Smith's annotated volumes of *Emma* establish him as the first known American enthusiast of Austen. Like fans today, he was eager to read more of her novels and to glean as much information as possible about her life. Much less appreciative were the circulating-library readers, whose annotations confirm that, decades before Twain, Austen's writings simply did not appeal to some Americans.

In their physical condition, the du Pont, Smith, and circulating library copies of *Emma* range from beautifully preserved, to damaged, to nearly destroyed. From them, we glimpse the full spectrum of early American readers' responses to Austen, from apparent indifference, to great interest, to distaste.

Lovers of books, if not of Austen: the du Pont sisters of Delaware

The du Pont copy of *Emma*, which is now held by Winterthur Library, is in excellent condition both externally and internally (see figure 2.1). The volumes are bound in two-tone calf leather: medium brown on the spines, with a darker, marbled-looking calf leather covering the boards (the front and back covers). A very delicate pattern of blind-stamping decorates the edges of the lighter leather. A volume number is stamped in gilt in the middle of each spine, among seven pairs of narrow gilt horizontal lines. The first volume of this copy retains a spine label in a dark red leather, which reads "EMMA" in gilt capital letters.[3] Signatures on the top right of both volumes' title pages identify the first owner: "E. I. Du Pont."[4] In a similar, but perhaps not identical hand, "Du Pont." also appears on the top of each left-hand endpaper. The only other indication of use is a green

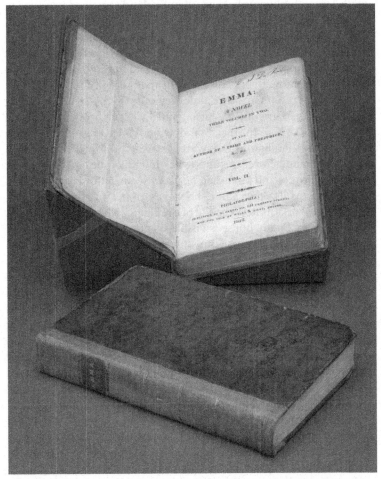

FIGURE 2.1 *E. I. du Pont's copy of* Emma. *Courtesy of the Winterthur Library: Printed Book and Periodical Collection.*

three-cent US stamp bearing the head of George Washington, which is stuck between pages 262 and 263 of volume two.[5]

In the mid-twentieth century, these two attractive volumes were put on display in one of the many period rooms at Winterthur Museum that were painstakingly furnished and decorated by Henry Francis du Pont, who transformed the site from a historic family home to a museum. The significance of this rare copy of *Emma* was hidden in plain sight from the American museum-going public, while Austen bibliographers based in England remained unaware of this copy's existence.[6]

The elegant signatures in this copy of *Emma* are those of Éleuthère Irénée du Pont (1771–1834), who was known as Irénée to his compatriots and as "Papa" to his eight children. In the wake of the French Revolution, Irénée emigrated from France in 1800 along with his father, Pierre Samuel du Pont de Nemours (1739–1817), a leading member of the Paris intelligentsia, and his elder brother Victor du Pont (1767–1827). In the Brandywine Valley, just beyond the outskirts of Wilmington, Delaware, Irénée established himself as a successful manufacturer of gunpowder. In France, he had worked for a time as a printer and publisher; he was also an enthusiastic botanist. Eleutherian Mills, the name he gave to his family home and gunpowder works, is now the site of the Hagley Museum and Library. There, Irénée's family house is visible, as are some of his gardens. E. I. du Pont de Nemours and Company, which he founded in 1802, still exists as the international conglomerate widely known as DuPont.[7]

In France, Pierre Samuel, the family patriarch, had developed an interest in books as part of his self-transformation from the son of a watchmaker to a writer praised by Voltaire. For him, as for his sons, an extensive family library represented the most important possible investment in intellect and culture. Together, the three du Pont men formed an impressive book collection of approximately twenty-two hundred titles, *Emma* among them. According to Ewald Rink, who has reconstructed the extent and nature of the du Ponts' family library, about a third of the titles personally owned by Irénée were literary in nature, and of those, half were in French and half in English.[8] Since, as Rink points out, Irénée never became fluent in English, the latter group of books most likely served to "satisfy the wishes of his family for educational and recreational reading."[9]

Recreational reading *Emma* could certainly have been, especially for Irénée's daughters. Yet this copy's extraordinarily good state of preservation, together with its lack of markings beyond the owner's signature, raises suspicions. Was this *Emma* ever, in fact, read by a member of the du Pont family?

That Irénée's daughters were keenly interested both in reading and in the preservation of beloved books is evident from marks of ownership they added to some of the other copies bearing their father's signature. On the right-hand flyleaf of the first volumes of the novels *Rhoda* (1816) and *Discipline* (1815), the signature "V. E. Bauduy—" appears in the upper right, as does, in the middle of the page, the following dedication:

Victorine E. Foster
        from aunt Sophie

        Louviers
        Jany 17th 1878[10]

"V. E. Bauduy" was Irénée's eldest daughter Victorine Elizabeth (1792–1861), who was born in France and emigrated, with her father, to the United States in 1801. Figure 2.2 shows the portrait of her painted by Rembrandt Peale in 1813, the year Victorine married Ferdinand Bauduy, a fellow French émigré. After her husband died in early 1814, only a few months into their marriage, Victorine returned to her family home, Eleutherian Mills, where she lived for the rest of her life. In loco parentis during the indisposition of her mother, Sophie Madeleine Dalmas, Victorine directed the education of her many younger siblings; she also ran a Sunday school for children of her father's employees.[11] Following French custom, Victorine was respected as the matriarch of the family after the deaths of her mother in 1828 and her father in 1834. A dedicated reader and the most intellectual of the sisters, Victorine listed six hundred titles in her possession in 1846.[12]

"Sophie" was Irénée's youngest daughter Sophie Madeleine (1810–1888), named for her mother and born in the United States. In 1833, Sophie married her first cousin, Victor's son Samuel Francis (1803–1865), and moved to Victor's family estate, Louviers, which was located across the Brandywine Creek from Eleutherian Mills. Samuel Francis, known as Frank, subsequently became Rear Admiral of the US Navy. The Victorine E. Foster to whom Sophie dedicated the copies of *Rhoda* and *Discipline* was her niece Victorine

FIGURE 2.2 *Victorine du Pont Bauduy (Mme Ferdinand Bauduy), portrait by Rembrandt Peale (1813), Delaware, oil paint on canvas. Courtesy of Winterthur Museum; bequest of Henry Francis du Pont, 1961.709.*

(1849–1934), daughter of Irénée's second-youngest son, Henry (1812–1889).

Sophie's dedication of these two books to the younger Victorine is consistent with her interest, late in life, in the preservation and distribution of family papers.[13] Sophie's concern with the dispersal of family books also contributed to the exceptional survival rate of the du Ponts' original library. This outcome Rink has attributed to the family in general having "taken good care of its heritage," without acknowledging the important role played by the du Pont women in particular.[14]

The presence of Victorine's signature and Sophie's dedication in *Rhoda* and *Discipline* indicates that the two sisters, at separate times and perhaps in different ways, valued these particular novels. The lack of comparable markings in the du Pont *Emma* is a less definite sign. Perhaps *Emma* was unread by the sisters; perhaps it was read by them, but unloved, or merely forgotten.

Aside from the commitment to learning represented by his library, Irénée was a notoriously frugal man who put his profits back into his business and was often in debt.[15] Why would he pay to buy a novel that no one in his family seems to have been especially interested in reading? The answer lies in Irénée's network of acquaintances among fellow businessmen in the Wilmington-Philadelphia area, prominent among whom was Mathew Carey. As Rink has observed, Irénée "had a close relationship with the publishing firm of Mathew Carey and its successor, and received a substantial part of their publications."[16]

When and how the du Pont copy of *Emma* reached Eleutherian Mills is unknown. The volumes may have been sent by Carey or brought home from Philadelphia by a family member. All the du Ponts frequently traveled to Philadelphia, which was an easy trip by steamboat from Wilmington unless the river was frozen.[17] Many of the children also received some formal schooling in Philadelphia.

Irénée's account books and receipt files include some entries for book purchases and binding costs. Almost never, however, are titles, authors, or specific recipients listed. A rare exception is a receipt for goods purchased in 1815 from Mathew R. Lockerman, which includes entries for "Binding 2 Small books . . . 50 [cents] each," for a "Volume Blairs Sermons (<u>Victorine</u>)," and for a "Drawing book (<u>Evilinia</u>)."[18] (Evelina, who lived from 1796 to 1863, was Irénée's second eldest surviving daughter.) More typically, an entry in Irénée's July 1817 accounts for "Sundries" lists a $2.75 payment for "des livres reliés," that is, for unbound books.[19]

Most likely, the du Pont *Emma* was bought already bound, as one of the fifty "full bound" copies prepared for Carey by Wakeling & Allen and sold for $2.50, as opposed to the copies in boards priced at $2 (see Chapter 1). As befits a man who valued knowledge more than show,

Irénée did not rebind his books. The copies of *Rhoda* and *Discipline* that bear his signature are even more plainly bound than his *Emma*: both have black leather spines and corners, minimal gilt decoration, and marbled boards. Since binding "2 small books" cost a dollar, as given on the 1815 Lockerman receipt, the parsimonious Irénée would surely have opted for a bound version of *Emma* that cost only fifty cents more than a copy in boards. Strongly supporting the hypothesis that Irénée's copy of *Emma* arrived fully bound is the presence of a twenty-four-page sales catalogue of Carey's dated October 1816, at the back of volume two: an element that is unique among the surviving six copies of this edition. An owner sending out volumes for custom rebinding would be unlikely to request that such a catalogue be retained.

The family culture that this copy of *Emma* entered was cosmopolitan in outlook, in spite of the country retirement of Eleutherian Mills. As members of the new American manufacturing class, Irénée's daughters enjoyed conversation with their father's many prominent acquaintances, as well as with their large extended family. In addition to excursions to Philadelphia and New York, Washington and Baltimore, the sisters "traveled the world in books," in the words of Betty-Bright Low and Jacqueline Hinsley, authors of a study of Sophie's youthful writings and drawings.[20]

Crucially, Irénée—"Papa"—encouraged his daughters' intellectual curiosity. Central to their education was their access to the abundant family library, which in Hinsley's judgment "probably compared favorably with the few good American university libraries and the even fewer private collections" at the time.[21] In this sense, the du Pont sisters were even more fortunate than Jane Austen herself, whose father—atypically for the time—allowed his daughters full access to his 500-book collection.[22]

The domestic scene in which the du Pont daughters read is best glimpsed through the many surviving drawings and watercolors of the youngest daughter, Sophie, which date principally from 1823–1833. As evident in figure 2.3, Sophie's "carics" (caricatures) show intimate, lively scenes full of the activities familiar to us from Austen's life and novels: sketching, writing, embroidery, piano-playing, dancing, amateur theatricals, and, of course, reading.[23] In typical early nineteenth-century multi-tasking, one sister often read aloud to the others while they drew or sewed.[24]

Given the family's origins, French books played a significant role in the sisters' reading. Victorine and Evelina, both born before the family's

FIGURE 2.3 *"The Pleasures of Society," drawing by Sophie M. du Pont (1827). Courtesy of Hagley Museum and Library.*

emigration, read French with native fluency, while all of the siblings conversed and corresponded in French with their parents and older relatives. The du Pont book collection reflects the family's bilingualism, with copies of Samuel Richardson's novels *Clarissa* and *Sir Charles Grandison* in French translation, and some titles—including Frances Burney's very popular novel *Evelina*—in both French and English.[25]

Their exceptional French aside, the sisters' literary knowledge and tastes were comparable to those of the best-informed women reading in English at the time. According to Hinsley's comprehensive study, the du Pont sisters' reading during the period 1810–1835 encompassed the novels of Samuel Richardson, Maria Edgeworth, Frances Burney, Hannah More, and many other authors, in addition to prose, poetry, and plays. American authors too the sisters read, among them James Fenimore Cooper. Their reading was made possible both by the books at home and also by membership in circulating libraries. Through subscriptions to periodicals, the sisters kept up with current ideas about literary tastes and trends, not all of which they shared. To quote Hinsley, in spite of the "quiet seclusion" in which they lived, the sisters were fully on par with "their male contemporaries of similar intelligence and privilege," and thus deserve to be considered members of the American intellectual elite of the day.[26]

The du Pont sisters' self-cultivation did not lead, however, to ambitions for public display. Instead, the sisters embraced, with intention, a contemporary idea regarding the purpose of women's intellectual and moral education: to exert positive influence on their families and communities. As Hinsley puts it, the sisters defined "for themselves their role as agents of social and moral uplift": the knowledge that they "gained from formal schooling and avid reading, besides enriching their private lives, found expression in a sense of responsibility for the material success and moral uprightness of the men of their family and a concern for the instruction of the children of their father's workmen."[27]

Discussions of reading and book purchases in the sisters' letters vividly convey the importance that their choices held for them, regarding both what to read and in what form to read it. Their literary tastes were decided and well known to each other. "Since you cannot bear Mrs Radcliffes descriptions, how should you relish mine?" wrote Victorine to Evelina in 1812.[28] Victorine herself strongly disliked Shakespeare. "I believe we go tonight to the play," she wrote Evelina from New York in December 1813, shortly after her marriage. "It is Shakespeare's comedy of Much a do about nothing and Cinderella. I would far sooner prefer one of Diamond's plays, I do not like Shaks—."[29] Years later, Sophie, whose literary tastes were shaped by Victorine's, described how "disgusted and shocked by the mass of absurdities, & worse" she was by reading Shakespeare.[30] More acceptable to the sisters, perhaps, was their family's copy of *Beauties of Shakespeare*, an ornately bound book of excerpts that was typical of early nineteenth-century efforts to purge objectionable portions of Shakespeare, especially for female readers.[31]

Victorine viewed literature as a source of inspiration for women and men alike. To her naval cousin (and future brother-in-law) Frank, she wrote in 1818:

> I was reading some time ago one of Lord Byron's poems and I was struck with some handsome lines on a ship, which I think so applicable to the Franklin that I send them to you thinking you will be pleased with them __
>
> > [How] gloriously her gallant course she goes!
> > Her white wings flying—never from her foes.
> > She walks the waters like a thing of life
> > And seems to dare the elements to strife __
> > Who would not brave the battle fire __ the wreck __
> > To move the monarch of her peopled deck?___
>
> I have never heard you say whether you were fond of poetry but I thought the above description would strike you as fine & I am

certain you enter into the sentiments of the last two lines. Have
you an opportunity of procuring books and do you feel inclined
to read often? I fear that you are so situated as to make it
inconvenient to read much, yet I would recommend you to
cultivate a taste for litterature [*sic*], you will have the more merit
if you surmount the difficulties you have to encounter.[32]

Victorine's quotation is from the first canto (section) of Byron's
very popular poem *The Corsair* (1814), which Jane Austen too
read.[33] In the next chapter, we will see another perspective from
1818 on the value of reading for military men, courtesy of Lord
Dalhousie.

While Victorine advised her cousin Frank to read, she overtly
directed the reading of her younger sisters. As the eldest daughter of
an often indisposed mother, she took a quasi-maternal role in this
respect. Her monitoring of Eleuthera (1806–1876), who was fourteen
years Victorine's junior, demonstrated particular concern. In 1818,
when Eleuthera was twelve, Victorine instructed Evelina to tell
their younger sister that "she may read Corneille's tragedy of
Pompey & Voltaire's Brutus or the death of Cesar_ Some of the
tragedies such as Le Cid and Zaire I had rather she should not read
till she is older."[34]

Eleuthera's exposure to fiction raised especially strong worries
for Victorine, as is evident in an agitated sequence of letters between
the two sisters from late March to early April 1821, when the
younger girl was at school in Philadelphia. Eleuthera reported
that she had been asked by a teacher to read aloud from a novel, a
genre that she knew her elder sister thought inappropriate for a girl
in her mid-teens. Eleuthera's trepidation is evident in her many
crossings-out:

Yesterday afternoon Mrs Hughs made all the young Ladies read
to her in a novel called Kenilworth. I read like the rest for you
know I could not refuse ~~well~~. I am sure you will not be displeased
for I only read one page. Mrs Hughs is a great admirer of Scott's
novels. She asked me if I had ever read any of them. I told her no.
She asked if I would like to read some as she was going to get
Rob Roy and two or three others but I said I never read any
books but those you chose for me. She said she was sure you
could have no objections but she has not spoken about it since

and I am sure ~~it will~~ I dont want to read any ~~so~~ ^in the meantime
one page out of 300 ~~will~~ can not do me the least harm.[35]

As I noted in Chapter 1, *Kenilworth* was published by Mathew
Carey on 10 March 1821. Mrs. Hughs evidently lost no time in
obtaining a copy, as one would expect from a "great admirer of
Scott's novels."
As Eleuthera anticipated, Victorine objected strongly.

I am rather surprized that Mrs H. should chose [*sic*] to make her
scholars read out of novels when so many more useful books
might be found _ Scott's novels are certainly among the very best
and I intend you shall read them, though not at present, because
I think some time hence you will enjoy them more therefor I
hope you will not think of reading any of them now, even if M^rs
H. should have them in the house and have them at the young
Ladies' disposal _ you know my love I have nothing so much at
heart as your own good, therefore I make no doubt you will
willingly follow my advice _ as to the page you may have to read
aloud now and then I cannot of course object to it, though I must
own I believe you will reap but little amusement and no
instruction whatever from it _ If Mrs H. were to request you to
read aloud one of these novels regularly, I would have you tell
her frankly that you cannot because you know I would not
approve of it. Let not false shame or a fear of giving offense ever
prevent you from doing what you feel to be right . . .[36]

Victorine's homily continued for several more lines. She reiterated
her opposition in a subsequent letter: "I do not like M^rs H_'s plan of
making her scholars read novels to her and I beg you to let me
know if she continues it regularly, because if it was necessary I
should write to her on the subject."[37] Fortunately, the contretemps
was soon at an end: Eleuthera assured her sister that she "need not
be in the least afraid of Mrs Hughs making us read novels for the
books she expects are on their way."[38]
    In her own reading, too, Victorine considered it essential to
balance "amusement" and "instruction": that is, pleasure and moral
improvement. Her moral exertion in reining in her own imagination
comes across clearly in an 1814 letter to Evelina about her responses
to Maria Edgeworth's writings:

I am reading Miss Edgeworth's Moral Tales, they are very pretty indeed__ I was disappointed in the tales of Wonder _ it is generally the case when we form high expectations _ It should be our constant endeavor in this world to check that enthusiasm which paints every thing in too glowing colours_ Nothing matches our expectations, and in all our pursuits we are baffled if we listen too eagerly to the suggestions of fancy_ I have found this to be the case in every thing.[39]

Victorine's vigorous abjuration here of "fancy"—imagination— differentiates her decisively from Austen's "imaginist," Emma Woodhouse.[40] Indeed, given the moral discipline that Victorine worked to cultivate in herself and her siblings, it is hard to conceive of her liking the self-involved Emma.

Yet Victorine was no Mary Bennet of *Pride and Prejudice*, always moralizing. To Evelina, Victorine confessed how thrilled she was by *Glenarvon* (1816), a novel written by Byron's former lover Lady Caroline Lamb:

I have been reading with Anna a part of the new novel Glenarvon . . . . I cannot tell you the feelings this work excites, would you believe it? The interest is excep[illegible] although all the principal characters are so vicious that the very soul revolts from such depravity_ The heroin [sic] is something in the style of Rhoda but far far worse _ The Hero, and can it possibly be "Lord Byron," the hero is such as your imagination never could paint! . . . . Evelina I know you are ready to scold me for reading such a book, indeed I will not finish it, & Anna & I have just looked to the end because we would not read the 2ᵈ. Volume_ yet the language is extremely fine indeed the book has no other recommendation, and it is a pity to see such talents as those of the author wasted in such a manner __[41]

In this letter, Victorine sounds more like the thrill-seeking female readers in Austen's *Northanger Abbey* than like her usual restrained self, the source of improving recommendations for her siblings.

In contrast to the moral weight of decisions about what to read, the sisters' choices about book purchases depended chiefly on taste. Writing from Washington in 1812, Victorine told Evelina that

Papa bought us some letters on <u>Washington city</u> for us to read upon the road .... Papa has also purchased me the exiles of Siberia, a pretty novel translated from the French, and a volume of poems by Walter Scott which we never saw before, I intend to present it to you my dear sister, at my return; it was for you I requested papa to buy it as I well know your partiality for that author, what will charm you the most is that <u>his</u> picture is at the beginning, but for gracious sake dont form too high expectations ~~for~~ or you will be disappointed.[42]

Evident here is both Victorine's intimate knowledge of her sister's literary preferences and Irénée's willingness to buy books selected by his daughters.

On other occasions, the sisters determined their own book purchases, in which decisions about binding played an important role for the sake of both appearance and price. To Evelina, Victorine wrote from Philadelphia in 1821:

I went this morning in several book stores and enquired for Scott's poems ~~but~~ I did not find any bound but I could easily bespeak them in whatever way you wish to have them. They are dearer however than what Wilson had told me, and the price is from $1.75 to $2 per volume_ I saw a great variety of handsome bindings, but I am really at a loss what choice to make as I am afraid not to hit yours & brother's tastes_ Would you like them stained dark red like Eleuthera's edition of Cowper or else bright yellow something like the small edition of La Fontaine I have in my little library? I wish you would write to me on the subject dear sister, and tell me what you would prefer.[43]

When selecting an edition of Wordsworth as a gift for a sister-in-law, too, Victorine pondered the various costs of American versus English editions and of different levels of elegance in binding before settling on a relatively inexpensive option, the English edition bound in blue muslin. Among the bookshops Victorine visited in her quest was that of Mathew Carey.[44]

Victorine kept lists of her yearly reading. Several of these survive, the earliest dated 1813. On only one does an Austen novel appear: *Mansfield Park*, in 1857, the year Victorine turned sixty-five.[45] In the same year, she recorded having read Elizabeth Gaskell's newly published *Life of Charlotte Brontë*; Victorine had read Gaskell's novel *North and South* in 1855. In the following two years, 1858–1859, Victorine read Brontë's novels *The Professor* (published posthumously in 1857) and *Jane Eyre* (1847), along with George Eliot's brand-new novel *Adam Bede* (1859). Victorine's reading of the works of Austen, Brontë, Gaskell, and Eliot all together is oddly similar to the experience of a present-day student or aficionado of the nineteenth-century English novel.

Mansfield Park's story of "cousins in love, &c." would surely have struck a chord with Victorine, given her youngest sister Sophie's marriage to their first cousin, Frank.[46] We can guess, too, that the potent morality of this particular Austen novel would also have been a good fit with the strict, devout Victorine. But *Emma*? Perhaps the best conclusion to draw from the suspiciously well preserved du Pont copy is that the sisters, like the majority of contemporary readers on both sides of the Atlantic, were more engrossed by the bestsellers of the day than by the works of the lesser-known "author of *Pride and Prejudice*." In America as in England, Austen did not benefit from the buzz that attended the newest work of Scott or scandalous works like *Glenarvon*. Her readers had to discover for themselves the pleasures of reading her less sensational works.

A careful and curious reader: Jeremiah Smith of New Hampshire

Proof that Austen's novels did appeal to at least some American readers of the late 1810s and early 1820s can be found in the copy of *Emma* owned by Jeremiah Smith (1759–1842). Born in New England, Smith was a Harvard graduate and judge who served as chief justice and, briefly, as the ninth governor of his natal state, New Hampshire. He was sufficiently distinguished in his own day to merit both a portrait (see figure 2.4) and a full-length biography, published a few years after his death.[47] Smith's 601-item collection of books and pamphlets, including his copies of *Emma* and of other Austen novels, was given to the Dartmouth College Library in 1972.[48]

FIGURE 2.4 *Jeremiah Smith, portrait by Francis Alexander (1835). Courtesy of Hood Museum of Art, Dartmouth College, Hanover, New Hampshire; gift of Dr. George C. Shattuck, class of 1803.*

The volumes of Smith's *Emma* are in much poorer shape physically than those of the du Pont copy. On each volume, the covers bulge outward from the spine, and groups of pages ("signatures," in book parlance) are fully or partly detached from the stitching: hallmarks of overly tight binding.[49] At some point, someone took needle and thread to try to stabilize the first signature in the first volume. Viewed endwise, the edges of the pages look as if they have been chewed. Individual pages show significant damage, too, including horizontal tears and erosion along the outer margin; a few pages are missing altogether. To blame, apparently, is not any mishandling by Smith or his descendants, but rather the cheap production values of Carey's edition. Smith's copy, with its black leather spine and corners over marbled covers, is evidently one of the 450 copies "in boards" that Carey sold for $2.[50] (see figure 2.5).

On the inside, in striking contrast, Smith's copy of *Emma* indicates the great care he took with his books. In black ink, he documented the date of his purchase, 8 March 1817, as well as from whom—"Bot. of Mr Foster"—and the format and price: "bds 1.75." (see figure 2.6).[51] Smith's is the only copy of the surviving six

FIGURE 2.5 *Exterior of Jeremiah Smith's copy of* Emma. *Courtesy of Dartmouth College Library.*

of which any of these facts is known. His bookseller was most likely John Welsh Foster (1789–1852) of Portsmouth, New Hampshire.[52] Why Foster sold *Emma* at $1.75 rather than Carey's own price of $2 is uncertain. Below Smith's notation of the price he paid was added in a different ink (but apparently the same handwriting), "2 Vols $2.50": presumably a price he gleaned from a Carey catalogue.[53]

Smith's attentiveness as a reader is evident from his markings in the text of *Emma*. As befits a lawyer, he read with pen in hand, correcting all the printers' errors that he noticed. His corrections range from the obvious—e.g., striking out an extra "o" from "loooked"—to the more thoughtful, as when he rightly discerned that the word "plot" was a misprint for "blot."[54] Austen did stump Smith on one occasion, however: with her coinage of the word

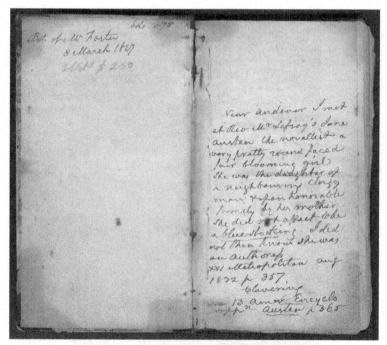

FIGURE 2.6 *Endpapers of volume 1 of Jeremiah Smith's copy of* Emma, *showing his notes on the purchase and on Austen's life, as well as repair stitches. Courtesy of Dartmouth College Library.*

"imaginist" to describe *Emma*. He gamely, and equally inventively, changed the spelling to "imaginast."

Beyond these corrections, Smith put a few vertical lines in the margins and underlined the occasional phrase. By far his most revealing annotations are to be found on the first volume's endpapers (the blank pages that precede the title page). There, he copied information about Austen's life and works gleaned from periodicals and reference works; the citations he diligently included identify the sources as variously American and English (see figures 2.6 and 2.7). These painstakingly copied quotations not only demonstrate Smith's interest in Austen's life and authorship but bring to light previously unknown mentions of Austen in the contemporary US press.

Smith's first set of notes, chronologically speaking, appears opposite the title page of volume one of his copy of *Emma*. It

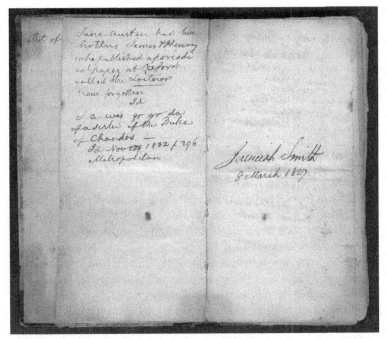

FIGURE 2.7 *Pages preceding the title page of volume 1 of Jeremiah Smith's copy of* Emma, *showing his further notes on Austen's life and his signature. Courtesy of Dartmouth College Library.*

consists of Austen's name (misspelled), a list of her other novels, and a few comments on them and on her life:

> By Miss Austin
> See Nᵒ 48 QuRev. 362 357 8 __ she died in the prime of life.__
> ——works—
> __Sense & Sensibility
> __Pride & prejudice
> __Mansfield Park
> __Emma
> 820__Northanger Abbey x
> _____Persuasion xx_____
> x her first__inferior to the rest
> xx last—posthumous__superior to rest

Smith derived these brief notes on Austen, including the erroneous spelling of her surname, from an unsigned review of *Northanger Abbey* and *Persuasion* that was printed in the January 1821 issue of John Murray's periodical the *Quarterly Review*. Subsequently identified as the work of Richard Whately, Archbishop of Dublin, this review is considered to be "the most important early nineteenth-century statement on Jane Austen" after Walter Scott's unsigned review for the March 1816 *Quarterly Review*, which I discussed in Chapter 1.[55]

Before Smith transcribed this list, however, he had already made further purchases of Austen's novels. On 1 June 1820, he acquired both Egerton's second edition of *Sense and Sensibility* (1813) and Egerton's third edition of *Pride and Prejudice* (1817). As with *Emma*, Smith added the dates of his acquisition of these volumes under his signature in them. His last Austen purchase occurred on 28 February 1824: Murray's second edition of *Mansfield Park* (1816). (Because Smith did not own *Northanger Abbey* and *Persuasion*, he may never have seen the "Biographical Notice" appended to Murray's 1818 edition of those novels, which treated Austen's life and authorship at some length.) In none of these volumes did Smith write, as he did in *Emma*, the price he paid or the bookseller's name. Nor did he make any corrections to these novels; evidently, their printing did not gall him as did that of Carey's *Emma*.

The earliest mention of Austen in the periodical press that Smith recorded appears as the lone note in his copy of *Sense and Sensibility*, where it serves to amplify the title page's identification of the work as "BY THE AUTHOR OF 'PRIDE AND PREJUDICE.'" To the left of that phrase Smith marked a handwritten "x," which corresponds to another "x" on the facing endsheet preceding the following transcribed quotation:

> "at Winchester died Miss Jane Austen youngest daughter of Rev George Austen Rector of Steventon Hants authoress of 'Emma', 'Mansfield Park', 'Pride & Prejudice' and 'Sense and Sensibility' Athenaeum Vol II p 488
> (1819)

In addition to neglecting to include closing quotation marks and getting the issue's 1818 date wrong, Smith misspelled the periodical's title: it was *The Atheneum*, the Boston publication that, as I discussed in Chapter 1, reprinted the obituary for Austen that had originally appeared in the *Gentleman's Magazine*. Smith's transcription from *The Atheneum* is valuable in establishing that at least one contemporary American reader took note of this obituary and connected its subject to a novel he had already read.

The rest of Smith's notes on the endsheets of volume one of *Emma* assemble information about Austen from sources dated in the early 1830s. On both sides of the Atlantic, interest in Austen's works was resurging in those years, thanks to the publication of the first complete American edition of her works by Carey & Lea in Philadelphia in 1832–1833 and the re-publication of her novels in affordable one-volume editions, with the first-ever illustrations, by Bentley in London in 1833. From the London publication *The Metropolitan: A Monthly Journal of Literature, Science, and the Fine Arts*, Smith recorded the following personal description of Austen:

> Near Andover I met at Rev. Mr Lefroy's Jane Austen the novellist a very pretty round faced fair blooming girl[.] She was the daughter of a neighbouring clergy man & of an honorable family by her mother[.] She did not affect to be a <u>blue-stocking</u>. I did not then know she was an Authoress.
> XVI Metropolitan Aug 1832 p 357
>   Clavering

Smith's source was serialized excerpts of a work titled "Clavering's auto-biography." "Clavering" was actually Sir Samuel Egerton

Brydges (1762–1837), a bibliographer and genealogist, and a founding member of the Roxburghe Club, an exclusive bibliophiles' society established in 1812. "Rev. Mr Lefroy" was the husband of Brydges' sister, Austen's great friend Anne Lefroy.[56] From a subsequent excerpt of "Clavering's auto-biography" in the November 1832 issue of the *Metropolitan*, Smith extracted two more facts about Austen's family: "Jane Austen had two Brothers James & Henry who published a periodical paper at Oxford called the <u>Loiterer</u> now forgotten" and "JA was gr gr da [great-granddaughter] of a sister of the Duke of Chandos."

Below Smith's August 1832 quotation from "Clavering" he wrote an additional note: "see 13 Amer. Encyclo opp^{te}<u>Austen</u> p. 365." This reference takes us to a hitherto unrecognized early American source on Austen: the *Encyclopædia Americana*, a reference work in thirteen volumes published from 1829–1833 by Henry Carey and his business partners. In thirteen volumes, it was the largest American-authored encyclopedia to date.[57] The inclusion of Austen in the last volume (1833) made sense, given that Carey & Lea were promoting their new complete edition of her novels. In full, the entry reads:

> AUSTEN, Jane, a gifted novelist, was born Dec. 16, 1775, at Steventon, in the county of Hants, of which parish her father was rector. Upon his death, his widow and two daughters retired to Southampton, and ultimately, in 1807, to Chawton. During her residence in the last-mentioned place, Miss Austen composed the novels, which for ease, nature, and a complete knowledge of the features which distinguish the domestic life of the English country gentry, are very highly esteemed. The principal of these productions are Sense and Sensibility; Pride and Prejudice; Mansfield Park; and Emma. Two more were published after her death, entitled Northanger Abbey, and Persuasion, which were, however, her most early attempts. The object of Miss Austen, in all her works, was to advocate the superiority of sound principle, unsophisticated manners, and undesigning rectitude, to showy and artificial pretensions. Her discrimination was acute, her humor easy and spontaneous, and her power of creating an interest in her characters by slight and reiterated touches, extraordinary. This amiable and accomplished lady, whose personal and mental attractions were of a high order, died of a decline, on the 18th of July 1817, in her forty-second year.[58]

With only slight emendations and no attribution, this description of Austen was republished the following year, 1834, in Samuel Knapp's *Female Biography*: the source that B. C. Southam cites in his *Jane Austen: The Critical Heritage* as the first American reference work to feature Austen. Spying "hints of Scott, Whately," and another British critic in the judgments rendered, Southam explains that "there was at this time little that could be identified as a distinctively 'American' school of fiction reviewing and criticism. Until the 1860s and 1870s a large proportion of literary journalism in American periodicals was simply a reprinting of material that had originally appeared in British journals."[59] Generally true that may be, yet the anonymous author of the *Encyclopædia Americana* entry deserves credit as the first American writer to describe Austen for an American audience. Notable too is the praise not only for Austen's depiction of the "domestic life of the English country gentry" but also for her "power of creating an interest in her characters": a power that, we can infer, could transcend the Englishness of her subject matter. It seems highly likely that the author of this entry was Henry Carey himself. Given his involvement in the printing of and publicity for the 1816 Philadelphia *Emma*, no one in the US was better acquainted than he with Austen's novels and their critical reception.

Since Smith's book collection was kept together, it is possible to form a sense of where *Emma* fits in the scheme of his reading. He owned relatively few novels overall, including some works by Burney, as well as Maria Edgeworth's *Castle Rackrent* and Scott's *Rob Roy*. In none of them did he write information about the author as he did for Austen—a sign, perhaps, of his particular regard for her writings. Like many readers of the time, he may have borrowed much of his pleasure reading from a subscription or circulating library.

Smith's reading and literary interests are mentioned only in passing by his biographer. John H. Morison did note that Smith, while serving as a selectman for his native town of Peterborough, New Hampshire, founded a "small social library" in 1787. And when Smith returned from stints traveling as a circuit judge, recalled Morison, "he usually refreshed himself for a week or two, by reading novels, or any other species of light literature that might be within his reach."[60] Morison's characterization of novel-reading as "refreshment" from work stands in contrast to the intriguing argument recently made by legal historian Alison L. LaCroix concerning the centrality of fiction-reading to citizenship, in the eyes of lawyers and judges of the early American republic.[61]

In the absence of firm evidence, it is possible only to speculate what drew a reader to a particular novel or author. In Smith's case, however, strong suggestions do exist regarding what interested him in Austen's writings. Morison describes Smith as having been morally serious, yet possessing a notable sense of humor: a combination shared with Austen herself and the majority of her admirable characters. Of Smith's family, Morison writes, "They were a serious and devout people. . . . And yet there was a love of merriment and wit mingling strangely with the most serious concerns. Judge Smith used to say, that they went to meeting on Sunday, practiced all that was good in the sermon through the week, and laughed at all that was ridiculous." Morison elaborates, "It is impossible for those who did not know him in his own house, to have any idea how much amusement he could extract from the most trifling events. . . . If there was anything in which he showed himself a man of genius, it was in the humor which flashed out through every feature of his mind and face."[62] It is certainly easy to imagine such a person appreciating Austen's writings.

Furthermore, Morison's biography portrays Smith as a man of deep feeling with an equally profound sense of privacy. Such traits are visible in Austen's characters ranging from Elinor Dashwood of *Sense and Sensibility*, to Mr. Knightley of *Emma*, to Anne Elliot of *Persuasion*. Morison best captures this aspect of Smith in his recounting of the lawyer's courtship of his first wife, Eliza Ross. Upon meeting her in 1794 and learning that she was already engaged, Smith penned what Morison refers to as "the only attempts at poetry that I have found among his writings," which he characterizes as expressions of "ardent admiration, devotedness and affection, such as might overwhelm with confusion any but a lady educated in the school of Sir Charles Grandison and Lady Harriet." Morison notes further that "Mr. Smith, near the close of his life, had his correspondence with her [Eliza] bound in a volume, which he very justly described: 'These letters show real fervor and attachment, and marks both of strong affection and passion; but they are little suited to the general eye.'"[63]

In keeping with his characteristic reticence, Smith did not annotate his copies of Austen's novels with personal responses.

Nevertheless, his careful recording, over many years, of information about the author's life unmistakably attests to his great interest in her. The 1816 Philadelphia *Emma* introduced Smith to Austen. His fortunately rediscovered copies of this and other Austen novels, including his quotations from now-forgotten US publications, offer the fullest evidence available of a devoted American reader of Austen before the 1830s.

Unimpressed by *Emma*: subscribers to a Rhode Island circulating library

For comments on the experience of reading *Emma*, we must look to the most astonishing survivor among the six remaining copies of the 1816 Philadelphia edition: the one now held by the New York Society Library, a private membership library founded in 1754. These volumes' level of disintegration is well conveyed by Gilson's description of them: "spines decayed and broken, pages much worn and decayed throughout, parts of many pages missing."[64] The title page, dedication, and first several pages of volume one are all in tatters (see figure 2.8). As a bookplate on the inside front cover makes clear, this copy was formerly owned by James Hammond's Circulating Library in Newport, Rhode Island, which touted itself as "the Largest *Circulating* Library in New England," with "over 8000 volumes," the great majority of which—5,000—fell into the category of "*Novels—Tales and Romances.*"[65] Thanks to a trustee, the New York Society Library acquired 1,850 volumes from the Hammond Library in 1868, among them this annotated *Emma*.[66] The sheer physical deterioration of this copy indicates that its volumes, still in the original publishers' boards, were not up to the rigors of library members' use. The exact year or years in which the annotations were added is unknown.

Careful though Gilson was to account for the external physical condition of this copy, he made no mention in his *Bibliography* of the historically valuable marginalia penciled by anonymous readers into the second volume. These responses first came to public view in 2015, as part of an exhibit titled "Readers Make Their Mark: Annotated Books at the New York Society Library." In an accompanying blog post about the 1816 Philadelphia *Emma*,

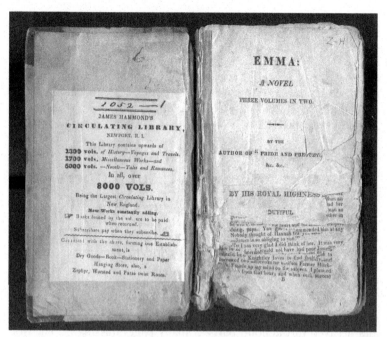

FIGURE 2.8 *James Hammond's Circulating Library copy of* Emma.
Courtesy of the Hammond Collection, New York Society Library, New York.

exhibit co-curator Madeline McMahon highlighted the importance
of comments "by an ordinary reader, for a book about ordinary
life."[67]

McMahon attributes all the marginalia to a single reader, whom
she guesses is female, based on the handwriting. To my eye, however,
two distinct hands are visible, neither obviously belonging to a man
or a woman. One writer pressed firmly with the pencil, wrote in a
formal cursive, and inserted only a few responses; the other scrawled
thoughts with light pressure on the pencil and commented
frequently. Some of the annotations, especially by the latter, are very
faint and require significant deciphering; here, too, my guesses
differ from McMahon's. Both readers responded strongly to
particular moments in volume two and also recorded summary
judgments on the final page.

The reader with the more formal handwriting focused throughout
on the novel's heroine. At the bottom of the page on which Emma

"smiled her acceptance" of Frank Churchill's agreeing to join the Box Hill expedition, this reader wrote, "Highty tighty" (a variant of hoity toity).[68] At the bottom of the page on which Mr. Knightley and Emma agree that they are not "really so much brother and sister as to make it at all improper" to dance together, this reader wrote—sagely, though with different spelling than Austen's—"I expect Emma is going to marry Mr. Knightly."[69] On the last page of the novel, directly over the printed word "FINIS," this reader wrote "I am delighted to get through with Emma Woodhouse or Mrs Knightly*".

Even more critical was the other reader, who alternated between global comments on the novel and responses to individual characters. An almost completely illegible comment on the inside flyleaf of the second volume is headed "Silly Book," and that sentiment pervades this reader's responses. Following Frank Churchill's invitation of Emma to dance, this reader recorded the following judgment: "This book is not worth reading whoever the author, as their time had better been spent in reading than inventing. By one who has read this."[70] A similar, though more concise, thought—"I wonder who likes this book"—appears at the top of the page on which Mrs. Elton declares that "without music, life would be a blank to me."[71]

This reader's especial dislike of Mrs. Elton is evident in two further annotations. "How disagreeable Mrs Elton is" appears at the top of the page opposite Mrs. Elton's declaration, apropos of the strawberry-picking expedition to Donwell Abbey, "I wish we had a donkey."[72] Similarly, "Mrs Elton is a goose" is the judgment recorded after Mrs. Elton states, at Box Hill, "I do not pretend to be a wit."[73] In contrast, this reader made only one comment on Emma: at the end of the page on which "Emma doubted their [her guests] getting on very well," this reader remarked, "Emma is always doubting."[74]

On the final page, rotated clockwise, appears this reader's greatest gift to reception history, in the form of summary judgments of Austen's characters, laid out in a chart:

Mr. Knightley ___ tolerable
Emma ___ intolerable
Harriet ___ very pleasant
Frank ___ delightful
Jane ___ enchanting

> Woodhouse ___ grouty
> Miss Bates ___ Full of Gab
> El[ton] ___ d—d sneak
> [Mrs. Elton?] ___ vulgar woman

The very unusual word "grouty" confirms beyond any doubt that these adjectives were chosen by an American reader. According to the *Oxford English Dictionary*, this word (meaning "sulky, cross, ill-tempered") exists only in a few instances of nineteenth-century usage, all from the United States.[75] "D—d," of course, is an abbreviation for "damned"—so Mr. Elton, in the eyes of this reviewer, was a "damned sneak." The name below that of Elton, while so faint as to be illegible, must logically be that of his certainly "vulgar" wife.

Both this concluding list and the marginal annotations invite comparisons to the "Opinions of *Emma*" that Austen herself solicited from her friends and family, comments that have long been valued for the insight they give into the reactions of everyday English readers.[76] Austen's informants, too, concentrated on responses to particular characters and comments about how much they enjoyed, or did not enjoy, reading this novel. While several of Austen's acquaintances shared the American annotator's dislike of Emma ("intolerable"), the English readers responded more positively to Mr. Knightley than did the American, who found him only "tolerable."[77] None of Austen's circle agreed with the American's approving view of Harriet, Frank, or Jane.[78] And no one among Austen's sources mentioned Mr. Woodhouse, while all praised the characterizations of Miss Bates and Mrs. Elton, which the American did not appreciate.

The American annotators' low opinion of *Emma* overall was shared by a few of Austen's informants. One, Mrs. Digweed, candidly remarked that she "did not like it [*Emma*] so well as the others, in fact if she had not known the Author, could hardly have got through it." Another, Mr. Cockerell, "liked it so little," Austen recorded, that her niece "Fanny w[d]. not send me his opinion." Yet another, Mr. Fowle "read only the first & last Chapters, because he had heard it was not interesting."[79] At least the American readers *did* make it all the way to the end of this novel, even if they celebrated their relief in having finished it!

Of course, these two sets of comments differ in several ways beyond the readers' nationality alone. Austen's informants summarized their thoughts after completing *Emma,* while the Americans responded as they read. Most of Austen's sources were familiar with her other works and drew comparisons with them, which the American readers did not (or could not) do. With the exception of the few readers whose ideas were forwarded to Austen by mutual friends, her informants were speaking to her in person, as opposed to writing anonymously in a borrowed copy. (Addressing Austen directly does not seem, however, to have especially inhibited those of her acquaintance who candidly expressed dislike for *Emma.*) Most significantly, Austen collected thoughts from many more than just two readers.

Given how little has been known about the responses of Austen's early American readers, however, even two anonymous, contrarian annotators of a single novel make a valuable contribution to reception history. There is no better reminder than these unvarnished comments of how much dislike Austen's novels elicited, in and shortly after her own lifetime, from some readers on both sides of the Atlantic.

Only when the 1830s American editions of Austen's novels reached a new generation of eager young women readers would her writings inspire adoration. Before we meet those devotees, however, a further owner of the 1816 Philadelphia *Emma* awaits our attention: a woman whose wide reading, spirit of adventure, and intellectual achievements inspire comparisons to Austen herself.

Notes

1 The book historian David Pearson notes that "a book can be written in, defaced, altered, beautified, or cherished, to produce a preservable object with an individual history." *Books as History,* rev. edn (London and New Castle, DE: The British Library and Oak Knoll Press, 2012), 22. Pearson refers to the effects of owners' rebinding, adding of bookplates, etc. as a "customisation cycle" (23).

2 See Emma Smith, *Shakespeare's First Folio: Four Centuries of an Iconic Book* (Oxford: Oxford University Press, 2016) and Owen Gingerich, *The Book Nobody Read: Chasing the Revolutions of Nicolaus Copernicus* (New York: Walker, 2004). Especially pertinent to my investigation is Smith's assertion of how her work bridges "interest in the material lives of books as objects; and more interpretive histories of literary reception" (20). See too Cathy N. Davidson, "The Life and

Times of *Charlotte Temple*: The Biography of a Book," in *Reading in America: Literature & Social History*, ed. Cathy N. Davidson, 157–79 (Baltimore: Johns Hopkins University Press, 1989).

3   Whether the binding now visible on the du Pont copy of *Emma* is that of Carey's binder, Wakeling & Allen, or of a later rebinder is not known. A full bibliographic description of this copy, including a collation of pages and accounts of binding and repairs, has yet to be recorded.

4   My observations of this copy were made on 6 October 2014, at Winterthur Library. Following present-day convention, I will render the family name as "du Pont"; spelling and capitalization in period sources are original.

5   The stamp is identifiable as having been produced in the early 1870s. *Scott Standard Postage Stamp Catalogue*, 141st edn, volume 1 (New York: Scott Publishing, 1985), 4.

6   The Winterthur Library catalogue entry for the du Pont *Emma* includes a note that the volumes were "transferred from [the] Powell Room, 4/79": http://library.winterthur.org:8001/lib/item?id=chamo: 66240&theme=winterthur.

7   For a brief overview of the lives of Pierre Samuel, Irénée, and Victor, see Ruth Lord, *Henry F. du Pont and Winterthur: A Daughter's Portrait* (New Haven: Yale University Press, 1999), 12–17. See also Betty-Bright Low and Jacqueline Hinsley, *Sophie du Pont, A Young Lady in America: Sketches, Diaries, & Letters 1823–1833* (New York: Abrams, 1987), 13. The present interior of the Eleutherian Mills house reflects the redecoration of a twentieth-century descendant; no original drawing room or library remains. For insight into family life at Eleutherian Mills and the history of the house, I gratefully acknowledge historian Laura Beardsley, who by good fortune was my tour guide at Hagley on 16 March 2016.

8   Rink records "2258 titles in about 5400 volumes" in the combined collection of the three men. Ewald Rink, "A Family Heritage: The Library of the Immigrant du Ponts" (unpublished MS., 1980s [?]), 9. "The largest category in Irénée's library was literature, almost 30% of total holdings," notes Rink, including "the works of Jane Austen, Lord Byron, Oliver Goldsmith, John Milton, Thomas Parnell, and Sir Walter Scott, among others" (37). Rink differentiates between Pierre Samuel and Victor, who were true book collectors, and Irénée, who acquired books for "practical" reasons (39). I am thankful to Max Moeller, Curator of Imprints at the Hagley Library, for sharing Rink's article with me.

9   Rink, "Family Heritage," 33.

10 According to its title page, the 1816 edition of *Rhoda: A Novel*—"from the second London edition"—was published jointly by Wells and Lilly, Boston; A. T. Goodrich, New York; and M. Carey, Philadelphia. On the authorship of *Rhoda* and the popularity of this title in its day, see Chapter 3. *Discipline*, a reprint of Mary Brunton's 1814 novel, was published by Wells and Lilly. I observed these copies on 14 March 2016, thanks to access to the rare book stacks at Hagley that was kindly granted by Max Moeller. According to Rink, 77% of the du Pont men's books are housed today at Hagley; only 6% of their original collection is at Winterthur. Rink, "Family Heritage," 45. The Hagley Library catalogue does not include documentation of inscriptions in rare books.

11 John Beverley Riggs, *A Guide to the Manuscripts in the Eleutherian Mills Historical Library: Accessions through the Year 1965* (Greenville, DE: Eleutherian Mills Historical Library, 1970), 280. Thumbnail descriptions of Victorine and her siblings are given in Low and Hinsley, *Sophie du Pont*, 10–11. For more about Victorine's role as tutor, see Hinsley, "Reading Tastes," 13–15.

12 Rink, "Family Heritage," 42.

13 Low and Hinsley, *Sophie du Pont*, 181. Charmingly, the then-teenage Sophie reported the birth of her niece Victorine on 13 August 1825 as follows: "The baby is called Victorine she has dark eyes and hair and is very pretty. . . . Little Victorine does nothing but sleep now, but I expect she will be much improved in September. Lilly [nickname for her brother Alexis Irénée] is delighted, it is something so new to have a niece!!!!!!!!" Quoted in Low and Hinsley, *Sophie du Pont*, 11.

14 Rink, "Family Heritage," 10.

15 Rink, "Family Heritage," 34; Low and Hinsley, *Sophie du Pont*, 13.

16 Rink, "Family Heritage," 36.

17 Low and Hinsley, *Sophie du Pont*, 49.

18 Receipt from Mathew R. Lockerman to E. I. Dupont, 1813–1814, Longwood MSS., Hagley Museum and Library (hereafter HML), 3/B. All spelling and punctuation original.

19 E. I. du Pont, account book for 1815–1818, Longwood MSS., HML, 3/B.

20 Low and Hinsley, *Sophie du Pont*, 17. Notably, the du Pont sisters' cultivated existence took place at very little physical remove from the work that supported it. Located just down the hill from their house was their father's gunpowder works, which produced noise, smells, dirt, and—too often—dangerous explosions. Irénée's youngest son, Alexis, died in one such gunpowder explosion in 1857. Low and Hinsley, *Sophie du Pont*, 10.

21 Hinsley, "Reading Tastes," 4.

22 See David J. Gilson, "Jane Austen's Books," *Book Collector* 23 (1974):
    547–50, reprinted in Gilson, *Jane Austen: Collected Articles and
    Introductions*, 73–89 (privately printed, 1998); Katie Halsey, *Jane
    Austen and Her Readers, 1786–1945* (London: Anthem, 2012), 17.

23 The sisters' collaborative writing projects included a newspaper, the
    Tancopanican Chronicle. Evelina's writings, including her self-
    illustrated poem "The Battle of Erie" and countless prayers and
    meditations, are preserved in Winterthur MSS., HML, 6/B/16. "The
    Brandywine languishes in the absence of its poetess," Victorine wrote
    to Evelina in 1813. Victorine du Pont to Evelina du Pont, 27 April
    1813, Winterthur MSS., HML, 6/A/2.

24 Low and Hinsley, *Sophie du Pont*, 66; Hinsley, "Reading Tastes," 17.

25 Copies observed on 14 March 2016. *Emma* was translated into
    French by Isabelle de Montolieu as *La Nouvelle Emma* and released
    in March 1816 by the bookseller Arthus Bertrand. As Gillian Dow
    points out in "Translations," in *The Cambridge Companion to* Emma,
    ed. Peter Sabor, 166–85 (Cambridge: Cambridge University Press,
    2015), this three-month period from Murray's December 1815
    London edition of *Emma* represents "a remarkable turnaround"
    (169). *La Nouvelle Emma* would not, however, been available in the
    American marketplace.

26 Hinsley, "Reading Tastes," 85. On the scope and influence of the du
    Pont sisters' reading in general, see Hinsley, "Reading Tastes," 20–77;
    on their membership in circulating libraries, 5; on British novelists,
    22–7; on American writers, 66–9; on subscriptions to periodicals,
    71–4. Hinsley's "Appendix" (127) lists all the titles in the Hagley
    Library (then the Eleutherian Mills Historical Library) known to have
    been read by the du Pont sisters between 1810 and 1835; Austen is
    not on the list.

27 Hinsley, "Reading Tastes," 86. Low and Hinsley point out that Sophie
    in particular felt the collision between French ideals of womanhood
    promulgated by their parents and the English customs that influenced
    American society at the time, and which the sisters felt obligated to
    adopt as part of their effort to become "Americanized" (*Sophie du
    Pont*, 19).

28 Victorine du Pont to Evelina du Pont, [20 June 1812], Winterthur
    MSS., HML, 6/A/2. Ann Radcliffe was the bestselling Gothic novelist
    whose works Austen's characters read, avidly, in *Northanger Abbey*.

29 Victorine Bauduy to Evelina du Pont, 7 December 1813, Winterthur
    MSS., HML, 6/A/2.

30 Sophie du Pont to Henry du Pont, 11 February 1832, quoted in
    Hinsley, "Reading Tastes," 38.

31 Observed on 14 March 2016. The *Beauties of Shakespeare* volume
    bears the bookplate of Pierre S. du Pont of Longwood, a
    contemporary of Henry Francis du Pont's. Pierre S. (1870–1954) was
    descended from Irénée's son Alfred Victor (1798–1856). The du Pont
    family papers were long divided between Longwood and Winterthur,
    a distinction that is preserved in the Hagley Library's catalogue
    system.

32 Victorine Bauduy to Francis du Pont, 9 August 1818, Winterthur
    MSS., HML, 6/A/2. A hole in the paper renders the first word of the
    Byron quotation illegible.

33 "Do not be angry with me for beginning another Letter to you. I have
    read the Corsair, mended my petticoat, & have nothing else to do."
    Jane Austen to Cassandra Austen, 5 March 1814, in *Jane Austen's
    Letters*, 4th edn, ed. Deirdre Le Faye (Oxford: Oxford University
    Press, 2015), 268.

34 Victorine du Pont to Evelina du Pont, 10 October 1818, Winterthur
    MSS., HML, 6/A/2. Hinsley notes that "Victorine had a great
    curiosity about pedagogical methods," which she fed both by reading
    and through firsthand observation of Philadelphia teachers. Hinsley,
    "Reading Tastes," 15–16.

35 Eleuthera du Pont to Victorine Bauduy, [March 1821], Winterthur
    MSS., HML, 6/C/18. A probable date of April 1821 has been added
    by an archivist, but this undated letter obviously precedes Victorine's
    letter dated 28 March.

36 Victorine Bauduy to Eleuthera du Pont, 28 March 1821, Winterthur
    MSS., HML, 6/A/2.

37 Victorine Bauduy to Eleuthera du Pont, 30 March 1821, Winterthur
    MSS., HML, 6/A/2.

38 Eleuthera du Pont to Victorine Bauduy, [1 April 1821], Winterthur
    MSS., HML, 6/C/18.

39 Victorine Bauduy to Evelina du Pont, 10 August [1814], Winterthur
    MSS., HML, 6/A/2.

40 Jane Austen, *Emma*, ed. Richard Cronin and Dorothy McMillan
    (Cambridge: Cambridge University Press, 2005), 362. Cronin and
    McMillan describe "imaginist" as "probably a coinage of Austen's,
    certainly according to *OED* the first usage of the word" (584).

41 Victorine Bauduy to Evelina du Pont, 29 October 1816, Winterthur
    MSS., HML, 6/A/2.

42 Victorine du Pont to Evelina du Pont, [21 June 1812], Winterthur
    MSS., HML, 6/A/2.

43 Victorine du Pont to Evelina du Pont, 7 March 1821, Winterthur
    MSS., HML, 6/A/2.

44 Victorine Bauduy to Evelina Bidermann, n.d., quoted in Hinsley,
    "Reading Tastes," 110 n. 11.

45 Winterthur MSS., HML, 6/A/2. Victorine's post-1835 book lists,
    which fall outside the scope of Hinsley's study in "Reading Tastes,"
    merit fuller examination.

46 Jane Austen, *Mansfield Park*, ed. John Wiltshire (Cambridge:
    Cambridge University Press, 2005), 6.

47 John H. Morison's *Life of the Hon. Jeremiah Smith, LL.D.* (Boston:
    Charles C. Little and James Brown, 1845) identifies its subject on the
    title page as having been "a member of Congress during Washington's
    administration, judge of the United States Circuit Court, Chief Justice
    of New Hampshire, etc." (i). In his preface, Morison notes that he had
    access to Smith's papers, including letters and commonplace books
    (iii); if those papers have survived, their current whereabouts is
    unknown.

48 Jay Satterfield, Special Collections Librarian at Rauner Library, notes
    that "in 1972 Mrs. Delmar Leighton of Cambridge, Massachusetts,
    presented to the Library as a gift in memory of Elizabeth Hale Smith
    the library of Miss Smith's grandfather, the jurist and statesman
    Jeremiah Smith. Comprising over six hundred items, it includes
    many pamphlets and other sources of prime importance to the study
    of New Hampshire and the young nation" (email message to author,
    30 October 2014).

49 My observations of books in Jeremiah Smith's collection were made
    on 29 June 2015 at Rauner Library. I am grateful to Morgan Swan,
    Special Collections Education and Outreach Librarian at Rauner, for
    sharing his judgment about the tight binding of these volumes
    (personal conversation with author, 29 June 2015).

50 The spine is horizontally ruled in gilt, with seven sets of double lines,
    somewhat differently spaced than on the du Pont copy. The title
    "EMMA." is stamped between the second and third sets of lines, with
    the volume number below. Like the du Pont copy, the Smith copy has
    yet to receive a full bibliographic description.

51 Smith recorded his date of acquisition both on the flyleaf and under
    his signature on another endsheet preceding the title page. Volume
    two of Smith's copy includes a piece of personal ephemera tucked
    inside the back cover: an engraved invitation card, embossed with

Harvard and Radcliffe seals, for a "College Tea" on Saturday, January twenty-sixth, year unspecified.

52 According to the Portsmouth Public Library, which holds albums of watercolors created by his daughter Sarah Haven Foster, John Welsh Foster was "a bookseller and printer" whose businesses "dealt with printing, book selling, and bookbinding." "Sarah Haven Foster Watercolors: Collection Description," Portsmouth Public Library, accessed 3 October 2016, http://www.portsmouthexhibits.org/collections/show/3.

53 Smith's copy of Burney's novel *Geraldine Fauconberg*, published by "M. Carey and Son" in 1817, includes a twenty-four-page catalogue of Carey's titles dated March 1817. In the category "NOVELS, &c." *Emma* is listed directly after *Geraldine Fauconberg*; however, no price for *Emma* is given in this catalogue, so Smith must have had access to another that did.

54 The passage in question conveys Mrs. Weston's reaction to hearing of Frank Churchill traveling to London to get his hair cut: "With the exception of this little blot, Emma found that his visit hitherto had given her friend only good ideas of him." Austen, *Emma*, ed. Cronin and Macmillan, 221.

55 B. C. Southam, ed., *Jane Austen: The Critical Heritage* (London: Routledge & Kegan Paul, 1968), 87; see also David Gilson, *A Bibliography of Jane Austen*, new edn (New Castle, DE: Oak Knoll Press, 1997), 85.

56 See Nicolas Barker, *The Roxburghe Club: A Bicentenary History* (Cambridge: Roxburghe Club, 2012). On the Austen-Brydges-Lefroy connection, see Janine Barchas, *Matters of Fact in Jane Austen: History, Location, and Celebrity* (Baltimore: Johns Hopkins University Press, 2012), 20; and David Gilson, "Jane Austen and Sir Egerton Brydges," *Jane Austen Society Report for 1976*, 9–11, reprinted in *Jane Austen: Collected Articles and Introductions* (privately printed, 1998), 135–7. *The Metropolitan: A Monthly Journal of Literature, Science, and the Fine Arts* was published in London from May 1831 to 1850; its name changed to simply *The Metropolitan* in 1833. A table of contents of *The Metropolitan* has been compiled by Gary Simons: "Metropolitan Magazine," March 2014, victorianresearch.org/MetropolitanMagazine2014.pdf.

57 Drake De Kay, "Encyclopedia Americana, First Edition," *The Journal of Library History* 3.3 (July 1968): 201–20.

58 *Encyclopædia Americana: A Popular Dictionary of Arts, Sciences, Literature, History, Politics and Biography, Brought Down to the Present Time; Including a Copious Collection of Original Articles in*

American Biography, ed. Francis Lieber, assisted by E. Wigglesworth and T. G. Bradford, vol. 13 (Philadelphia: Carey, Lea, & Blanchard, 1833), 365. In the entry, "Hants" is an abbreviation of "Hampshire." Two factual inaccuracies are present: the move to Chawton took place in 1809, not 1807, and *Persuasion* was a late, not an early, work.

59 Southam, ed., *Critical Heritage*, 27. Charles Beecher Hogan had earlier identified Knapp's *Female Biography* as the first "formal notice, and criticism, of Jane Austen to be published in book form" in either England or America. "Jane Austen and Her Early Public," *The Review of English Studies* n.s. 1 (1950): 54.

60 Morison, *Life*, 35, 168.

61 Alison L. LaCroix, "The Lawyer's Library in the Early American Republic," in *Subversion and Sympathy: Gender, Law, and the British Novel*, ed. Martha C. Nussbaum and Alison L. LaCroix, 251–73 (Oxford: Oxford University Press, 2013).

62 Morison, *Life*, 7, 168, 170.

63 Morison, *Life*, 102, 103–104.

64 Gilson, *Bibliography*, 101.

65 My observations of this copy were made on 9 January 2014, at the New York Society Library. Hammond's Circulating Library catalogued *Emma* as #1052; the title was later joined by Austen's other works, evidently in the 1832–1833 Carey & Lea editions, according to the *Catalogue of James Hammond's Circulating Library* (Newport, R. I.: Power Press of Coggeshall and Pratt, 1858). In addition to the large quantity of novels, Hammond's contained 1,300 volumes of "*History—Voyages and Travels*" and 1,700 of "*Miscellaneous Works*," according to the label on the copy of *Emma*. Like many circulating libraries of the time, Hammond's was operated by a businessman who also retailed other goods, in this case dry goods and stationery. See Kenneth E. Carpenter, "Libraries," in *A History of the Book in America vol. 2: An Extensive Republic: Print, Culture, and Society in the New Nation, 1790–1840*, ed. Robert A. Gross and Mary Kelley, 273–85 (Chapel Hill: American Antiquarian Society/University of North Carolina Press, 2010).

66 The trustee, Robert Lenox Kennedy, described the Hammond Collection as "a very curious memorial of the taste, manners, and lighter literature of the country from the period of 1783 until about or near 1830." Quoted in *The New York Society Library: 250 Years*, ed. Henry S. F. Cooper, Jr. and Jenny Lawrence (New York: The New York Society Library, 2004), 76. Kennedy also presciently remarked

that "[a]s specimens of the class of works in circulation some years ago and of the style of printing and binding, in various parts of our Country, they may prove of increasing interest as time rolls on" (86).

67   Madeline McMahon, "Jane Austen's *Emma* in Early America," The New York Society Library *Library Blog*, 4 May 2015, accessed 10 October 2016. McMahon points out that the annotations in this *Emma* extend beyond comments on the text: jottings include a brief stretch of musical notation penciled in one margin, doodles of Hammond's name, and the names apparently of library patrons. Also written in cursive on the inside cover of the second volume is the name "Jane"; whether this refers to the character Jane Fairfax, to the author, or to a reader is unknown. On the value of marginalia in general and in Romantic-era books in particular, see H. J. Jackson, *Marginalia: Readers Writing in Books* (New Haven: Yale University Press, 2001) and *Romantic Readers: The Evidence of Marginalia* (New Haven: Yale University Press, 2005). That writing in library copies was a common circumstance is evident from such institutions' guidelines. For instance, the Boston Library's catalogue—the same one that identified *Emma* as "a Novel, by Miss Austin" (discussed in Chapter 1)—included the following observation: "The frequent *marks*, either of the pen or the pencil, which disfigure, and exceedingly injure the pages, are not made by persons of literature and taste, but by the thoughtless." *Catalogue of Books in the Boston Library, June 1824* (Boston: Munroe and Francis, 1824), 6, *GoogleBooks*. For examples of crotchety annotations added by members of the Library Company of Pennsylvania to travel narratives with whose depiction of America they vehemently disagreed, see Joseph Rezek, *London and the Making of Provincial Literature: Aesthetics and the Transatlantic Book Trade* (Philadelphia: University of Pennsylvania Press, 2015), 157–60.

68   All page references to this copy will give first the volume, chapter, and page number in Carey's edition—which is accessible to all via the digital facsimile http://www.emmainamerica.org—then, in parentheses, a corresponding reference to the Cambridge edition. This annotation appears on Volume II chapter 15, p. 141 (volume III chapter 7, p. 398). On the challenges of transcribing annotations and their context, see Jackson, *Marginalia*, 262–3.

69   Volume II chapter 11, p. 202 [misprint for 102] (volume III chapter 2, p. 358).

70   Volume II chapter 2, p. 20 (volume II chapter 11, p. 276).

71   Volume II chapter 5, p. 43 (volume II chapter 14, p. 299).

72   Volume II chapter 15, p. 131 (volume III chapter 6, p. 386).

73 Volume II chapter 15, p. 147 (volume III chapter 7, p. 404).

74 Volume II chapter 9, p. 81 (volume II chapter 18, p. 336).

75 "grouty, adj.2," *OED Online*, Oxford University Press, accessed
    11 October 2016.

76 Jane Austen, "Opinions of *Emma*," in *Later Manuscripts*, ed. Janet
    Todd and Linda Bree (Cambridge: Cambridge University Press, 2008),
    235–9; subsequently quoted parenthetically in endnote text. On the
    significance of these responses of everyday readers to Austen
    reception, see Laura Fairchild Brodie, "Jane Austen and the Common
    Reader: 'Opinions of Mansfield Park,' 'Opinions of Emma,' and the
    Janeite Phenomenon," *Texas Studies in Literature and Language* 37.1
    (1995): 54–71.

77 Austen's beloved niece Fanny Knight "could not bear <u>Emma</u> herself,"
    while Mr. Ben Lefroy "[d]id not like the Heroine so well as any of the
    others"—a sentiment he did not share with his wife, who preferred
    Emma "to all the heroines" of prior novels (235, 237, 238). Fanny
    Knight considered Mr. Knightley to be "delightful"; he was "liked by
    every body," according to Fanny's father, Austen's brother Edward;
    and was an "excellent Character," in the view of Austen's aunt and
    uncle the Leigh Perrots (235, 236).

78 Of the few of Austen's informants who mentioned Harriet, one said
    there was "too much" of her and the other, that she liked "all the
    people of Highbury in general, except Harriet Smith" (236). Rather
    than Frank's being "delightful," he struck the Leigh Perrots—the only
    acquaintance of Austen's who mentioned him—as "better treated than
    he deserved" (236). Jane Fairfax, whom the American reader found
    "enchanting," left Austen's friend Anne Sharp "dissatisfied," and was
    "pitied" by the Leigh Perrots (235, 236).

79 "Opinions of *Emma*," 237, 238.

3

An Accomplished Scotswoman Reads Austen Abroad:

Christian, Countess of Dalhousie in British North America

Like so many nineteenth-century women, Christian Broun Ramsay, Countess of Dalhousie (1786–1839) is chiefly remembered today in relation to two distinguished men.[1] Her husband George Ramsay (1770–1838), 9th Earl of Dalhousie in the Scottish peerage, was a decorated British army officer who fought in the Battle of Waterloo; head of the British government in colonial Canada and India; the founder of Dalhousie University in Halifax, Nova Scotia; and a patron of the arts and of learned societies in Canada.[2] The youngest of Lady Dalhousie's three sons, James Andrew Broun Ramsay (1812–1860), was created first Marquess of Dalhousie in the English peerage for his service to Queen Victoria as governor-general of British India.[3]

In her own right, Lady Dalhousie was recognized in her lifetime for her pioneering, extensive collections of plants from North America and India, many of which still survive.[4] The countess was elected the first female honorary member of the Botanical Society of

Edinburgh. She was celebrated, too, by the naming of the genus *Dalhousiea* and several individual plant species, plus a long-tailed broadbill bird.[5] In commemoration, the bird and one of the plants are featured in the life-size oil portrait of the countess created in 1829 by Scotland's foremost portraitist, Sir John Watson Gordon.[6] A more intimate likeness of her by Watson Gordon, believed to be a preparatory sketch, appears as figure 3.1.[7]

Lady Dalhousie's ownership of the 1816 Philadelphia *Emma* now held by Goucher College invites consideration of her life from a new angle: her literary interests. Both volumes of the countess's copy of *Emma* bear her signature, "C B Dalhousie," vertically on the title page; the first volume also contains a small bookplate reading "COUNTESS OF DALHOUSIE"—similar in appearance to a calling card—on the inside front cover. The title page reproduced in figure 1.1 is that of Lady Dalhousie's copy and shows her signature. Her bookplate can be seen in the open-access digital facsimile of her copy created by Goucher College Library, at www.emmainamerica.org.

That the countess cherished her copy of *Emma* can be inferred from the elegant, evidently expensive binding she chose for it: brown calf leather with hand-stamped gilt decorations on the covers and spines.[8] Today, the volumes show their age, especially at the hinges (where the covers meet the spine). Even so, of the six surviving copies of the 1816 Philadelphia *Emma*, Lady Dalhousie's is by far the most beautifully bound.

The Austen bibliographer David Gilson guessed, reasonably, that the countess bought her copy of *Emma* while she was living in North America with her husband, but no definite information about her book ownership or reading has been known.[9] Fortunately for posterity, Lady Dalhousie noted her daily reading in her diaries, which reveal where and when she read Austen's novels, as well as what else she was reading at the time. The countess's responses as a reader emerge more fully from her letters, which convey her often delightfully witty observations in a very appealing voice.

Like Jane Austen, her near contemporary, Lady Dalhousie was a highly cultured, enthusiastic theatergoer who read widely in poetry, novels, and nonfiction prose, in French, English, and Italian. In other important ways, however, the two women's lives diverged considerably. By birth and by marriage, Lady Dalhousie possessed social and economic advantages far exceeding Austen's, though comparable to those of Austen's most fortunate heroines. (The most elevated female characters in Austen's novels are Lady Catherine de Bourgh, daughter of an earl, in *Pride and Prejudice*, and Lady Dalrymple, a dowager viscountess, in *Persuasion*; neither one is admirable.) Austen's family is often described as well connected, thanks both to her mother's family, the landed Leighs, and to the

FIGURE 3.1 *"Christian Broun, 1786–1839. Wife of the 9th Earl of Dalhousie," by Sir John Watson Gordon [1829]. Courtesy of the Scottish National Gallery.*

adoption of her brother Edward by wealthy, childless relations, the Knights.[10] The social circles in which Lady Dalhousie and her family moved were far more exalted, however, due to her husband's rank in the Scottish peerage, his high government positions, and his military connections. Indeed, when Lord Dalhousie was named governor-in-chief of British North America in 1820, he reported directly to King George IV: the man to whom, under his former title of Prince Regent, Austen had reluctantly dedicated *Emma*.[11]

Significantly, Lady Dalhousie was personally acquainted, as Austen was not, with some of the literary greats of her age. In particular, Walter Scott (1771–1832), whose unsigned review of *Emma* proved so pivotal to Austen's literary reputation (see Chapter 1), had been a schoolmate of Lord Dalhousie's at the Royal High School in Edinburgh.[12]

In terms of travel, too, the countess enjoyed many more advantages—and adventures—than did Austen, whose journeys were constrained by finances and by social convention requiring unmarried gentlewomen to travel accompanied.[13] Lady Dalhousie toured England and Wales as a young woman (chaperoned, of course) and lived abroad for much of her adult life, as a result of her husband's posts in the colonial administration of the British Empire. She served as Lord Dalhousie's first lady in Halifax, where he held appointment as lieutenant governor of Nova Scotia from 1816 to 1820; in Quebec City, where he was governor-in-chief of British North America from 1820 to 1828; and in India, where he was commander-in-chief from 1828 to 1832.[14]

With respect to women's roles, on the other hand, Lady Dalhousie was more conventional than Austen in both private and public life. The countess followed the path of marriage and motherhood that Austen depicted in her novels but did not choose for herself. Moreover, while Austen envisioned herself as a published author in her early teens, an aspiration finally gratified by the printing of *Sense and Sensibility* in 1811, Lady Dalhousie evidently had no such ambition to be recognized.[15] Rather than seeking to publish under her own name, she followed accepted practice for scientifically minded women at the time by contributing to the work of professional male botanists. Most notably, she corresponded with and sent extensive collections of specimens to leading scientists, including Sir William Jackson Hooker (1785–1865), and to institutions including the Royal Botanic Garden Edinburgh.[16]

In addition, Lady Dalhousie earned herself a place in the history of Canadian literature by encouraging an aspiring novelist, Julia Catherine Beckwith Hart, who dedicated *St. Ursula's Convent, Or, The Nun of Canada* to "The Right Honourable, The Countess of Dalhousie ... with profound respect." Published by subscription in Kingston in 1824, *St. Ursula's Convent* was the first novel published in Canada by a Canadian-born author, male or female. Of approximately two hundred copies printed, only "six or seven" remain.[17]

Lady Dalhousie's privilege and social status made possible both the extent of her reading and the survival of sources that convey it. She could afford to buy plenty of books and subscribe to libraries. She had leisure time in which to read and to write about her reading. Likenesses were made of her and reminiscences recorded. And, after her death, her personal papers were preserved by family members as part of a multi-generational private archive.[18] To the benefit of both American and Scottish reception on Austen, these extraordinary documents make it possible to trace the countess's evolving literary interests from her girlhood reading, through the love of books she shared with her husband, to her book ownership and encounters with Austen's novels—most thought-provokingly, *Persuasion* and *Emma*—in North America.[19]

Plants, drawing, reading, riddles: girlhood education

The daughter of Charles Broun, Esq., a wealthy Scottish advocate (comparable to an English barrister), Christian grew up at Coalstoun House, an extensive estate about twenty miles from Edinburgh.[20] There, as a child, she began collecting plants, some of which she preserved and interleaved between the pages of her personal diaries and scrapbooks, a practice she continued throughout her life (see figure 3.2).

Her parents' only child, Christian was named for her mother, who lived for just two days after the birth.[21] Letters written by her father show that, to him, she was "Christy" or "Christie," a nickname that would later be used by her husband as well.[22] While elsewhere in the world "Christian" is a given name exclusively for boys, in Scotland at the time it was relatively common for girls.[23]

FIGURE 3.2 *Page from Christian Broun's commonplace book, with interleaved plant specimen. Courtesy of private owner.*

Like Austen, Christian was educated both at home and, for a few years, at a private girls' residential academy.[24] At the Misses Carvers' school in Doncaster, in southern Yorkshire, the teenaged Christian was tutored in the subjects then considered essential for a gentlewoman: "French, Music, drawing and the writing of figures, English reading and Geography of the globe," according to a 1799 letter from one of the Misses Carver to Mr. Broun.[25] (Readers of *Pride and Prejudice* will note how much less extensive is this list of accomplishments than the one promulgated by Caroline Bingley.[26]) Whether botany was a subject of study or a private enthusiasm for Christian during these years is not known. It might have been either, since the gathering of plants and flowers was then considered an appropriate pastime for women, as was the drawing of collected specimens with the "feminine" media of watercolor or chalks (not oils, a medium restricted to professional artists, nearly all of whom were men). Of course, the profession of botany—like all academic professions—was closed to women.[27]

In this era, as readers of Austen's novels know well, the accepted purpose of education for young women of leisure was preparation for marriage and motherhood, not a profession. Even as Mary Wollstonecraft and others advocated for less superficial, more academic education for girls, feminine accomplishments remained valued because it was thought that such training equipped a woman in four important ways. A woman could amuse herself during time alone with artistic or musical pursuits, as Anne Elliot does at the piano in *Persuasion*, and as Austen herself did in adulthood.[28] She could entertain family members and guests—including, during her marriageable years, potential suitors—in the domestic circle, as do many Austen heroines, including Jane Fairfax and Emma Woodhouse in *Emma*. Once a mother, she could apply her artistic skills to illustrating lessons for her young children, boys and girls alike, and could instruct her daughters in all the accomplishments. Finally, in case of financial ruin or spinsterhood, she could support herself by teaching other young women, typically as an in-home governess, as Jane Fairfax is prepared, but reluctant, to do. Some fathers did encourage their daughters' aspirations to achieve in the arts beyond these accepted outlets, as Rev. George Austen did by offering Jane's novel, then titled *First Impressions*, to the London publishers Cadell and Davies in 1797; famously, the firm "declined by Return of Post" even to receive the manuscript.[29] But such cases were relatively rare.

As an heiress to her father's considerable land and fortune, Miss Broun of Coalstoun was in a position very different from Austen's own, and very similar to that of the fictional Emma Woodhouse: that is, she did not need to excel in accomplishments in order to be considered a desirable match. Unlike the self-aggrandizing Emma, however, Christian fell short of the ideal of an effortlessly accomplished woman, according to her own charmingly unaffected accounts. Of her attainments in needlework, she apprised her father in 1803, "I am now Netting a purse for my uncle but as soon as it is finished I shall net you a Coarse one w^h I declare I shall be quite Affronted if you do not Wear." Of her progress in drawing, she noted that she was sending "the two Landscapes I have finished which I thought you would like to have tho' they are not very beautiful. I have likewise sent the head which I have done by myself. I assure you it is all my own doing as Mr Hough did not see it till it was finished."[30] Given norms of women's art education in this era, the "Landscapes" and the portrait "head" Christian mentions in this letter were most likely copies rather than drawn from life, much as the young Charlotte Brontë later produced during her own training in the 1830s and subsequently described in her novels.[31]

"Not very beautiful" Christian's drawings may have been, but in other realms, her interests and enthusiasms exceeded what was expected of young women. Her letters to her father show both her strong interest in literature and the lively, original manner in which she expressed her reactions to what she read. Urged by her father to take medicine for her "Hooping Cough," she joked in 1802, "I had much rather read my Histoire Romaine at Night than take an Emetic." More seriously, Christian wrote, "I am Affraid I shall not get Ptolemy Aulites finished so he must just be sent some other time . . . I am now reading the twentieth & last Volume of the Roman . . . I hate Tiberius with all my heart."[32] (Several concerned letters to the school during an earlier period of illness in 1799 further attest to Mr. Broun's caution regarding his daughter's health: a minor point of contact with Emma Woodhouse's experience with her own widowed, anxious father.)

Such a passionate reader required a constant infusion of new books, which Christian relied upon her devoted father to supply. "We finished Sophocles and Aeschylus last night," she announced in January 1803. "If—you have a mind to spend so much money, and if—the whole party would be so much obliged to you. Nobody can read them so well as Miss Margaret—in short, if you would but send us Potter's Euripides you would delight the whole family."[33] On another occasion, she requested, with evident chagrin, that he return to her a volume that she was in the middle of reading and had sent him by mistake. "I am certainly the foolishest creature in the world . . . I sent you two books yesterday which I thought were my Journal, but I find today that I have sent you only one Book and a French one which I have not finished however I have now sent you the first Volume of the Journal and will be very much obliged to you to send me back my <u>poor</u> <u>travelled</u> <u>Contes</u> by the very first opportunity as I am in the very act of finishing a story."[34]

That Christian, in her mid-teens, sent her journal to her father to read might surprise us today. Such an act was fully in keeping, however, with the essential goal of education for young women at this time: the formation of the moral mind and the feeling heart. Through carefully directed reading of "improving" texts, as well as reflective writing on her daily life, a girl would develop virtue and self-regulation, it was thought. (Austen's readers will be reminded of the quality of "sense" shown by Elinor Dashwood in *Sense and Sensibility*.) By opening her journal to her father, Christian allowed him to assess her progress in the realm of moral education. Rather than stressing the dutifulness of her sharing, however, she conveyed her trust that he would appreciate her work in writing as much as in other subjects. "I have sent you my Journal as a <u>New</u> <u>Year's</u> <u>Gift</u>," she told him, with her pride evident in her underlining.[35] (That journal has not survived.)

Of course, keeping a journal offered practice for a would-be writer, too. In *Northanger Abbey*, which Austen originally attempted to publish in 1803, Henry Tilney half-mockingly celebrates "this delightful habit of journalizing which largely contributes to form the easy style of writing for which ladies are so generally celebrated."[36]

No evidence comparable to Austen's juvenilia remains to suggest that Christian aspired to write fiction or poetry. Very conventionally, she kept a commonplace book: a scrapbook of hand-copied excerpts from literature, in this case mostly verse. The blank volume she used is beautifully leather-bound, gilt-stamped, and fastened with a clasp.[37] Most of the entries are highly sentimental: "Lines on a lost infant" is a typical title. One set of lines, poignantly, includes the note "from a MS book of my mother's"—that is, copied from a similar commonplace book kept by the mother Christian never knew. Some authors' names are recognizable today. Christian identified one except as "the first poetical composition of Walter Scott Esq[r] written when a boy during a Thunder Storm," and she included too a short prose passage, in French, attributed to "Mme. Genlis," an author to whom Emma Woodhouse refers in *Emma*.[38] Many interleaved plants are present, as well as two miniature watercolors of birds. (While the copied verses end about a third of the way through the volume, the plants continue.)

Also surviving among Christian's personal papers is a paperbound, handwritten book of riddles.[39] Unlike her commonplace book, she created a title page for this volume, which reads:

Riddles—&c &c &c
    C B Dalhousie 1809

Carefully numbered, the riddles total 445 items, ranging from single-line puns in the form of questions to elaborate verses and ciphers. With no solutions included, the modern reader can only guess at the answer to puzzles such as #26, "Why is a handsome woman like an oatcake?". Less enigmatic is #30, "Why is a person in bed like an unbound book?": the answer must have something to do with "sheets" (see Chapter 1).

Readers of *Emma* will recognize the great similarity between this manuscript compilation of riddles and the one on which Emma Woodhouse and Harriet Smith collaborate: the effort that represents the closest that Austen's "imaginist" heroine Emma ever comes to actual authorship.[40] Furthermore, one of Christian's entries offers a tantalizing connection to *Emma*. Her riddle #158 is a shortened, altered version of the riddle of which Emma Woodhouse's father, despite repeated attempts, can recall only the first line: "Kitty, a fair but frozen maid," a verse authored by the actor and poet David Garrick (1717–1779).[41]

A literary marriage

As its title page makes plain, when Christian began her book of riddles in 1809, she was no longer Miss Broun of Coalstoun but "C B Dalhousie." Following her father's death in 1803, she married George Ramsay, 9th Earl of Dalhousie on 14 May 1805.[42] Born in October 1770, Lord Dalhousie was fifteen years Christian's senior— by coincidence, very close to the sixteen-year age difference between Mr. Knightley in *Emma* (whose first name the earl shares) and Emma Woodhouse. According to the *Canadian Dictionary of National Biography*, the young George Ramsay "received his primary education from his mother" Elizabeth. After further study at the Royal High School of Edinburgh and the University of Edinburgh, he inherited his property and title at the age of seventeen and entered the British Army in the following year.[43] His choice of a military profession, unusual for an eldest son, may indicate an inclination to public service; it also suggests a need for earned income to supplement the proceeds of his family estate. Located eight miles from Edinburgh, the old and distinguished Dalhousie Castle was then in need of extensive upkeep and renovation, for which Christian's inheritance from her father, including the Coalstoun property, was doubtless most welcome. The need for funds to support the continued renovation of Dalhousie Castle was one of two deciding factors in the earl's decision to take up his first administration post in Canada, the other being his desire for advancement in military rank.[44]

Did love as well as money bring together Miss Broun of Coalstoun and Lord Dalhousie of Dalhousie Castle, as would have been the case if they were an Austen heroine and hero? Whether or not theirs was initially a love match, "Lord D." and "Lady D.," as they designated each other in their respective journals, evidently became very attached. His letters to her from his various army postings are full of warmth: "My dearest Christie," begins a typical one, which concludes, "God bless you. Kiss my boys for me and believe me Ever and Always your most truly affectionate D."[45]

An especially fond series of letters from 1813 traces the earl's evolving responses to a portrait of the countess that she had sent to him. (The portrait has not survived.) "I received your letter this morning and the picture, a thousand thanks for it, but it is a sad performance, I cannot trace a feature of your face in it, but perhaps by looking long and long at it, it may improve," he wrote in an undated letter. "Such as it is I shall carry it wherever I go—the best that could have been made would have but poorly replaced the happiness of being with you."[46] His next letter, also undated, confirmed his hope: "The more I look at yourself the more it improves; it is a hurried and faulty drawing but he has hit the features and it will I assure you be a most agreeable companion to me when I can find an hour of solitary society."[47] Finally, he concluded as follows a letter dated 13 October 1813:

I was sitting one evening with your picture keeping me company and reading Burns 1st Epistle to Davy, the 8th and 9th Stanzas applied vividly that I read them over and over, but as the 4 lines of grief did not suit, I changed them to

> "Now, Honour, Duty and my King
> Have called me from my home
> Her penciled picture comfort brings
> And cheers me when alone."

You may laugh now as much as you please, but pray keep them to yourself.

God bless you my ever Dearest Christie again and again
Yours most affectly
D.[48]

For a Scotsman, there could hardly be a more appropriate source of literary comfort than verses by Robert Burns (1759–1796), the enormously influential Scottish poet and nationalist.

The Dalhousies' shared literary sensibility is most apparent in the virtuoso performance with which she celebrated his award of the Order of the Bath earlier in 1813. The countess's undated letter consists entirely of a multi-page sequence of quotations from Shakespeare, which begins, suitably, with references to *Macbeth*: "All hail, Dalhousie, hail to the Peer of Scotland! All hail, Dalhousie, that may be Peer of England! All hail, Dalhousie, that shall be Knight hereafter!"[49] (Readers of *Emma* will note with amusement that, like Emma Woodhouse, the countess did not address her husband as "George."[50]) Clearly both touched and impressed, the earl responded,

> Your Shakespeare is delightful and quite beautified this time. You not only improve but already write masterly, in this way, for it seems all one to you whether you quote as a Witch in Macbeth, a Noble Dame of Rome, or from the gay and gallant days of our own Henrys. Caesar, Timon, the Moor, or Petruchio, they are all in your mind's eye, and ready at your wit's call. To read your letter and its high sounding praises I could tell the Peer of Wellington to cast his ribbon to the winds; I have one valued friend at home whose praise makes trash of that, and of all the Princes or Powers in Christendom; but tho' that is my feeling, I fear for it the world and even my Shakespeare witty wife would call me fool.[51]

Lord Dalhousie's appealing description of the countess as his "Shakespeare witty wife" makes it clear that he appreciated both her intellect and her way with words. For his own part, he concluded a series of thoughts on rereading *Julius Caesar* and *Coriolanus* with the self-deprecating comment, "Recollect only I am not a <u>reviewer of books</u>."[52]

That Shakespeare stood at the apex of the Dalhousies' literary pantheon is confirmed by an undated "Coalstoun Glossary" written by the countess. Among her definitions are:

One of us . . . . Flighty and Voluble.
Not one of us . . . . Quiet, decent and well disposed.
Clever . . . . Ourselves.
Stupid . . . . All the world besides . . .
Wit . . . . Our own books and sayings.
Literature . . . . Quoting Shakespeare, writing nonsense and admiring John Kemble.
Shakespeare . . . . The summum bonum.[53]

The Dalhousies were far from unique in their devotion to Shakespeare, whose popularity surged two centuries after his death.[54] Nor were they unusual in their admiration of John Philip Kemble (1757–1823), a celebrated actor who was also manager of the Theatre Royal at Covent Garden from 1803–1817; his sister was the famous actress Sarah Siddons.[55]

In her own diaries, Lady Dalhousie frequently noted what her husband was reading, typically a sermon on Sundays and verse or a biography on other days of the week. Only very rarely did he read a novel. In one of his army letters, he observed, "William Stuart beat all hands at Chess, & I read Don Quixote—Idle fellows both, you will say—."[56]

Just how conventional were Lord Dalhousie's views on novel-reading for men, particularly army men, comes across clearly in a December 1818 letter he wrote regarding the Halifax Garrison Library, a subscription lending library he had established the previous year for officers. "The great want of Books of good reading, & the difficulty in procuring them in the present state of Halifax, pointed out to me the inestimable advantages, the comfort, the lasting pleasure to be derived from such an Institution," he recalled, before urging

that the Collection of Books be kept select . . . if once trash or
novel reading takes the lead, the object is equally defeated.
Reading of that sort is always obtained abundantly in circulating
libraries, but the intention of this Institution, is to furnish elegant,
instructive, classical reading and amusement, so that while as
officers we are serving our country at a distance from home, we
may at the same time devote our leisure hours in fitting ourselves
for any station in life in which Fortune may place us.[57]

To an Austen reader, of course, a reference to "trash or novel
reading" instantly recalls the passionate defense of novels by the
narrator in chapter five of *Northanger Abbey*, which includes the
statement, "Let us leave it to the Reviewers to abuse such effusions
of fancy at their leisure, and over every new novel to talk in
threadbare strains of the trash with which the press now groans."[58]
   The earl's own collection of books, however, indicates that his
views on novel reading actually fell closer to those of Henry Tilney
in *Northanger Abbey*, who proclaims to Catherine Morland that
the "person, be it gentleman or lady, who has not pleasure in a good
novel, must be intolerably stupid."[59] A manuscript volume titled
"Library Catalogue of Dalhousie Castle" lists approximately 1,500
titles, in which novels are well represented, among them Scott's
Ivanhoe, *Rob Roy*, *Guy Mannering*, and *Kenilworth*, as well as
Richardson's *Sir Charles Grandison*, one of Jane Austen's own
favorite novels.[60] No works by Austen appear in this catalogue;
evidently, *Emma* was part of the countess's personal collection. The
Dalhousie Castle library was also rich in poetry—Milton's *Paradise
Lost*, Scott's *Lady of the Lake*, "Byron's Life & Works" in sixteen
volumes—and in what we would call nonfiction, including,
understandably, an extensive group of titles pertaining to North
America.
   The catalogue of Lord Dalhousie's collection was prepared in the
early 1830s, when he initiated and oversaw the renovation of the
physical space of the Dalhousie Castle library. A plan drawn on
the endpapers of the beautifully bound catalogue delineates a
spacious layout and well-proportioned arched alcoves, along with
numbered shelves. As befits an inventory designed to support
reinstallation of a collection, the catalogue identifies each book
only by its title and the number of volumes, not by the author's
name or publication details. Nor is genre noted, with a few rare

exceptions, e.g. "The Gaurds [*sic*] a Novel." The design of the library room, and the hardwood the earl is said to have imported from Canada for the shelves, are still visible today in what is now the Dalhousie Castle Hotel.[61]

The earl's commitment to building his family's book collection is evident too in sources that document his purchases and payments for book-binding. Substantial payments to tradesmen identified as booksellers—£25 5s 16d to "White Bookseller," £48 7s 9d to "Ballantine Bookseller"—appear in an estate account book for Dalhousie Castle from 1813–1816, just before the family moved to Nova Scotia.[62] Clearly, Lord Dalhousie shared the sentiments articulated by Mr. Darcy in *Pride and Prejudice* regarding the obligation of a gentleman to the library of his family estate:

> "I am astonished," said Miss Bingley, "that my father should have left so small a collection of books.—What a delightful library you have at Pemberley, Mr. Darcy!"
>
> "It ought to be good," he replied, "it has been the work of many generations."
>
> "And then you have added so much to it yourself, you are always buying books."
>
> "I cannot comprehend the neglect of a family library in such days as these."[63]

In extent, however, Lord Dalhousie's collection was significantly more modest than the finest private libraries of his contemporaries. Seven thousand volumes were shelved in the purpose-built, double-height library room at Newhailes, the estate owned by Lady Dalhousie's cousin Miss Christian Dalrymple; the Newhailes collection, now housed at the National Library of Scotland, is considered the finest intact library of the Scottish Enlightenment.[64]

Evidence of the financial value of the Dalhousie Library collection can be found in an inventory of Lord Dalhousie's belongings prepared by an appraiser in 1838, following the earl's death in March of that year.[65] The collective category "Books, Prints, & Pictures" includes records of 3,622 volumes. (Most works were multi-volume, hence the difference between this number and the approximately 1,500 titles in the library catalogue.) About a third of the titles, including a set of Scott's *Waverley Novels*, are individually named and appraised; the other two-thirds are grouped together under the heading

"Miscellaneous Works, additional volumes, Pamphlets, Imperfect Works, Portfolios, etc." Altogether, the estimated value of Lord Dalhousie's books was £270—much less than his holdings of "Wine and other liquors," which were appraised at £686. The total value of his possessions was given as £4,341 14s 6d.

Encounters with Austen's novels during a "transatlantic life"

Both Lord Dalhousie's dedication to stewarding his book collection and his interest in reading works that he considered worthwhile befitted his social position as a landowning peer, especially one who, as a proud Scot, valued knowledge greatly. Lady Dalhousie's devotion to reading, however, went well beyond what one might expect for a noblewoman of her time and place, as her daily diary entries make clear.[66]

Externally, Lady Dalhousie's diaries are unprepossessing: slim blank books, some bound fully in leather, other with boards for covers and minimally decorated leather binding and corners. (Volumes survive covering September 1811 through 1839, the year of her death.) On the inside, the volumes contain a wealth of data about the countess's reading. She recorded, by title, what works she began, continued, and finished each day, along with any travels, visits paid or received, and plays attended. In addition, several lists of her book collection, with titles and numbers of volumes, are preserved within her diaries, written either onto the pages or on separate, inserted sheets. Her diaries do not contain reflections on her reading; these thoughts she put into her letters, relatively few of which have survived.[67]

Lady Dalhousie's diaries are a challenge to consult. Though her handwriting is generally very clear and readable, as one would expect from an educated gentlewoman, she often wrote vertically and diagonally over her horizontal daily entries. She rotated each page clockwise to record, vertically, the names of correspondents from whom she had received letters, and counterclockwise to record those to whom she sent letters. Diagonally, she notated literary works read in addition to those she listed daily. As a result, some portions of pages are almost impossible to decipher. Further increasing the difficulty—and, from another perspective, the charm—of reading Lady Dalhousie's diary volumes are the many pressed flowers and leaves, along with the occasional insect and feather, preserved between pages.

The Dalhousies' relocation to Halifax, where the earl was to become lieutenant governor of Nova Scotia, took place in the summer of 1816, just as, in Philadelphia, the printing of Carey's *Emma* began (see Chapter 1). "Heard that the appointment to Halifax was decided," Lady Dalhousie noted in her diary on 20 July 1816. "Pack'd books," she recorded on 14 August 1816, a week before embarking on the multi-stage journey from Dalhousie Castle to Halifax.[68] Lord and Lady Dalhousie brought with them their youngest son, four-year-old James; the two elder sons, Ramsay and Charles, remained at school in London. Having sailed from Portsmouth on the *Forth* on 8 September, the Dalhousies arrived in Halifax on 25 October.[69]

The earliest surviving portrait of the countess dates from this year, when she was thirty years of age. A modest-sized image of her with little James, it is, in René Villeneuve's words, "a graceful pencil drawing enhanced with watercolour depicting a mother tenderly resting a hand on her youngest son's shoulder."[70] Lady Dalhousie's elaborately curled hair and empire-waisted white dress follow the fashions of the day, which are well known to aficionados of Austen films. Her large, dark eyes are the most expressive part of her face, which bears a neutral expression. As portrayed by the artist, the countess's face, especially her prominent nose and small chin, bears some resemblance to that of Jane Austen, as recorded in Cassandra Austen's smaller-scale c. 1810 portrait, likewise a pencil drawing with face and hair rendered in watercolor.[71]

Readers of Austen's novels know all too well the value accorded to a woman's perceived beauty during this period. Judging by this likeness of the countess, she would not have been considered beautiful by the standards of the day; neither was Austen.[72] Contemporary comments about Lady Dalhousie's appearance bear out this supposition. Joseph Howe, a journalist and noted Nova Scotia politician, observed that "[n]othing could be more correct and refining than the tone given to society by Lady Dalhousie who, without being handsome, was remarkable for the plainness of her dress and the elegant simplicity of her manners."[73] The fullest description of the countess, which conveys evident admiration, appeared in Edward Bannerman Ramsay's widely read posthumous memoirs: "a very remarkable person . . . eminently distinguished for a fund of the most varied knowledge, for a clear and powerful judgment, for acute observation, a kind heart, a brilliant wit."[74] Along the same lines, Walter Scott, Lord Dalhousie's old schoolfellow, recorded in his journal on 30 March 1829 that "Lady Dalhousie, formerly Miss Brown of Coalstoun, is an amiable, intelligent, and lively woman, who does not permit society to 'cream and mantle like a standing pool.'"[75]

For her part, the countess's excitement at visiting Scott at his renowned Scottish baronial estate is evident in her exuberantly punctuated diary entry for that day: "To Abbotsford!!!"[76] It is tempting to imagine that Lady Dalhousie and Scott discussed Austen's novels during this or other encounters. Scott's letters and journals indicate that he continued to think very highly of Austen, and to reread her works, throughout the 1820s, well after his unattributed review essay for John Murray's *Quarterly Review* in March 1816.[77] That Lady Dalhousie saw that very review also falls within the bounds of possibility, since she mentioned perusing the *Quarterly Review* in a 28 April 1818 diary entry, when she was in Halifax.[78]

The theory that Lady Dalhousie's first acquaintance with Austen's novels came via Scott, either in person or through his unsigned review, is not, however, well supported by her ownership of the 1816 Philadelphia *Emma*. Had she been intrigued by the review, she surely would have bought Murray's then-available London edition of *Emma*, published in late December 1815, rather than waiting a full year to obtain Carey's Philadelphia edition in North America. Moreover, if inspired by the review, she would likely have sought out the other two Austen novels mentioned in it: *Pride and Prejudice* and *Sense and Sensibility*. Instead, according to Lady Dalhousie's diary, the first Austen novel she read was *Persuasion*, in June 1818.

Lady Dalhousie read *Persuasion* while aboard ship, on a coastal voyage southwest from Halifax to Mahone Bay. Here are her relevant June 1818 diary entries (see figure 3.3):

> 24 Prepared to embark in the Forth—Wind contrary . . .—slept on Board.
> 25 Sailed but obliged to return by wind contrary.—read 1st Vol. of "Persuasion." . . .

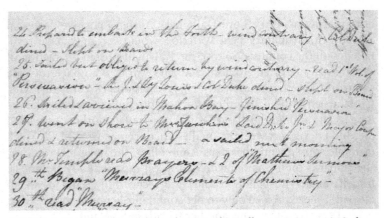

FIGURE 3.3 *Portion of page from Lady Dalhousie's June 1818 diary, showing her reading of* Persuasion. *Courtesy of private owner.*

> 26 Sailed & arrived in Mahon [*sic*] Bay—finished "Persuasion."[79]

While the countess made reading a regular part of her day no matter where she was, a sea journey would certainly have afforded welcome uninterrupted stretches for enjoying a novel.[80] A more appropriate choice could hardly be made for *Persuasion*, given Austen's focus in that novel on the British Navy.

Northanger Abbey too Lady Dalhousie chose to read while on a coastal journey, this time heading northeast from Halifax to Country Bay. Her entry for 24 September 1818 reads: "Sailed in the Leander. Read 'Northanger Abbey' & 'Marriage.'"[81] That the countess read *Northanger Abbey* next after *Persuasion* makes sense, given that the two novels were published together by John Murray in a four-volume set. (Both works were somewhat shorter than Austen's prior novels, hence the presentation of each in two volumes rather than the standard three.) Both titles, moreover, were still relatively new when the countess read them, having been published in December 1817 (with 1818 printed on the title page).

That Lady Dalhousie began her acquaintance with Austen via *Persuasion* and *Northanger Abbey* is significant for two reasons. The first is the subject matter of *Persuasion*, which would have held particular interest for the countess in several respects. Though the novel's hero Captain Frederick Wentworth was a naval officer, not an army man like Lord Dalhousie, Austen's positive portrayal of the British military post-Waterloo would certainly have resonated with the countess. So too, surely, would Austen's depiction of the mutually devoted Admiral and Mrs. Croft, who have traveled the world together and clearly enjoy each other's company. Mrs. Croft, when praised by others for her intrepidity, explains that as long as she and her husband "could be together, nothing ever ailed me, and I never met with the smallest inconvenience."[82] Mrs. Croft's example subsequently heartens Anne Elliot, the novel's heroine, as she embarks on life as the wife of a naval captain. Lady Dalhousie herself, in her husband's recollection, "cheerfully agree[d] to go abroad"; she expressed only to her confidants her distress at leaving behind her two older sons and her friends in Scotland.[83]

The countess's adventurous spirit during what she called her "transatlantic life" is abundantly evident in her diaries.[84] Ever curious, she sought out, collected, and sent to British institutions not only the native flora but also the distinctive minerals of North America.[85] In the most daring act recorded of her, she was the first person, male or female, to walk the length of a just-finished suspension bridge between Ottawa and Hull, over the Rideau Canal. Her own diary for 27 September 1827 notes only that she "walked across suspension bridge."[86] Lord Dalhousie, in his journals, told the story more fully: "Lady D. did walk across the whole line . . . even that trembling and very nervous part of it, the suspension bridge, which in fact Col. By [the army officer in charge of the bridge's construction] himself had not ventured to do, untill Lady D. called me back to accompany her over, and then he kept his own secret. I admit it was a bold thing for a lady, but I was satisfied before of the safety of it."[87]

The steadying influence of Mrs. Croft on her husband the Admiral in *Persuasion* represents further common ground with Lady Dalhousie's experience. Austen shows Mrs. Croft "judiciously" assisting her husband in steering their carriage, which causes Anne Elliot's "amusement at their style of driving, which she imagined no bad representation of the general guidance of their affairs."[88] In a situation with much higher stakes, when Lord Dalhousie was initially passed over as the next head of British Canada, the countess persuaded him not to send a bitter letter of resignation. "At Lady D.'s particular desire this letter was not sent," reads a note in the earl's handwriting on the surviving document.[89]

Austen's sensitive—and uncharacteristic—depictions in *Persuasion* of affectionate parent-child relationships in the Musgrove family would also have appealed to the countess. A devoted mother, Lady Dalhousie found it "a very severe trial" to leave her two elder sons behind in England when departing for Halifax.[90] She must have been especially moved by the grave injury of one very young Musgrove boy and Mrs. Musgrove's mourning of the recent death, as a teenager, of another. In August 1817, just under a year before she read *Persuasion*, a ship's arrival from England brought "Lady D. flying down all joy for her letters," as Lord Dalhousie vividly recalled, only to receive the tragic news that their eldest son, Charles, had died of an illness.[91] The Dalhousies' profound grief is evident in their private writings, as is the staunch Scottish Presbyterian faith that offered them consolation. They found comfort, too, in sending for the other son they had left in England, Ramsay, who then remained in North America with them for several years.

By remarkable and sad coincidence, bereavement for a child connects Lady Dalhousie and *Persuasion* with an earlier occasion of British women reading Austen in Nova Scotia. As Sarah Emsley and Sheila Johnson Kindred have discovered, Lady Sherbrooke—wife of Sir John Coape Sherbrooke, Lord Dalhousie's predecessor as lieutenant governor—read *Mansfield Park* aloud over five days in July 1815 with Mary Wodehouse, the wife of a naval captain, who was grieving the recent death of her firstborn child, a son, at three months of age.[92] The two women's purposefully consolatory reading, as Emsley and Kindred persuasively describe it, took place at Birch Cove, the Sherbrookes' country retreat eight miles from Halifax. The copy of *Mansfield Park* they read was on loan from a naval captain, Sir Robert Cavendish Spencer, who was visiting from England.

Beyond these parallels in *Persuasion* to Lady Dalhousie's own experience, her encounter with *Northanger Abbey* was significant because it acquainted her with Austen's life, via the "Biographical Notice" prefaced to the first volume. This brief account—authored by, but not attributed to, Austen's brother Henry—was both the first widely public identification of Austen as the author of her works and the first published description of her as a person.[93] Thanks to the "Biographical Notice," the countess had access to information about Austen and her authorship that had not been available to Scott when he wrote his review essay in 1816, or to Mathew Carey when he published his Philadelphia edition of *Emma*.

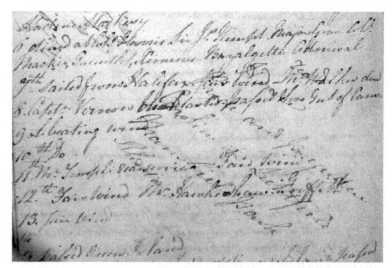

FIGURE 3.4 *Portion of page from Lady Dalhousie's June 1820 diary, showing her reading of* Pride and Prejudice *and* Mansfield Park. *Courtesy of private owner.*

Lady Dalhousie did not rush to read further works by Austen. Two years later, in June 1820, *Pride and Prejudice* and *Mansfield Park* appear among a list of five titles that the countess wrote diagonally over her entries beginning 7 June (see figure 3.4). Once again, she was on a voyage, this time from Halifax to the Dalhousies' new residence at Quebec, where they arrived on 18 June.[94] Coincidentally, the order in which Lady Dalhousie read these two Austen novels reproduces the sequence of their original publication in 1813 and 1814, respectively, and also of the order in which they are mentioned on the title pages of *Northanger Abbey* and *Persuasion*: "BY THE AUTHOR OF 'PRIDE AND PREJUDICE;' 'MANSFIELD-PARK,' &C."[95]

The other titles on this list give some indication of the range of Lady Dalhousie's literary reading, in terms of genre, language, and publication date. *Home: A Poem*, by Ann Cuthbert Knight (1788–1860), was published in 1815 after the author emigrated from her native Scotland to Montreal.[96] *Caroline de Lichtfield, ou Mémoires d'une Famille Prussienne* (1786), was a bestselling novel by the Swiss author Isabelle de Montolieu (1751–1832).[97] *Rhoda*, a didactic novel published anonymously in 1816 by the Englishwoman Frances

Margaretta Jacson (1754–1842), was more popular in its day than Austen's *Emma*.[98] That Lady Dalhousie read *Pride and Prejudice* and *Mansfield Park* in the company of works by three other women authors is certainly notable. Overall, however, she read many works by male authors, as well as extensively in history, philosophy, biography, and other non-literary subjects; the full range of her reading deserves much more investigation than is possible here.

When exactly Lady Dalhousie read *Emma* cannot, unfortunately, be determined with absolute certainty. I have scrutinized repeatedly all the pages of her diary volumes from 1817 through 1824, both in the original and in digital photographs. On a diary page overwritten vertically and diagonally, a word as short as "*Emma*" can disappear, especially if the ink is faded or deteriorated, as is true of several portions of Lady Dalhousie's 1819–1824 diary volume.

Nevertheless, the general time period during which Lady Dalhousie read *Emma* can be established with relative confidence, thanks to the book list she included at the back of the diary volume she began on 1 September 1819. While the titles in the first two-thirds of this 141-item list are alphabetized, those in the last third are not, implying that the countess added them in the order that she acquired the books.[99] The title *Emma* appears in the unalphabetized portion, amid a group of titles—*Rhoda* among them—that can be cross-referenced with diary entries ranging from 7 June 1820 to November 1821. Lady Dalhousie listed the number of volumes per title, which suggests that she prepared the alphabetized portion of this book list to aid with packing for her move from Halifax to Quebec in June 1820. She continued to note the number of volumes throughout the list. *Emma*, of course, has two.

That Lady Dalhousie read *Emma* during July through September 1820 seems especially probable because this period was, by her account, one of intense reading. In a 26 September 1820 letter written from Sorel, in the countryside outside Quebec, the countess explained that she has "had little to do but to draw & to read while here" and that her "reading has been various."[100] A final, tempting possibility for a more exact dating for the countess's reading of *Emma* appears opposite her diary entries for 8 to 9 September 1820: a diagonal notation so thoroughly illegible that it could refer to any title of approximately the same length as *Emma*.

Whether the countess read *Emma* shortly after leaving Halifax or did so at a greater remove, she would have recognized how much the provincial social hierarchy of Austen's fictional village of Highbury had in common with the bustling British colonial port city in Nova Scotia. As a newcomer, Lady Dalhousie described Halifax as "exactly what any country society is at home, the amazing influx of Navy and Army has tended much to polish the people, nor are they in any respect behind us in civilization. There are several most uncommonly pleasant men—the ladies are of sundry kinds—prudes, Coquettes etc., etc."[101] Lady Dalhousie's sketches vividly convey her amused impressions of her new compatriots (see figures 3.5 and 3.6).[102] In his journals, Lord Dalhousie recorded his own equally wry observations: "Last night Lady D. gave a Ball to the better class of the society. About 200 people came to it, not powerful in either beauty or good dancing, but on the whole it showed a very good set of people, very much inclined to be pleased, at same time extremely civil & attentive."[103]

Of this society Lady Dalhousie, as the wife of the lieutenant governor, was the female leader, much as Emma Woodhouse, thanks to her family's social position and wealth, is queen bee of the comparatively minuscule Highbury.[104] Unlike the self-satisfied Emma, however, Lady Dalhousie was alert both to the personal dangers of her position and to its effects on her social inferiors.

FIGURE 3.5 *Watercolor by Countess of Dalhousie [1819]. Courtesy of the Nova Scotia Museum.*

FIGURE 3.6 *Watercolor by Countess of Dalhousie [1819]. Courtesy of the Nova Scotia Museum.*

"[E]very person," she reported, "is evidently acting a part with me. The young Ladies never speak at all, and the elder ones seem to think it necessary to be always of my opinion; then they always flatter me—some well and some ill—and if I was not well aware of, and on my guard against this, I should certainly run much risk of fancying myself very near perfection."[105] Emma Woodhouse, of course, does indeed fancy herself very near perfection, an endeavor abetted by her doting father and her former governess—and, crucially, counteracted by the moral guidance of her brother-in-law and eventual husband, Mr. Knightley.

The probity that Emma learns only in adulthood the young Christian Broun had cultivated, along with other feminine virtues, in her girlhood. How carefully Lady Dalhousie monitored her self-regard in midlife is evident from her response to the elevation in her status resulting from her husband's promotion to governor-in-chief of British North America. To her dear friend Mrs. Anderson, she wrote,

> One fear—one <u>terror</u> possesses me now—that you will find me dreadfully changed on my return—accustomed here to be <u>second</u> only to one I tremble lest I be taught to expect & to insist that all <u>except</u> <u>that</u> <u>one</u>, ~~must~~ ^ shall bow & yeild [*sic*] to my sovereign

will & pleasure, & that I therefore on returning to you my equals, render myself hateful to you & miserable to myself—However—as I am aware—nay <u>feel</u> the approaches of this Villainous inclination, & am armed against it, surely I shall be able to counteract its <u>worst</u> effects—if not to escape altogether –[106]

Lady Dalhousie's "<u>terror</u>" of becoming insufferable contrasts directly with Emma Woodhouse's complacent enjoyment of her own privilege. Rather than become, in the countess's words, "<u>second</u> only to one," namely, her husband, Emma prefers to remain unmarried. As she observes to her protégée Harriet Smith, "without love, I am sure I should be a fool to change such a situation as mine. Fortune I do not want; employment I do not want; consequence I do not want: I believe few married women are half as much mistress of their husband's house as I am of Hartfield; and never, never could I expect to be so truly beloved and important; so always first and always right in any man's eyes as I am in my father's."[107]

With respect to feminine companionship, too, Lady Dalhousie's choices accorded more with expectations of sensible, virtuous behavior than do Emma's. After the departure of her governess, Emma enlists the beautiful but dim Harriet, who offers her no challenge or support of any kind, intellectual or moral. Lady Dalhousie, by contrast, rejoiced to find in Halifax a young woman who shared her literary interests and artistic tastes. "One most uncommonly pleasant young woman, Miss Cochrane, I see more of than of any other: our pursuits are in many respects similar," she explained to her Scottish cousin Miss Christian Dalrymple. "I think I should have loved her even at home, but here she is invaluable. I take the greatest care not to show her more attention than others when in company, yet the mornings wch she spends here in reading together (and wch by the bye would tire the others as much of me as I should tire of them), has excited much jealousy."[108] In addition to reading and drawing with Lady Dalhousie at Government House (the official residence of the lieutenant governor), Isabella Cochrane accompanied the countess on expeditions in and around Halifax. Lord Dalhousie noted in his August 1818 journal how "happy" had been "Lady D. and Miss Cochrane in their reading & studies in Chemistry & Mineralogy" while in Mahone Bay.[109]

Lady Dalhousie and Emma Woodhouse differ most thought-provokingly in the extent to which each used her extensive leisure time for intellectual and artistic self-cultivation. Throughout *Emma*, Austen stresses how incompletely Emma has developed her considerable artistic talents and intellectual gifts. Her portfolio of drawings contains only "many beginnings," not completed works:

> Miniatures, half-lengths, whole-lengths, pencil, crayon, and water-colours had been all tried in turn. She had always wanted to do everything, and had made more progress both in drawing and music than many might have done with so little labour as she would ever submit to. She played and sang;—and drew in almost every style; but steadiness had always been wanting; and in nothing had she approached the degree of excellence which she would have been glad to command, and ought not to have failed of. She was not much deceived as to her own skill either as an artist or a musician, but she was not unwilling to have others deceived, or sorry to know her reputation for accomplishment often higher than it deserved.[110]

Especially striking is the explicit judgment by Austen's narrator that Emma has fallen short not only of her potential but of her duty: she "ought not to have failed of" achieving excellence.

In contrast, Lady Dalhousie brought dedication and enthusiasm to bear on all her pursuits, whether artistic or botanical. "My miniatures progress (as our neighbors the Americans say), but want of good Copies [i.e., originals from which to copy] prevents my improvement," she lamented soon after the move to Quebec.[111] In addition to her satiric portraits in the Halifax portfolio, two colorful miniatures, one of a man wearing a turban, another of a woman in an exaggerated mobcap, are tucked into her 1811–1819 diary volume. Most significantly, of course, she educated herself as a botanist, chiefly through self-directed reading, and attained considerable technical skill in the preservation of plants.[112]

In the realm of reading, too, Austen makes plain that Emma has not lived up to her promise. As the clear-eyed Mr. Knightley observes,

> "Emma has been meaning to read more ever since she was twelve years old. I have seen a great many lists of her drawing up at various times of books that she meant to read regularly through— and very good lists they were—very well chosen, and very neatly

arranged—sometimes alphabetically, and sometimes by some other rule. The list she drew up when only fourteen—I remember thinking it did her judgment so much credit, that I preserved it some time; and I dare say she may have made out a very good list now. But I have done with expecting any course of steady reading from Emma. She will never submit to any thing requiring industry and patience, and a subjection of the fancy to the understanding."[113]

The difference between Emma's aspirational reading lists and Lady Dalhousie's documentation of her extensive, near-daily reading could not be more obvious.

While similar in privilege, the fictional Emma and her historical reader, Lady Dalhousie, are each unconventional in opposing ways: by achieving less and more, respectively, than was expected of British gentlewomen. Emma lacks motivation to occupy herself with the pursuits considered appropriate for young ladies; she concentrates instead on matchmaking and, within the tight confines of Highbury, exercising her considerable imagination. Lady Dalhousie, in addition to fulfilling her duties as a wife, mother, and political hostess, explored the natural world with curiosity and intrepidity, creating collections that greatly exceeded those of a typical botanizing lady.

Reading tastes and book acquisition

Comments by Lady Dalhousie on her reading of Austen's novels have not survived. Nevertheless, her recorded thoughts on other authors, together with what can be determined about her book ownership, provide valuable further contexts for her reading of Austen and her possession of the 1816 Philadelphia *Emma*.

In her great enthusiasm for the works of Scott and Byron in particular, Lady Dalhousie was a woman of her time. As Annika Bautz has shown, the literary reputations of Scott and Austen form inverse trajectories: Scott's international fame was immense in his own day, when Austen's was very modest, and the reverse is true today.[114] Lady Dalhousie's diaries make clear that she kept up with every new Scott release and that she regularly reread her favorites. The works of Byron too recur in her entries, some read by her, others aloud by "Lord D." These preferences Lady Dalhousie would have seen reflected in *Persuasion*, in which Austen depicts Anne Elliot and Captain Benwick "talking as before of Mr. Scott and Lord Byron, and still as unable, as before, and as unable as any other two readers, to think exactly alike of the merits of either."[115]

Like so many contemporary readers, including the du Pont sisters, Lady Dalhousie both adored Scott's novels and confidently guessed his identity as author. (He put his name to his published poems but concealed his identity when turning to novels, lest his reputation as a poet be tarnished.[116]) "Are you not delighted with Old Mortality?" she wrote to her friend Mrs. Anderson in June 1817. "I think 'tis <u>above</u> and beyond all the rest, (for—convince me that it is not by the same author as Waverley is, or that <u>that</u> Author was not Walter Scott)."[117] Austen too esteemed Scott's fiction, albeit with some writerly envy of his great success in two literary genres. As she wrote to her niece Anna Austen, an aspiring novelist, in 1814, "Walter Scott has no business to write novels, especially good ones.—It is not fair.—He has Fame & Profit enough as a Poet, and should not be taking the bread out of other people's mouths.—I do not like him, & do not mean to like Waverley if I can help it—but fear I must."[118]

Equally typically, Lady Dalhousie read Byron's poetry avidly while deploring many of his poetic techniques and much of his subject matter. "Are you, my dear M^rs A, a great admirer of Lord Byron's fourth canto?" she wrote to Mrs. Anderson in August 1818, referring to the recently published section of *Childe Harold*. "To my shame (I suppose) I must own being very much disappointed in it. It is a very strange performance and from the desultory manner in which he has treated his subject he has contrived to make it very far from interesting. Granted that some of the stanzas are truly magnificent, but others are not even poetry or sense. His egotism is peculiarly disgusting."[119] The countess's dislike intensified a year later, as she read the first portions of *Don Juan*. "What a sad prostitution of talent is it, in Lord Byron, to bestow his upon beautifying irreligion & immorality," she observed. "He ought to be ashamed of doing—& the world of receiving it."[120] Austen's novels, of course, posed no such problems either of "desultory" construction or of celebrating immorality; perhaps, if they had, they would have enjoyed more popularity.

As a devout Scottish Presbyterian, Lady Dalhousie had a strongly moral orientation in general and as a reader in particular. She had patience neither with salacious literary works nor with suggestive interpretations. Hearing an acquaintance's insinuations about Scott's

1823 novel *Peveril of the Peak*, the countess "loudly protested I was either too <u>wicked</u> or too <u>innocent</u> to discover where the wickedness lay. When told that it is in the intention of making Alice Charles's mistress, I entered an especial Memo in my Journal never to converse alone with my <u>delicate</u> friend . . . [lest she] corrupt my Morals—for she must be desperately vicious."[121] This conversation may remind Austen's readers of the interactions in *Mansfield Park* between the powerfully moral Fanny Price and the beautiful Mary Crawford, whose self-display, bold comments, and eventual countenancing of adultery mark her as the most vice-prone female character in Austen's published novels.[122]

Of Lady Dalhousie's literary reading beyond Scott and Byron, some titles will be recognizable to readers of Austen, including *Mysteries of Udolpho* (mentioned in *Northanger Abbey*) and *Elegant Extracts* (mentioned in *Emma*).[123] In September 1822, the countess read *Precaution*, the anonymously published Austen-inspired first novel by James Fenimore Cooper.[124]

The countess's literary interests and artistic pursuits were a challenge to supply in North America. Lord Dalhousie lamented that "there is not a Bookseller's shop in Halifax, nor is there an individual possessed of anything that can be called a Library"—that is, an extensive private collection of books, as opposed to a subscription-based circulating library, which did exist in the city.[125] In a detail that readers of *Emma* will savor, he noted appreciatively in his journal that his predecessor in Halifax "left us a Piano Forte, which was a thing not to be got here."[126]

Lady Dalhousie's diary entries refer to many more titles than her book lists contain. Very little, however, can be determined about those books she read in Canada but did not own. She likely borrowed some volumes from friends, as her Halifax predecessor, Lady Sherbrooke, did with *Mansfield Park* in 1815. Payments for subscription fees and late penalties show that both the countess and the earl were members of multiple libraries in North America. They patronized circulating libraries while living in Halifax and Quebec, respectively. During their Quebec years, too, both Dalhousies continued to subscribe to the Garrison Library that the earl had founded at Halifax, and the collection of which he endeavored to preserve against the "trash" of novels.[127]

Some of the books that Lady Dalhousie acquired while in Nova Scotia and Quebec were sent to her by friends and acquaintances in

Britain. On 18 July 1822, thanks to an Edinburgh friend, Miss Isabella Houstoun, she read Scott's novel *The Fortunes of Nigel*, published less than three months before (on 29 May 1822).[128] "I long to hear how you like it," Miss Houston wrote in September, assuring the countess that "Wakefields [*sic*] Introduction to Botany goes [illegible] tomorrow."[129]

Even her sons' tutors were pressed into service to send Lady Dalhousie books. Rev. Mr. J. Temple, one of James's instructors at Harrow, informed the earl on 26 January 1824, "I have purchased St Ronan's Well for Lady Dalhousie, as a matter of course, though in my mind little better than a common novel. It will be sent by the Halifax Mail of next month."[130] While Rev. Temple's lack of enthusiasm was palpable, his speed was impressive: *St Ronan's Well* was published on 27 December 1823. Through the efforts of Temple and others, Lady Dalhousie remained as au courant with Scott as one could be living across the Atlantic.

Clearly, the Dalhousies continued in North America their practice of spending a substantial amount of money on books. Frequent payments for book purchases and binding appear in Lord Dalhousie's account and cash books during the family's years in Halifax and Quebec. During their Halifax years, the Dalhousies bought primarily from New York sellers, with some purchases from Philadelphia.[131] In Quebec, the Dalhousies were able to patronize local merchants and artisans, including "Lodge the bookbinder," "Cary Book Seller," and "Neilson Book Seller."[132]

Titles of specific books, however, are not listed in the cash and account books, and only rarely are entries for purchases and binding attributed to the countess in particular. Thus, in addition to the uncertainty about when in 1820–1821 Lady Dalhousie read *Emma*, many fundamental questions remain about her copy of the novel, including when and from whom she bought it, and who bound it and when. While further research may shed more light, as of now we can only guess whether Carey's *Emma* might be among the "Books bought from N.Y. for Lady Dalhousie in 1817 £1.18.9" referred to in an 8 February 1820 entry, or whether *Emma* was the very title concerned in the 24 January 1821 payment "To Lodge the Bookbinder a book for L^y D 3 | 6."[133]

In terms of binding and personalization, Lady Dalhousie's copy of *Emma* does not resemble the relatively few books of hers that remain to this day in the possession of her descendants.[134] Most of the surviving volumes are half-bound in leather rather than fully bound, and none are decorated like *Emma*. Nor do any of the other volumes contain a bookplate comparable to the apparent calling card the countess inserted into her copy of *Emma*; instead, some bear a large square bookplate with the family crest, and others a small square plate with a crown over the initials "CBD." The vertical signature on the title page with which Lady Dalhousie further marked her ownership of *Emma* is, however, apparent on several of the other volumes, including an 1823 New York *Reginald Dalton* and an 1820 Edinburgh *Ivanhoe*.

After two hundred years and many changes at Colstoun House— including years of tenant occupation, a destructive fire in 1907, and a series of sales of the most valuable books to raise funds—it is a wonder that any of the countess's collection remains at all. Knowledge of the family's sales of books does solve one mystery, however, related to the provenance of her copy of *Emma*: how it came to be in the possession of a Salisbury rare book dealer, from whom the noted First World War poet Siegfried Sassoon purchased it in the early twentieth century. From Sassoon, the volumes were bought by the American bibliophile Frank J. Hogan; after Hogan's death, they were acquired by Alberta H. Burke, who gave them to Goucher College in 1975 as part of her distinguished Austen collection.[135]

Notably, Lady Dalhousie kept track of which books she owned in American editions, designating them with the abbreviation "Am^n" on the list of her collection included in her 1819–1824 diary volume.[136] (Apparently through an oversight, her listing of *Emma* is not so marked.) A letter to her friend Mrs. Anderson also demonstrates that the countess considered North American printings of English titles to have novelty value. "You did not answer a query I put as to whether you possessed a copy of Lord Byron's 'English Bards and Scotch Reviewers,' but taking it for granted that one printed in America will be considered a kind of curiosity, I send one," Lady Dalhousie wrote from Halifax.[137]

The countess's decision to have her copy of *Emma* beautifully rebound strongly suggests that she valued this novel as more than "a kind of curiosity." Certainly her investment in rebinding had far-reaching consequences. Her stewardship of this book ensured the volumes' soundness through all the journeys on which they accompanied her, as well as enhancing the book's value for subsequent owners. Indeed, only because this *Emma* was sold from Colstoun House were book collectors and bibliographers prompted to speculate about this copy's first possessor and, more broadly, about the origins of the edition itself. Thanks to the care Lady Dalhousie took with her books, even American editions, it has been possible to rediscover the full story of the 1816 Philadelphia *Emma* and its readers, including the countess's own fascinating life as a well-traveled reader and a counterpart to Austen.

Notes

1 In personal and legal documents from Lady Dalhousie's lifetime, her family name is spelled alternately as "Brown" and "Broun"; the second spelling is currently in use by her descendants, the Broun-Lindsay family. Some published sources incorrectly render Lady Dalhousie's first name as "Christina." According to Andrew Sharp, steward of the Dalhousie Castle Hotel, the second syllable of the earl's family name (like that of the Canadian university) is properly pronounced to rhyme with "house" rather than "moose," as a Scottish Highlands accent would render it. Personal conversation with author, 6 July 2016.

2 For contrasting accounts of Lord Dalhousie's career as an administrator, see Peter Burroughs' unsparingly critical assessment in "Ramsay, George, 9th Earl of Dalhousie," *Dictionary of Canadian Biography*, vol. 7, 722–33 (Toronto: University of Toronto Press, 2007) and the sympathetic introductions by Marjory Whitelaw to her edition of *The Dalhousie Journals*, 3 vols. (Ottawa: Oberon Press, 1978–1982). In *Lord Dalhousie: Patron and Collector* (Ottawa: National Gallery of Canada, 2008), René Villeneuve makes a compelling case for considering Lord Dalhousie "Canada's first great patron and art collector" (9). Among the cultural institutions inaugurated and supported by the earl was the Literary and Historical Society of Quebec (Burroughs, 725). Mine is the first treatment of Lord Dalhousie in his private, domestic character.

3 David J. Howlett, "Ramsay, James Andrew Broun, first marquess of Dalhousie (1812–1860)," *Oxford Dictionary of National Biography*, online edn, January 2011.

4 See James S. Pringle, "Canadian Botanical Specimens Collected 1826–1828 by the Countess of Dalhousie, Acquired by the Royal Botanical Gardens," *Canadian Horticultural History/Histoire de*

l'horticulture au Canada 3.1 (1995): 1–21. Conservation and
digitization of this collection has recently been overseen by David A.
Galbraith, Head of Science at the Royal Botanical Gardens, which are
located near Hamilton, Ontario (email to author, 6 January 2016).
Dr. Galbraith apprised me that the Herbarium at the Royal Botanic
Garden Edinburgh also holds specimens collected by Lady Dalhousie,
especially from India.

5   Deborah Anne Reid, "Unsung Heroines of Horticulture: Scottish
    Gardening Women, 1800 to 1930" (PhD diss., University of Edinburgh,
    2015), 118. Reid's dissertation features the most extensive account to
    date of Lady Dalhousie's life and botanizing. Reid notes that although
    the countess "did not collect species of *Dalhousiea*, the name for this
    genus of tropical leguminous shrubs was proposed by Robert Graham
    to commemorate her botanical prowess and it is a higher mark of
    respect that he chose to name a genus after her rather than just a
    species" (118). Reid also lists the several species of plants and one
    species of bird collected by Lady Dalhousie in British India that were
    named for her (118, 123). See also Catherine Horwood's brief treatment
    of Lady Dalhousie in *Gardening Women: Their Stories from 1600 to
    the Present* (London: Virago, 2010), which includes the observation,
    apropos of the genus *Dalhousiea*, that "one feels she deserved better
    than this not particularly interesting leguminous plant" (27).

6   Reid, "Unsung Heroines," 123.

7   This portrait is reproduced close to its original size, though in black
    and white rather than the delicate "black, white, and red chalk on buff
    paper" used by the artist. The portrait's medium is identified in the
    item's entry (D 3671) in the Scottish National Gallery's catalogue,
    which was kindly supplied to me by Hannah Brocklehurst, Curator of
    Prints and Drawings at the Scottish National Gallery. I am very grateful
    to her for her help, and most especially for allowing me extended time
    with the portrait itself. Its dating is possible thanks to the following
    notation in the countess's diary for 21 May 1829: "Sat for picture."
    Personal diary of [Christian, Countess of Dalhousie], 1 June 1824 – 30
    June 1830, Broun-Lindsay papers, via National Register of Archives for
    Scotland (hereafter NRAS) 2383/3/62. The Watson Gordon oil portrait
    of the countess is in private hands. A silhouette of the countess
    attributed to Jarvis Hankes is in the collection of Libraries and Archives
    Canada, catalogued as MIKAN No. 2885745. I am grateful to Jessie
    Moolman of the Reference Services Division for this confirmation
    (email to author, 30 December 2015).

8   In his *Bibliography of Jane Austen*, new edn (New Castle, DE: Oak
    Knoll Press, 1997), David Gilson describes this copy as bound in "full

diced calf gilt" and bearing the countess's "engraved booklabel" (100). A narrow gilt border alternating crosses and lozenges appears on the front and back covers of both volumes, while gilt ornaments— including images of plants and birds—are placed vertically on the spines. The volumes contain no binder's mark or label. On the expense of binding in this period, see Chapter 1. That Lady Dalhousie, rather than a later owner, commissioned the binding can be inferred from the placement of her bookplate in the first volume.

9   Gilson, *Bibliography*, 101.

10 All biographers of Austen grapple with the family's complicated status in the English gentry; see, for example, Jan Fergus, *Jane Austen: A Literary Life* (New York: St. Martin's, 1991), 47–50.

11 On the dedication of *Emma* to the Prince Regent, see Juliette Wells, Introduction to *Emma*, by Jane Austen (New York: Penguin Classics, 2015), xviii–xix.

12 "I was Lord Dalhousie's companion at school," Scott recalled in his 23 December 1827 journal. Walter Scott, *The Journals of Sir Walter Scott*, ed. W. E. K. Anderson (Edinburgh: Canongate, 2009), *EBSCOhost*.

13 On Austen's travels, see Hazel Jones, *Jane Austen's Journeys* (London: Robert Hale, 2015). Until 1815, the Napoleonic Wars prevented travel by all Britons to the Continent.

14 Burroughs, "Ramsay, George," 722–32.

15 The fullest account of Austen's literary aspirations and publications is that of Fergus.

16 Reid, "Unsung Heroines," 109.

17 Julia Catherine Beckwith Hart, *St. Ursula's Convent, Or, The Nun of Canada*, 1824, ed. Douglas G. Lochhead (Ottawa: Carleton University Press, 1991), 1, xiii. On the nature of *St. Ursula's Convent* as a novel and its significance to Canadian literary history, see Lochhead's preface, in which he describes the work as having "suffered from misunderstanding and neglect" (xiii). Hart's dedication to the countess is noted by George Parker in "Courting Local and International Markets," in *History of the Book in Canada Vol. 1: Beginnings to 1840*, ed. Patricia Lockhart Fleming, Gilles Gallichan, and Yvan Lamonde (Toronto: University of Toronto Press, 2004), 346.

18 Only a very small fraction of the countess's letters are preserved in the group of personal papers maintained by her descendants: the Broun-Lindsay papers at Colstoun, which are to be transferred to the John Gray Centre, Haddington, East Lothian, Scotland. Further research may uncover relevant letters from the countess held in other archives.

19 For Austen's few references to Scotland and the Scots in her novels
    and letters, see David Groves, "Jane Austen and Scotland,"
    Persuasions 7 (1985): 66. A definitive account of the importance and
    influence of Austen's Scottish readers and critics has yet to be written.
    In addition to the roles of John Murray and Walter Scott in Austen's
    publishing and reception—the former reflected in the recent deposit of
    the Murray archives at the National Library of Scotland in
    Edinburgh—central topics would include the first full-length
    biography of Austen by a woman writer, *Jane Austen and Her Works*
    (1880) by Sarah Tytler, the pen name of novelist Henrietta Keddie
    (1827–1914), which has recently been reissued by Bloomsbury
    Academic; the influence of the Scottish-born R. W. Chapman, Austen's
    twentieth-century editor for Oxford University Press; and the two
    novels commissioned by HarperCollins' twenty-first-century "Austen
    Project" that have Scottish authors and settings: Val McDermid's
    Northanger Abbey (2014) and Alexander McCall Smith's *Emma: A
    Modern Retelling* (2015).

20 Now spelled "Colstoun," the house is owned by descendants of the
    Broun family and hosts a cooking school as well as private events:
    http//www.colstoun.co.uk.

21 Reid, "Unsung Heroines," 99–100.

22 Letters from Charles Broun to Miss Carver, 1799, Broun-Lindsay
    papers, NRAS 2383/3/132. All transcriptions from manuscript
    reproduce spelling, capitalization, formatting, and punctuation as
    exactly as possible.

23 One of Christian Broun's cousins, Miss Christian Dalrymple, inherited
    the estate of Newhailes from her father, an unusual circumstance at
    the time for an unmarried woman. Hilary Horrocks, *Newhailes*
    (printed for the National Trust for Scotland, 2014), 12.

24 On Austen's schooling, see Fergus, *A Literary Life*, 34–6.

25 Quoted in Reid, "Unsung Heroines," 100.

26 Jane Austen, *Pride and Prejudice*, ed. Pat Rogers (Cambridge:
    Cambridge University Press, 2013), 43. On Austen and feminine
    accomplishments, and ideas on women's education in general, see
    Juliette Wells, "'In Music She Had Always Used to Feel Alone in the
    World': Jane Austen, Solitude, and the Artistic Woman," *Persuasions*
    26 (2004): 98–110.

27 On opportunities for and constraints on women botanists during this
    time, see Ann B. Shteir, *Cultivating Women, Cultivating Science:
    Flora's Daughters and Botany in England 1760–1860* (Baltimore:
    Johns Hopkins University Press, 1996).

28 See Wells, "'In Music.'"

29 Fergus, *A Literary Life*, 12–13.

30 Christian Broun to Charles Broun, 1 January 1803, Broun-Lindsay papers, NRAS 2383/3/132.

31 See Juliette Wells, "'Some of Your Accomplishments Are Not Ordinary': The Limits of Artistry in *Jane Eyre*," in *The Brontës in the World of the Arts*, ed. Sandra Hagan and Juliette Wells, 67–80 (Houndmills, Basingstoke: Ashgate, 2008).

32 Christian Broun to Charles Broun, 22 December 1802, Broun-Lindsay papers, 2383/3/132.

33 Christian Broun to Charles Broun, 1 January 1803, Broun-Lindsay papers, NRAS 2383/3/132.

34 Christian Broun to Charles Broun, undated (apparently 1803), Broun-Lindsay papers, NRAS 2383/3/132.

35 Christian Broun to Charles Broun, 1 January 1803, Broun-Lindsay papers, NRAS 2383/3/132.

36 Jane Austen, *Northanger Abbey*, ed. Barbara Benedict and Deirdre Le Faye (Cambridge: Cambridge University Press, 2006), 19.

37 The NRAS catalogue for this commonplace book identifies it as containing "Extracts from various literary works with enclosed specimens of dried ferns and other plants," dated c. 1804 (Broun-Lindsay papers, NRAS 2383/3/58). The volume is not dated and the paper does not show a watermark; a later entry, not in Christian's handwriting, is marked June 1817, so evidently she continued to add to the compilation over the years. Neither entries nor pages are numbered.

38 Jane Austen, *Emma*, ed. Richard Cronin and Dorothy McMillan (Cambridge: Cambridge University Press, 2005), 503.

39 Collection of riddles made by Christian, Countess of Dalhousie, Broun-Lindsay papers, NRAS 2383/3/68.

40 "In this age of literature, such collections on a very grand scale are not uncommon," remarks Austen's narrator. "Miss Nash, head-teacher at Mrs. Goddard's, had written out at least three hundred." Austen, *Emma*, 74. Only "a thin quarto" in size, Emma and Harriet's volume is on a smaller scale than Christian's (74).

41 Copied in another handwriting than Christian's, her book's entry reads:

>   Kitty, a fair but frozen Maid
>   Kindled a flame I yet deplore.
>   The hoodwink'd boy I call'd to aid
>   Still of his near approach afraid.

So fatal to the suit before
At length the little urchin came.
From earth I saw him mount in air
And soon dispense with anxious care
The bitter reliques of the flame.
Say by what title & what name
Shall I this youth address?
Cupid & he are not the same.
Tho' both can raise and quench a flame.
I'll kiss you if you guess.

"A chimney sweeper" is the answer. Cronin and McMillan give the entirety of the verse, including the following salacious lines that are entirely absent from Christian's book: "To Kitty, Fanny now succeeds,/ She kindles slow, but lasting fires;/ With care my appetite she feeds;/ Each day some willing victim bleeds,/ To satisfy my strange desires." Austen, *Emma*, 550.

42 Reid, "Unsung Heroines," 101.

43 Burroughs, "Ramsay, George," 722.

44 Whitelaw, ed., *Dalhousie Journals*, 1:15 (June 1816).

45 Earl of Dalhousie to Countess of Dalhousie, 25 September 1813, Broun-Lindsay papers, NRAS 2383/3/15; typescript transcription by "E. C. B. L." of original in the Dalhousie family papers in the National Archives of Scotland, Edinburgh. Spelling, capitalization, formatting, and punctuation are those of the typescript.

46 Earl of Dalhousie to Countess of Dalhousie, [1813], Broun-Lindsay papers, NRAS 2383/3/15.

47 Earl of Dalhousie to Countess of Dalhousie, [1813], Broun-Lindsay papers, NRAS 2383/3/15.

48 Earl of Dalhousie to Countess of Dalhousie, 28 October 1813, Broun-Lindsay papers, NRAS 2383/3/15. The verses quoted are from Burns's "Epistle to Davie, a Brother Poet," first published in 1785.

49 Countess of Dalhousie to Earl of Dalhousie, [1813], Broun-Lindsay papers, NRAS 2383/3/15.

50 Not long after Emma accepts Mr. Knightley's proposal of marriage, she and he discuss what she shall now call him. He begins:

"'Mr. Knightley.'—You always called me, 'Mr. Knightley;' and, from habit, it has not so very formal a sound.—And yet it is formal. I want you to call me something else, but I do not know what."

"I remember once calling you 'George,' in one of my amiable fits, about ten years ago. I did it because I thought it would offend you; but, as you made no objection, I never did it again."

"And cannot you call me 'George' now?"

"Impossible!—I never can call you any thing but 'Mr. Knightley.'"

Austen, Emma, 405.

51 Earl of Dalhousie to Countess of Dalhousie, 25 September 1813, Broun-Lindsay papers, NRAS 2383/3/15.

52 Earl of Dalhousie to Countess of Dalhousie, 2 May 1813, Broun-Lindsay papers, NRAS 2383/3/15. Lord Dalhousie's thoughts on Shakespeare's military men in this letter are perhaps revealing of his own character: "I have read Julius Caesar and Coriolanus, the latter I greatly prefer of the two, but both are admirable and I think cannot fail to captivate young men's hearts as well as young <u>women's</u>. Brutus is greatly noble in that scene only with Cassius in 4th act. Coriolanus is equally noble and great in every scene he appears in. Manly, open, brave, and inflexible in his resolution, he is softened only in the irresistible and most amiable forces of our nature. I would feel with Coriolanus every sentiment he expresses towards the Mob, and his fury at being termed 'Traitor' by Aufisius is a fine example of Walter Scott's expression of 'bearding the lion in his den', tho' to be sure its a sinking in poetry in my bringing a whole scene of Shakespeare into one line of Walter Scott."

53 "Coalstoun Glossary," undated, Broun-Lindsay papers, NRAS 2383/3/15.

54 The comparative popularity of Shakespeare and Austen two hundred years after their respective deaths was examined in a 2016 exhibit titled "Will & Jane: Shakespeare, Austen, and the Cult of Celebrity," at the Folger Shakespeare Library in Washington, D.C. See Janine Barchas and Kristina Straub, "Curating Will & Jane," Eighteenth-Century Life 40.2 (April 2016): 1–35.

55 "Kemble, John Philip," in A Biographical Dictionary of Actors, Actresses, Musicians, Dancers, Managers, and Other Stage Personnel in London, 1660-1800, by Philip H. Highfill, Jr., Kalman A. Burnim, and Edward A. Langhans (Carbondale: Southern Illinois Press, 1982), 8:335–83. In Jane Austen and the Theatre (Cambridge: Cambridge University Press, 2002) Penny Gay judges it conceivable that Austen saw Kemble and Siddons in performance in Bath or London (6–7).

56 Earl of Dalhousie to Countess of Dalhousie, 25 September 1812, Broun-Lindsay papers, NRAS 2383/3/269. Considered one of the

earliest and greatest novels, Cervantes' *Don Quixote*, first published in 1605, was widely available in English translation.

57 Earl of Dalhousie to Col. Darling, 27 December 1818, Broun-Lindsay papers, NRAS 2383/3/380. Karen Smith points out that, after seventeen years, half of the holdings of the Halifax Garrison Library constituted "fiction, travel, and biographies." Karen Smith, "Community Libraries," in *History of the Book in Canada Vol. 1: Beginnings to 1840*, ed. Patricia Lockhart Fleming, Gilles Gallichan, and Yvan Lamonde (Toronto: University of Toronto Press, 2004), 151. The Halifax Garrison Library still exists; it is now called the Cambridge Library.

58 Austen, *Northanger Abbey*, 30.

59 Austen, *Northanger Abbey*, 107.

60 Catalogue of books in Dalhousie Castle Library, undated, Broun-Lindsay papers, NRAS 2383/3/113. The catalogue is written, in a copyist's hand—with some additions and emendations in Lord Dalhousie's handwriting—on paper that bears an 1831 watermark. On Austen and Grandison, see Austen, *Northanger Abbey*, 315 n. 9.

61 Sharp, personal conversation, 4 July 2016. In the twentieth century, Dalhousie Castle was leased to a school and stood empty before being reconfigured as a hotel and aqueous spa.

62 Accounts for various expenses and receipts relating to the Colstoun and Dalhousie Castle estates, 1813–1816, Broun-Lindsay papers, NRAS 2383/3/59.

63 Austen, *Pride and Prejudice*, 41.

64 Horrocks, *Newhailes*, 22–8.

65 Inventory of the furniture and personal property of the late George, Earl of Dalhousie, at Dalhousie Castle, 1838, Broun-Lindsay papers, NRAS 2383/3/115.

66 See Jacqueline Pearson, *Women's Reading in Britain, 1750–1835: A Dangerous Recreation* (Cambridge: Cambridge University Press, 2005).

67 In addition to Christian's girlhood letters to her father, the Broun-Lindsay papers contain letters the countess wrote from Canada to a dear, older friend: Mrs. Anderson of St. Germain, Tranent, East Lothian, wife of Lieutenant-General David Anderson. (Mrs. Anderson's death on 17 December 1824 was recorded in *The Scots Magazine and Edinburgh Literary Miscellany*, n. s. 95 [1825], 128.) A 1924 cover letter explains that a great-granddaughter of Mrs. Anderson's returned this group of letters to a great-granddaughter of Lady Dalhousie's. Broun-Lindsay papers, NRAS 2383/3/261. Typed transcripts of some of the countess's letters to her husband are also included

in Broun-Lindsay papers, NRAS 2383/3/15; originals of these letters are in the Dalhousie fonds, National Library of Scotland, GD-45.

68 Personal diary of [Christian, Countess of Dalhousie], 30 September 1811—1 April 1819, Broun-Lindsay papers, NRAS 2383/3/60.

69 Whitelaw, ed., *Dalhousie Journals*, 1:15, 1:20.

70 Villeneuve, *Lord Dalhousie*, 16. The artist is William Douglas (1780–1832), a Scotsman; the original is in private hands.

71 Cassandra Austen's portrait of her sister's face, which is the only authentic likeness of Jane Austen from her lifetime, has been widely reproduced; see for example Juliette Wells, *Everybody's Jane: Austen in the Popular Imagination* (New York: Bloomsbury Academic, 2011), 147.

72 For descriptions of Austen's looks recorded by her family members, see Wells, *Everybody's Jane*, 143.

73 Quoted in Whitelaw, ed., *Dalhousie Journals*, 1:7.

74 Edward Bannerman Ramsay, *Reminiscences of Scottish Life and Character*, 23rd edn. (Edinburgh: Edmonston & Douglas, 1874), 257, *GoogleBooks*.

75 Scott, *Journals*. The quotation is from Shakespeare's *The Merchant of Venice*.

76 Personal diary of [Christian, Countess of Dalhousie], 1 June 1824 – 30 June 1830, Broun-Lindsay papers, NRAS 2383/3/62. A site of literary tourism beginning in Scott's lifetime, Abbotsford is significant for preserving Scott's library, in its original room, with books in their original order, his copy of Murray's edition of *Emma* among them. See David McClay and Kirsty Archer-Thompson, *Rave Reviewer: Scott on Frankenstein, Emma, & Childe Harold* (printed for National Library of Scotland and Abbotsford, 2016).

77 Scott's observations on Austen are assembled in B. C. Southam, ed., *Jane Austen: The Critical Heritage* (London: Routledge & Kegan Paul, 1968), 106.

78 Personal diary of [Christian, Countess of Dalhousie], 30 September 1811 – 1 April 1819, Broun-Lindsay papers, NRAS 2383/3/60.

79 Personal diary of [Christian, Countess of Dalhousie], 30 September 1811 – 1 April 1819, Broun-Lindsay papers, NRAS 2383/3/60.

80 In Halifax, the countess reported, her friend and companion Miss Cochrane "reads to me in the morning while I draw." Countess of Dalhousie to Mrs. Anderson, 18 April 1817, Broun-Lindsay papers, NRAS 2383/3/261.

81 Personal diary of [Christian, Countess of Dalhousie], 30 September
    1811 – 1 April 1819, Broun-Lindsay papers, NRAS 2383/3/60. The
    novel *Marriage* was published anonymously in 1818 by Susan Ferrier
    (1782–1854), who is often called "the Scottish Jane Austen." It is
    notable that Lady Dalhousie read *Northanger Abbey* just three
    months before her husband's letter about keeping the Halifax
    Garrison Library free of "trash or novel reading."

82 Jane Austen, *Persuasion*, ed. Janet Todd and Antje Blank (Cambridge:
    Cambridge University Press, 2006), 77.

83 Whitelaw, ed., *Dalhousie Journals*, 1:15 (June 1816). Several years
    into the Dalhousies' residence in Quebec, Lady Dalhousie confessed
    that she worried that her sons, back in Britain, "may forget" her; she
    lamented not seeing the prospect of "an end to this banishment."
    Countess of Dalhousie to Mrs. Anderson, 20 May 1823, Broun-
    Lindsay papers, NRAS 2383/3/261.

84 Countess of Dalhousie to Mrs. Anderson, 5 June 1817, Broun-Lindsay
    papers, NRAS 2383/3/261.

85 "I am sending a very pretty collection of Minerals to the Edin.‑
    Museum and shall make worthy additions thereto in Canada," i.e.,
    Quebec. Countess of Dalhousie to Mrs. Anderson, 29 November
    1819, Broun-Lindsay papers, NRAS 2383/3/261. According to Peter
    Davidson, Senior Curator of Mineralogy at the National Museum of
    Scotland, that institution—successor to the Edinburgh Museum—
    holds a record of acquiring, in "1819–1820," a "collection of minerals
    made in North America by Lady Dalhousie and presented to the
    museum by her ladyship" (email to author, 9 September 2016).

86 Personal diary of [Christian, Countess of Dalhousie], 1 June
    1824 – 30 June 1830, Broun-Lindsay papers, NRAS 2383/3/62.

87 Whitelaw, ed., *Dalhousie Journals*, 3:117 (27 September 1827).

88 Austen, *Persuasion*, 99.

89 Earl of Dalhousie to Lord Melville, 15 September 1819, Broun-
    Lindsay papers, NRAS 2383/3/380.

90 Countess of Dalhousie to Miss Christian Dalrymple, 9 April 1817,
    Broun-Lindsay papers, NRAS 2383/3/14.

91 Whitelaw, ed., *Dalhousie Journals*, 1:44 (10 August 1817).

92 Sarah Emsley and Sheila Kindred, "Among the Proto-Janeites: Reading
    Mansfield Park for Consolation in Halifax, Nova Scotia, in 1815,"
    Persuasions On-Line 35.1 (Winter 2014). All facts in this paragraph
    are drawn from Emsley and Kindred's article, which is exceptional for
    its thoroughly researched, sensitive portrayal of a historical episode of

everyday reading. Captain and Mrs. Wodehouse remained in
Halifax and were often guests of the Dalhousies, who—shades of
Emma—sometimes rendered their name as "Woodhouse" in their
journals.

93   Henry Austen's portrayal of his sister in the "Biographical Notice" is
now widely considered less an accurate depection than an effort to
present her in a conventional light, as a good and pious woman who
did not seek fame. Austen's surviving letters contradict this and other
descriptions of her.

94   Personal diary of [Christian, Countess of Dalhousie], 1 September
1819 – 31 May 1824, Broun-Lindsay papers, NRAS 2383/3/61.

95   A facsimile of the title page is printed in Austen, *Persuasion*, lxxxvii.

96   Scott R. MacKenzie, *Be It Ever So Humble: Poverty, Fiction, and the
Invention of the Middle-Class Home* (Richmond: University of
Virginia Press, 2013), 259, n. 2.

97   Isabelle de Montolieu, *Caroline of Lichtfield*, ed. Laura Kirkley
(London: Routledge, 2016). Montolieu translated both *Sense and
Sensibility* and *Emma* into French: see Gillian Dow, "Translations,"
in *The Cambridge Companion to* Emma, ed. Peter Sabor
(Cambridge: Cambridge University Press, 2015), 169–70.

98   On the greater popularity of *Rhoda* versus *Emma* in 1816, see David
Gilson, "Jane Austen and *Rhoda*," *Persuasions* 20 (1998): 21–30.
Gilson subsequently uncovered that the novelist Maria Edgeworth in
particular preferred *Rhoda* to *Emma*: see "Jane Austen and *Rhoda*: A
Further Postscript to *Persuasions* 20 (1998)," *Persuasions* 22 (2000):
109–11.

99   Personal diary of [Christian, Countess of Dalhousie], 1 September
1819 – 31 May 1824, Broun-Lindsay papers, NRAS 2383/3/61.
Subsequent lists made by Lady Dalhousie show that her collection
grew significantly larger. Indeed, the personal library she formed in
British North America deserves consideration in comparison to the
list of "some of the most important personal libraries, 1650–1840"
compiled by Marcel Lajeunesse for *The History of the Book in
Canada, Vol. 1*, all of which involve men book owners. Marcel
Lajeunesse, "Personal Libraries and Bibliophilia," in *History of the
Book in Canada Vol. 1: Beginnings to 1840*, ed. Patricia Lockhart
Fleming, Gilles Gallichan, and Yvan Lamonde (Toronto: University of
Toronto Press, 2004), 204–5.

100 Countess of Dalhousie to Mrs. Anderson, 26 September 1820, Broun-
Lindsay papers, NRAS 2383/3/261. For a contemporary watercolor
of the view down to Richelieu River from the house at Sorel, see

Charles Ramus Forrest, "Sorel, from Government House," catalogue number 88 in Villeneuve, *Lord Dalhousie*, 121.

101 Countess of Dalhousie to Miss Christian Dalrymple, 9 April 1817, Broun-Lindsay papers, NRAS 2383/3/14 (typescript transcription).

102 Lady Dalhousie's Halifax portfolio is described by Marie Elwood in "Studies in Documents: The Discovery and Repatriation of the Lord Dalhousie Collection," *Archivaria* 24 (Summer 1987): 108–16.

103 Whitelaw, ed., *Dalhousie Journals*, 1:22 (16 November 1816).

104 On the scale of Halifax society, the countess recorded, "[t]here is a very large society—90 Civilians (independent of Military) who dine at Government house, and in all about 300 who are invited to the great Birthday Balls. We have dinners of 16 or 18 people twice a week, one Gentlemen the other a mixed party, then besides the great Ball on the 18th January at wch were all the shopkeepers in Halifax, I have given 5 private Balls to about 160 people." Countess of Dalhousie to Miss Christian Dalrymple, 9 April 1817, Broun-Lindsay papers, NRAS 2383/3/14.

105 Countess of Dalhousie to Miss Christian Dalrymple, 9 April 1817, Broun-Lindsay papers, NRAS 2383/3/14.

106 Countess of Dalhousie to Mrs. Anderson, 29 November 1819, Broun-Lindsay papers, NRAS 2383/3/261.

107 Austen, *Emma*, 90–91.

108 Countess of Dalhousie to Miss Christian Dalrymple, 9 April 1817, Broun-Lindsay papers, NRAS 2383/3/14.

109 Whitelaw, ed., *Dalhousie Journals*, 1:93 (5 August 1817). Isabella Cochrane was born in 1784 to Thomas Cochrane of Halifax; in 1829, she married Edward Bannerman Ramsay of Edinburgh, an eminent clergyman known as Dean Ramsay (and no relation to the earl's family) having been introduced to him as "a friend of Lady Dalhousie." Rev. Arthur Wentworth Hamilton Eaton, *The Cochran-Inglis Family of Halifax* (Halifax: C. H. Ruggles & Co., 1899), 13; Cosmo Innes, "Memoir of Dean Ramsay," in Ramsay, *Reminiscences*, xxxii. Lady Dalhousie's death in January 1839 took place at the Ramsays' home. She "died in the drawing-room in an instant," recorded Ramsay in his journal. "It was an awful visitation, and never to be forgotten." Innes, "Memoir," xxxviii.

110 Austen, *Emma*, 45–6.

111 Countess of Dalhousie to Mrs. Anderson, 26 September 1820, Broun-Lindsay papers, NRAS 2383/3/261.

112 Reid observes that the countess's "success in preserving and drying plant specimens from Penang and India and shipping them back to Scotland in a satisfactory condition is testimony to her practical skill, though the extent of her expertise is difficult to measure since details of the techniques she used to preserve these specimens were not recorded in her letters or journals." Reid, "Unsung Heroines," 115–16.

113 Austen, *Emma*, 37.

114 Annika Bautz, *The Reception of Jane Austen and Walter Scott: A Comparative Longitudinal Study* (London: Continuum, 2007).

115 Austen, *Persuasion*, 116. On Austen and Byron, see Rachel M. Brownstein, *Why Jane Austen?* (New York: Columbia University Press, 2011), chapter four. See too H. J. Jackson's provocative argument that Romantic authors who, like Austen, died at least relatively young with compact oeuvres were most likely to achieve enduring literary renown. H. J. Jackson, *Those Who Write for Immortality: Romantic Reputations and the Dream of Lasting Fame* (New Haven: Yale University Press, 2015).

116 See Ina Ferris, "Scott's Authorship and Book Culture," in *The Edinburgh Companion to Sir Walter Scott*, ed. Fiona Robertson, 9–21 (Edinburgh: University of Edinburgh Press, 2012).

117 Countess of Dalhousie to Mrs. Anderson, 4 June 1817, Broun-Lindsay papers, NRAS 2383/3/261. *Waverley*, Scott's first novel, was published anonymously in 1814.

118 Jane Austen to Anna Austen, 28 September 1814, in *Jane Austen's Letters*, 4th edn., ed. Deirdre Le Faye (Oxford: Oxford University Press, 2015), 289.

119 Countess of Dalhousie to Mrs. Anderson, 20 August 1818, Broun-Lindsay papers, NRAS 2383/3/2.

120 Countess of Dalhousie to Mrs. Anderson, 29 November 1819, Broun-Lindsay papers, NRAS 2383/3/261.

121 Countess of Dalhousie to Mrs. Anderson, 20 May 1823, Broun-Lindsay papers, NRAS 2383/3/261.

122 See Juliette Wells, "A Harpist Arrives at Mansfield Park: Music and the Moral Ambiguity of Mary Crawford," *Persuasions* 28 (2006): 101–14. Among the writings Austen left unpublished during her lifetime, Lady Susan, the eponymous heroine of an epistolary novella, significantly outdoes Mary Crawford in viciousness.

123 On Austen's reading, see Katie Halsey, *Jane Austen and Her Readers, 1786–1945* (London: Anthem, 2012) and two articles by Susan Allen Ford: "A Sweet Creature's Horrid Novels: Reading in *Northanger*

Abbey," *Persuasions On-Line* 33.1 (Winter 2012), and "Reading *Elegant Extracts* in *Emma*: Very Entertaining!," *Persuasions On-Line* 28.1 (Winter 2007).

124 Personal diary of [Christian, Countess of Dalhousie], 1 September 1819—31 May 1824, Broun-Lindsay papers, NRAS 2383/3/61.

125 Whitelaw, ed. *Dalhousie Journals*, 1:75 (6 December 1817). On book availability in British North America, see Fiona A. Black, "Importation and Book Availability," in *History of the Book in Canada Vol. 1: Beginnings to 1840*, ed. Patricia Lockhart Fleming, Gilles Gallichan, and Yvan Lamonde, 115–37 (Toronto: University of Toronto Press, 2004) and "Book Availability in Canada, 1752–1820, and the Scottish Contribution," PhD diss., Loughborough University, 1999.

126 Whitelaw, ed. *Dalhousie Journals*, 1:22 (11 November 1816).

127 In Lord Dalhousie's personal cash book, a payment for "5 days fine at Library Lady D 1*s* 8*d*" is recorded on 20 March 1822 and "To Lady Dalhousie at Library 16*s*" and "To d° [ditto] for fines at Ga^n [Garrison] Library 8*d*" on 24 October 1822. Cash book of Lord Dalhousie detailing personal and household expenses, 1820–1824, Broun-Lindsay papers, NRAS 2383/3/102. Smith notes that "although primarily intended to serve their own officers, garrison libraries extended membership privileges to the local community." Karen Smith, "Community Libraries," 147.

128 Personal diary of [Christian, Countess of Dalhousie], 1 September 1819 – 31 May 1824, Broun-Lindsay papers, NRAS 2383/3/61. William B. Todd and Ann Bowden, *Sir Walter Scott: A Bibliographical History, 1796–1832* (New Castle, DE: Oak Knoll Press, 1998), 561.

129 Miss Isabella Houston to Countess of Dalhousie, 20 September 1822, Broun-Lindsay papers, NRAS 2383/3/2. Of *Nigel*, "No one could have written it except Shakespeare or Walter Scott!!!" wrote Miss Houston. Priscilla Wakefield's *Introduction to Botany, in a Series of Familiar Letters* was first published in 1798 and was issued in many subsequent editions.

130 Rev. J. Temple to Earl of Dalhousie, 26 January 1824, Broun-Lindsay papers, NRAS 2383/3/2.

131 An entry in the earl's account books dated 15 April 1818 mentions "Books from N. York $27.75" and "Maps from Philadelphia"; "Books from N. York $37 ½ dollars" is listed on 24 August 1818 and "Mr Black for books from the States $15^s" on 21 August 1819. Account book of Lord Dalhousie detailing personal and household expenses, 1816–1820 [mistakenly catalogued as 1816–1817], Broun-Lindsay papers, NRAS 2383/3/453.

132 Cash book of Lord Dalhousie detailing personal and household
    expenses, 1820–1824, Broun-Lindsay papers, NRAS 2383/3/102.
    Respectively, these were Charles Lodge (dates unknown), one of four
    bookbinders in Quebec at the time and the only one with an English
    name; Thomas Cary (1751–1823), a bookseller and printer; and John
    Neilson (1793–?), a printer, publisher, and journalist. Claude
    Galarneau and Gilles Gallichan, "Working in the Trades," in *History
    of the Book in Canada Vol. 1: Beginnings to 1840*, ed. Patricia
    Lockhart Fleming, Gilles Gallichan, and Yvan Lamonde (Toronto:
    University of Toronto Press, 2004), 81; Marie Tremaine, *A
    Bibliography of Canadian Imprints, 1751–1800* (Toronto: University
    of Toronto Press, 1952), 501, 664. Fiona A. Black has identified
    Neilson as an importer of books who traveled to Britain and France
    to source stock. Black, "Importation and Book Availability," in
    History of the Book in Canada Vol. 1, 117. Very little is known
    about styles of binding in early nineteenth-century Canada: see
    Patricia Lockhart Fleming, "Bookbinding," in *History of the Book in
    Canada Vol. 1*, 109–12.

133 Cash book of Lord Dalhousie detailing personal and household
    expenses, 1820–1824, Broun-Lindsay papers, NRAS 2383/3/102.
    One intriguing possibility is that the countess bought *Emma* from
    Eastburn, one of Carey's partners who advertised the title beginning
    on 30 December 1818 (see Chapter 1). The Philadelphia *Emma*
    appears as item #2529 in *A Catalogue of Books for 1818; Including
    Many Rare and Valuable Articles in Ancient and Modern Literature,
    Now on Sale by James Eastburn & Co. at the Literary Rooms,
    Broadway, Corner of Pine-Street, New-York, at the Prices Affixed*
    (New York: Printed by Abraham Paul, May, 1818), 155. Also in this
    catalogue is the two-volume Boston edition of *Rhoda* (157): the
    novel that the countess read along with *Pride and Prejudice* and
    Mansfield Park and that directly follows *Emma* on the list of books
    in her 1819–1824 diary. As with *Emma*, the countess recorded the
    number of volumes in her copy of *Rhoda* as "2," which makes plain,
    even without the additional designation "Am[n]," that she owned this
    novel in the American edition. Further collation of the countess's
    book lists with contemporary booksellers' catalogues may yield more
    certain information.

134 I observed the countess's books on 6 July 2016. I am grateful to their
    owner for the opportunity of access, and to members of the family
    for contributing information about the history of Colstoun House.
    The 1907 fire, which resulted in the complete rebuilding of the house,
    was mentioned by them; it is also included in Charles Douglas's
    "Sumptuous Residence," *Scotland Magazine* 58 (August 2011): 10.

135 Gilson, *Bibliography*, 101. The subsequent owners of the countess's
    copy are listed in the Appendix. Images of the various owners'
    bookplates, as well as Sassoon's penciled annotations identifying
    Lady Dalhousie, can be seen in the digital facsimile at www.
    emmainamerica.org.

136 Personal diary of [Christian, Countess of Dalhousie], 1 September
    1819 – 31 May 1824, Broun-Lindsay papers, NRAS 2383/3/61.

137 Countess of Dalhousie to Mrs. Anderson, 29 November 1819,
    Broun-Lindsay papers, NRAS 2383/3/261. Byron's *English Bards
    and Scotch Reviewers* was published in Philadelphia in 1811,
    following its original 1809 London printing.

PART TWO

Transatlantic Austen Conversations

4

Enthusiasts Connected Through the "Electric Telegraph of Genius":

The Quincy Sisters of Boston and the Francis W. Austen Family of Portsmouth

A new generation of American readers gained affordable access to all of Austen's novels in the early 1830s, thanks to the complete edition published in Philadelphia by Carey & Lea. *Elizabeth Bennet; or, Pride and Prejudice*, released in August 1832, was followed by *Persuasion, Mansfield Park, Northanger Abbey, Sense and Sensibility*, and *Emma*, the last published in May 1833. Seven hundred and fifty copies were printed of *Elizabeth Bennet* and 1,250 of each other title. The 7,000 total copies represented a huge influx into a market that had previously contained only occasional imported volumes and the 500 copies of the 1816 Philadelphia *Emma*.[1]

In contrast to the 1816 Philadelphia *Emma*, all but the first of these 1830s reprints specified the novels' author—"Miss Austen"— on the title pages and spine labels of each volume. (The title page of *Elizabeth Bennet* identified Austen only as "THE AUTHOR OF 'SENSE AND SENSIBILITY,' &C."; it also described the edition as the "FIRST AMERICAN FROM THE THIRD LONDON EDITION," source information that was omitted on the subsequent reprints' title pages.) Further unlike the 1816 Philadelphia *Emma*, these self-proclaimed American editions did make purposeful changes to Austen's text, chiefly by eliminating (rare) profanities and altering occasions on which characters take the deity's name in vain.[2]

Editors of newspapers and periodicals promoted these reprinted novels as worthwhile reading for Americans.[3] Referring to *Elizabeth Bennet*, the New York *Evening Post* remarked that "[t]he mere fact of a novel running through three editions is pretty good evidence that it is not as trashy as the great majority of those productions."[4] The Philadelphia *National Gazette*, which identified "the late Miss Austin," with some exaggeration (and misspelling), as having "acquired great celebrity" through her six novels, provided a more thorough set of critical bona fides: "Miss Mitford styles Miss Austin the most correct of female writers; the London Quarterly Review extols *Persuasion* as 'one of the most elegant fictions of common life;' her works in general were commended in the warmest terms in all the principal British critical journals." This notice ended with a strong endorsement: "If the American world will read novels, let us have those of which the moral is good, the texture pure, and the instructiveness practical and domestic; entertaining and ingenious, but free from all poison."[5] Judging by that final remark, Carey & Lea were wise to bowdlerize Austen's text.

The *National Gazette* made clear, too, that Austen's novels had already gained passionate American readers, by including the following anecdote.

> A lady of our country requested a distinguished female correspondent who was on a visit to Sir Walter Scott, to ask him how it happened that in his Lives of the Novelists, he had omitted so celebrated a writer as Miss Austin. The correspondent wrote in reply—
>
> "I showed your letter to Sir Walter Scott, and he told me to tell you that if you would refer to his 'Lives of the Novelists,' you would perceive that the volume left off with Bage, a novelist who wrote prior to Miss Austin. That if the public had encouraged him—which was not the case—he would have put forth a second volume, wherein he should have done Miss Austin that justice which her extraordinary genius merited; that he considered her one of the first of female novelists."[6]

The identity of this American "lady" advocate for Austen is unknown. Fortunately, her sentiments were wholeheartedly shared by contemporaries in Boston who left abundant papers attesting to their ardent love of Austen's novels: Eliza Susan Quincy (1798–1884) and Anna Cabot Lowell Quincy Waterston (1812–1899).

The significance of the Quincy sisters to Austen reception history has been almost entirely overlooked. Eliza Susan has been dismissed by Kathryn Sutherland as nothing more than an "eager American autograph hunter," and Anna has been all but forgotten.[7] Yet the sisters' writings on Austen, which span from 1833 to 1870, afford the most extensive record of Austen appreciation by mid-nineteenth-century readers of any nationality. In the American context, the intense enthusiasm shared by Eliza Susan and Anna provides a valuable counterweight to the well-known critical remarks of contemporary male authors such as Longfellow and Emerson.

Uniquely among American readers of their time, moreover, the Quincys cultivated an acquaintance with members of Austen's family, via correspondence with and a personal visit by Anna to Admiral Sir Francis W. Austen (1774–1865), Jane's longest-surviving sibling. The earliest direct encounter between an American Austen enthusiast and the author's close relations, this was also the only recorded meeting between a lover of Austen's writings and a member of the author's own generation, as opposed to a nephew or niece.[8] The Quincys' conversations with Admiral Austen shed light on how Jane Austen and her literary legacy were spoken of on both sides of the Atlantic in the decades before J. E. Austen-Leigh's *Memoir* brought her international fame.[9]

I will begin with Anna's personal diaries from the 1830s, which recount her family's initial encounters with Austen's novels and her own especially vivid responses to them. I turn next to the sisters' first exchanges with the admiral, in 1852, including their ecstatic response to his presentation of a letter written by Jane: the only such complete document given by an Austen family member to a devotee of her novels, whether English or American. Augmenting the value of his gift, the admiral shared with the Quincys personal reminiscences of his sister. The following section treats Anna's 1856 visit to the admiral and his family in Portsmouth. At its center is a newly rediscovered manuscript: the travel journal in which Anna recounted that day in great detail for the benefit of her family in Boston. I conclude by considering the influence of the Quincys' enthusiasm on Austen's rising renown, especially through the remarkable article on Austen that Anna published in the *Atlantic Monthly* in 1863, which is virtually unknown today.

Recommended reading and fertile imaginations

On 14 March 1833, when she was twenty years of age, Anna began a diary volume, addressed to two of her sisters who were temporarily away from home. Within a week, she made her first reference to an Austen novel: *Sense and Sensibility*. Recounting an arrival during a stormy night, she noted parenthetically that "no Dashwood was at hand to receive—or rather to deceive us."[10] Anna's diary makes clear that reading Austen's novels was a family affair for the Quincys. Like many readers of the period, they enjoyed reading aloud—or, as Anna idiosyncratically spelled the word, "loud":

> Monday 8th [April] ... Eve[nin]ᵍ Read loud in Persuasion, which is certainly the most natural thing you can possibly imagine.— ...
> Wednesday 10 [April] ... Evᵍ—finished Persuasion,—& felt as if we could not bear to part with Anne Elliot & Capt Wentworth ...
> Tuesday 7th [May] ... Evenᵍ. read loud in Mansfield.— ...
> Tuesday 14 [May] ... Read loud in Northanger Abbey ...
> Wednesday 15th ... Evenᵍ—Finished Northanger—[11]

The Quincys were thoroughly up to date: they read *Persuasion*, *Mansfield Park*, and *Northanger Abbey* in the order of those titles' publication in 1833 by Carey & Lea. *Sense and Sensibility*, presumably, the family had obtained as soon as it was available in Boston.[12]

Living at home with Anna in 1833 were her parents and her three unmarried sisters, including Eliza Susan, known as Susan within the family, then aged thirty-five. Home was in Cambridge, Massachusetts, where Josiah Quincy III (1772–1864) was president of Harvard University, having previously served in Congress and as the first mayor of Boston. The Quincy family was wealthy, respected, and well connected, both intellectually and socially. Eliza Susan, Anna, and their sisters were educated at home along much the same lines as Lady Dalhousie and the du Pont sisters had been in their time. Of the four sisters, Eliza Susan was the most intellectually and artistically gifted. Proud of her distinguished family, she wrote several books about its history and, near the end of her life, helped ensure the survival of its historic house in Quincy, Massachusetts. Also an accomplished visual artist, Eliza Susan preferred landscapes and houses to people; no portraits of or by her survive. Anna's likeness exists only in a late-life photograph.[13]

Austen came to the Quincys' attention through word of mouth rather than advertising. Josiah's wife, Eliza Susan Morton Quincy (1773–1850), explained to a friend in 1835 that Austen's novels were "first mentioned" to them "by Judge Story, to whom they were recommended by Judge Marshall. High authority, certainly."[14] (Supreme Court Chief Justice John Marshall made Associate Justice Joseph Story aware of Austen following the latter's oration on women authors for Phi Beta Kappa at Harvard in 1826: see Introduction.) Josiah Quincy himself recalled in his memoirs two occasions on which he and Story discussed British women novelists, among them Austen.[15]

Story's engagement with Austen's works, as recorded by his son and biographer, William Wetmore Story, bears strong similarities to the Quincys' own. After recounting the Phi Beta Kappa episode, Wetmore Story stated that it

is due to my father to say, that he fully recognized the admirable genius of Miss Austen. Scarcely a year passed that he did not read more than one of them, and with an interest which never flagged. I well remember, in the year 1842, when I was engaged in finishing a bust of him in marble, for which he gave me several sittings, that "Emma" was read aloud at his request to beguile the time. With what relish he listened, his face lighting up with pleasure, and interrupting my sister continually to comment on the naturalness and vivacity of the dialogue, or the delicate discrimination of character,—to express his admiration of the author's unrivalled power of exciting and sustaining interest in groups of common and prosaic persons, merely through her truth and felicity of delineation,—and to draw parallels between the characters in the novel, and persons of our acquaintance . . . .

Our little family group was then enlarged by the addition of Emma, Mr. Knightley, Mr. Woodhouse and Miss Bates, who almost became real persons to us, as we read. But the ludicrous impatience with which my father always greeted the entry of Miss Bates, plainly showed that she was a fiction, for had she had an actual existence, he would have been sure to receive her with patience and kindness.[16]

Like the Quincys, Story relished reading Austen's novels aloud in family company, responded strongly to her characters, and enjoyed the sense of permeability between real and fictional worlds. Wetmore Story's characterization of his own "little family group" as "enlarged" by the characters of *Emma* is especially comparable to Anna's description in her April 1833 diary of her family as feeling that they "could not bear to part with Anne Elliot & Capt Wentworth."[17]

Austen's characters from *Emma* were vividly present to Anna in August 1834 during a journey to upstate New York with her father and sister Abigail, which she documented in another journal volume. Of a visit to a Mr. Delavan, owner of an estate called Delvale, near Saratoga Springs, Anna recorded on 12 August that they had "a very pleasant drive about 4 miles when the walls of <u>Donwell Abbey</u> rose to our view_ the seat of a real Mr Knightley."[18] Throughout her account, Anna insistently identified her American host with Austen's quintessential English landowner. Banished to the back seat of his carriage, she described herself as "really as much put out as I could be with Mr Knightley ... I consoled myself, however, with admiring Mr Knightley's horses and whole establishment, which, like everything about him, is just what a gentleman's should be."[19]

The transformative power of Anna's fiction-fueled imagination is strongly evident here. Edward C. Delavan (1793–1871) was a wine merchant who invested profitably in the Erie Canal before retiring from business. By the time Anna met him, he had, ironically, become a prominent temperance crusader.[20] Wealthy he certainly was, but whether he really resembled Mr. Knightley in any other way can hardly be ascertained—and is, essentially, beside the point. What matters is that Anna formed from *Emma* notions of what a gentleman, his house, and even his horses should be. These notions she was ready to see embodied in her own American landscape, in spite of all the many differences between her own world and that of Austen's fiction.

Much like Catherine Morland of *Northanger Abbey*, Anna delighted in superimposing ideas from novels on everyday life. While Catherine eventually learns to be careful in doing so, however, Anna retained a lifelong habit of equating her favorite characters and fictional places with real people and locations. An excerpt from the journal she kept on her first trip to England, more than twenty years later, captures well this aspect of her fertile imagination, which embraced all of literature, not only Austen: "We went into the room, where the Skeleton was found, and thro' many most mysterious passages 'just like what one reads about,' as Catherine Morland would say. . . . It is just the place for Hawthorne to write one of his eerie stories about, or which Jane Eyre would have described. A Mrs. Rochester might have been locked up in this old house, and nobody below been the wiser for it."[21]

Admirers, rewarded with a relic, envision a society of devotees

Eliza Susan's literary devotion took a different form from that of her youngest sister. While Anna encountered a "real" Mr. Knightley in upstate New York, Eliza Susan initiated correspondences with authors whom she admired in both America and Britain, with the dual aim of expressing her appreciation for their works and seeking autographs for her collection. She wrote over the course of several decades to, among others, John Greenleaf Whittier, Harriet Beecher Stowe, Oliver Wendell Holmes, Nathaniel Hawthorne, William Cullen Bryant, and Henry Cabot Lodge.[22] Among Eliza Susan's British correspondents, the novelist Maria Edgeworth was especially receptive: the two exchanged several letters from 1834 to 1847, many of which pertained to the Irish famine.[23]

Collecting signatures from living authors and searching for those of recently deceased famous authors was much in vogue in the mid-nineteenth century on both sides of the Atlantic.[24] After Charlotte Brontë's death, for instance, her father fielded many requests from eager readers for scraps of her handwriting.[25]

The earliest recorded appeal to a member of Austen's family for an item in Jane's handwriting was made in 1841 by the novelist Catherine Hutton (1756–1846) of Birmingham to Francis Austen, through mutual acquaintances.[26] Francis complied, albeit with some reluctance. As he wrote to the intermediary, "[t]he individual whose Autograph your friend is desirous to obtain was my Sister. I have several letters of hers in my possession, but not one that I could feel justified in parting with. I send you however her Signature such as she usually wrote it when she used (which she rarely did) more than her initials."[27] The scrap of paper read "Yours very affec: ly / J. Austen / Chawton Wednesday / Feb. 17." Hutton preserved it together with notes of her own on Austen's life and the following very personal comment on the meaning of Austen's writings to her: "I am inferior to Jane Austen in person, manners, and talents; but when she makes one of her characters speak her own mind, as she frequently does, I am delighted to think that I bear some resemblance to her."[28]

Eliza Susan, of course, was unaware of Hutton's earlier request when she first wrote to the admiral in 1852. From her experience with other authors, she had some reason to be confident that her expression of esteem for Austen's works would be warmly received by her brother. Nevertheless, she framed very carefully her request for a sample of Austen's handwriting. Her letter is worth quoting in its entirety so that her deliberate self-presentation and rhetorical strategies can be fully appreciated.

> Vice Admiral, Sir Francis Austen, K. C. B.
>
> Boston, Massachusetts, U. S. A.
> January 6. 1852
>
> Since high critical authority, has pronounced the delineations of character, in the works of Jane Austen, second only to those of Shakespeare, trans=atlantic admiration appears superfluous.— Yet it may not be uninteresting to her family to receive an assurance, that the influence of her genius is extensively recognised in the American Republic, even by the highest judicial authorities.—
>
> The late Mr Chief Justice Marshall, of the Supreme Court of the United States, and his associate M^r. Justice Story, highly estimated & admired Miss Austen, & to them we owe our introduction to her society.—For many years, her talents have

brightened our daily paths, & her name and those of her characters, are familiar to us, "as household words".—We have long wished to express to some of her family the sentiments of gratitude & affection she has inspired, and request more information relative to her life, than is given in the brief Memoir prefixed to her works.—

Having incidentally heard that a brother of Jane Austen, held a high rank in the British navy, we have obtained his Address from our friend Admiral Wormley, now resident in Boston.— And we trust this expression of feeling, will be received by her relative, with the kindness & urbanity, characteristic of the Admirals of <u>her</u> creation.—

Sir Francis Austen, or one of his family would confer a great favor by complying with our request.—The autograph of his sister, or a few lines in her hand=writing, would be placed among our chief treasures.—

The family who delight in the companionship of Jane Austen, & who present this petition, are of English origin. Their ancestor held a high rank among the first emigrants to New England, & his name & character have been ably represented by his descendants, in various public stations, of trust & responsibility to the present time,—in the colony and State of Massachusetts.

A letter addressed to

"Miss Quincy,

care of the Hon<u>ble</u> Josiah Quincy Sen.

Boston.

Massachusetts."—

U. S. A."

would reach its destination.[29]

The postmark and salutation of Eliza Susan's letter made her nationality clear. Rather than identifying herself right away, however, she opened her letter by flourishing her first credential as a knowledgeable appreciator of Austen's works: familiarity with criticism that had favorably compared Austen's works with Shakespeare's. Eliza Susan evidently took it for granted that a brother of Jane's would not need this attribution spelled out.[30]

Next, she broached the subject of "transatlantic admiration" by referring to Americans more prominent than herself, Marshall and Story. Only then did Eliza Susan explain to Francis Austen how she came to know of him and to obtain his address: "incidentally," through a Boston acquaintance of hers, a fellow member of the British Navy. To use the conventional spelling of his surname, Ralph Wormeley (1785–1852) was himself a transatlantic figure, having been born in Virginia and brought up in England. Like the Quincys, he was well connected in Boston society.[31] Of course, his willingness to give Francis Austen's address to Eliza Susan conveyed his own approbation of her, as all parties would have been fully aware.

Only after establishing her intellectual and social bona fides did Eliza Susan express to Francis the devotion to Jane Austen and her works that prompted her to write. Using the language of familial intimacy, she described her household as having been introduced not to Austen's writings but "to her society." Reading and rereading Austen's novels made them feel close to her, as if they lived with her and her characters: "For many years her talents have brightened our daily path, and her name and those of her characters are familiar to us as 'household words.'" (Certainly, Anna's travel journal bears out the latter assertion.) From this sense of deep attachment, Eliza explained, came the desire to convey "gratitude and affection" and to know more about Austen's life "than is given in the brief memoir prefixed to her works": that is, Henry Austen's 1818 "Biographical Notice," which Carey & Lea reprinted in their 1833 edition of *Northanger Abbey*.[32] Eliza presented almost as an afterthought her final request, for the "great favour" of a relic that would bring herself and her family members closer, in feeling, to their beloved author: an "autograph" or "few lines in her handwriting."

Eliza Susan closed her letter with a final set of credentials: the "English origin" of her family, the "high rank" of her emigrant ancestor, and the eminence of her current family—including the title, "Honorable," of the man whom the admiral would infer to be her father.

Eliza Susan was fortunate in which Austen brother Admiral Wormeley happened to know. Born in April 1774, Francis was the sibling closest in age to Jane. Only he, of the three Austen brothers still alive in January 1852, lived beyond that year. (Charles Austen and Edward Austen Knight died in October and November, 1852, respectively.[33]) Furthermore, alone among the Austen family, Francis had lived in North America, having commanded the North American and West Indies station of the British Navy from 1845 to

1848.[34] This experience perhaps helps explain his receptiveness to overtures from Boston.

His reply was swift and appreciative. "I can have no hesitation in assuring you," he wrote in a letter dated 31 January, "that it was most gratifying to me to receive such a testimonial to the merits of my late Sister's works, and thereby to learn that their celebrity had reached across the Atlantic."[35] He generously gratified Eliza Susan's request for more information about Austen than is available in the "Biographical Notice," in spite of his disclaimer that "there is little I could add to it of a nature to be interesting to strangers." Like his brother Henry before him, he viewed his late sister's life as essentially uneventful. As he put it, "[p]assing the greater part of her life if not in absolute retirement yet so much out of what is commonly meant by the world, rarely mixing with any but intimate Friends and near Relations, that it would be a matter of much difficulty to recall any circumstance worth relating." Regarding Jane's character, however, he offered the following rich description:

> Of the liveliness of her imagination and playfulness of her fancy, as also of the truthfulness of her description of character and deep knowledge of the human mind, there are sufficient evidence in her works; and it has been a matter of surprise to those who knew her best, how she could at a very early age and with apparently limited means of observation, have been capable of nicely discriminating and pourtraying such varieties of the human character as are introduced in her works.—In her temper she was chearful and not easily irritated, and tho' rather reserved to strangers so as to have been by some accused of haughtiness of manner, yet in the company of those she loved the native benevolence of her heart and kindliness of her disposition were forcibly displayed. On such occasions she was a most agreable companion and by the lively sallies of her Wit and good-humoured drollery seldom failed of exciting the mirth and hilarity of the party. She was fond of children and a favorite with them. Her Nephews and Nieces of whom there were many could not have a greater treat than crouding round and listening to Aunt Jane's stories.[36]

This recollection of Austen from the perspective of a brother who knew her well contributes significantly to our understanding of her.

Her virtue and piety, the qualities highlighted in obituaries and in the "Biographical Notice," were not Francis's main concern. Instead, he candidly stated that the Austen family recognized Jane's profound knowledge of humanity, though they could not really account for it. His intimate glimpse of a woman who opened up "in the company of those she loved" complements, too, the reminiscences of Jane's much younger nieces and nephews about how entertaining she was in the family circle.[37]

Francis was even more generous with respect to Eliza Susan's request for a sample of Austen's handwriting. Rather than a mere signature or a scrap of a few lines, he sent an entire letter: "the first Jane Austen manuscript to cross the Atlantic," as one historian has pointed out.[38] What's more, Francis chose a letter written by Jane to one of her own dear friends. As he explained,

> I have in my possession several of her letters written to an intimate friend, who subsequently became my wife and is now deceased. From these I select one to forward herewith in the confident belief that no improper use will be made of it. It will be at once a specimen of her hand-writing and of the playfulness of her mind. The incidents to which it adverts could be interesting only to those acquainted with the parties. All mentioned in it are dead with the exception of the one named "Charles." There is no date of year affixed, but from collateral circumstances it must have been written as early as 1798 or 99. I scarcely need observe that there never was the remotest idea of its' being published. I shall be glad to know that my letter arrives safely at its destination.[39]

Francis subsequently corrected to 1800 the date of his sister's letter.[40] Written from Steventon, the village in which Jane and her siblings grew up, it was addressed to "[m]y dear Martha": Martha Lloyd (1765–1843), who in 1809 joined Jane, Cassandra, and their widowed mother to live at Chawton Cottage. In 1828, Martha married Francis; it was his second marriage, her first.

Francis's choice of letter was thoughtful. While indeed the majority of it concerned minutiae of no particular interest, he rightly anticipated that the book-loving, close-knit Quincy sisters would enjoy his sister's friendly comments to Martha about reading, more than a decade before the publication of her own first novel,

Sense and Sensibility, in 1811. "You distress me cruelly," Jane wrote, "by your request about Books; I cannot think of any to bring with me, nor have I any idea of our wanting them. I come to you to be talked to, not to read or hear reading. I can do that at home; & indeed I am now laying in a stock of intelligence to pour out on you as my share of Conversation."[41]

Eliza Susan's grateful reply to Francis was a veritable performance of enthusiasm. She took care, first, to assure Francis of the document's safe arrival and that his desire for privacy would be respected: "Your letter and the valuable autograph you have entrusted to me, 'in the confident',—and just—'belief that no improper use will be made of it',—arrived safely by the last British Steamer." Next, she vividly depicted the excitement shared by her entire family at its receipt:

> A great sensation was excited in our family circle by the acquisition of a letter actually written and folded by Jane Austen!—Brothers and sisters, nephews & nieces, hastened to see it, and seized upon it with great delight.—In the evening my father whose eightieth birthday has just passed, walked to a distant part of the city, where my youngest sister resides, to give, himself, the agreeable intelligence.—I enclose the note he brought me on his return. Some passages will amuse you, and never being intended for your eye, it evinces more vividly, than any acknowledgments of my own, the sentiments excited by your kind compliance with our request.—Like Mr Collins we can truly say "you could not have bestowed your favour on more grateful objects."—[42]

What made the Austen letter "valuable" to the Quincys, Eliza Susan conveyed, was not its monetary or exchange value but rather its personal importance as a relic of their beloved author. She stressed, too, the sense of personal connection with Austen that the letter afforded. Calling its contents "most characteristic," she singled out three details as "seem[ing] like passages from the novels of the writer" and commented that these, "together with the traits of character you mention bring us, as it were, into [her] society."

The "note" of Anna's enclosed by Eliza Susan shows that even before seeing the precious letter itself, she responded even more ecstatically to the power of a document that, in her words, was "written by the very hand to which we owe so much." Anna's postscript reads, "if the house takes fire to night save the letters. I cannot 'die without the sight'." She shared, furthermore, Eliza Susan's impulse to celebrate the letter's arrival with Austen allusions and quotations, likening her excited father to Miss Bates of *Emma*, herself to Mrs. Jennings of *Sense and Sensibility*, and even deciding that Admiral Austen "must have been like Captain Wentworth when he was young—and just like what the Captain would have been at eighty years of age. He has replied to your letter with true 'naval alacrity,' & evidently deserves to be Miss Austin's brother."[43] (Anna used the spelling "Austin" throughout.) Though almost twenty years older than when she equated Mr. Delavan with Mr. Knightley, Anna clearly retained her enthusiasm for relating real people to fictional characters.

Remarkably, Anna's hasty note ended with a fervent vision of a society of Austen devotees. "I never expected we should get so near Miss Austin in this world;—though I have always hoped to find some 'little coterie in Heaven,' where I might catch a glimpse of her!" She signed off "[w]ith love and congratulations to all true lovers of Miss Austin."[44] Anna's conception of an exclusive "little coterie" composed only of "true lovers" of the author anticipated by many decades Kipling's 1924 short story "The Janeites" and by almost a century the founding of the Jane Austen Society of the UK, the first official organization of Austen aficionados, in 1940.[45] Of course, Kipling's fictional Janeites are all English and all male. And when he imagined Austen in the afterlife, as he did in the poem "Jane Austen in Heaven" appended to the story's book publication in 1926, he focused on a romantic future for the author rather than an opportunity for her to commune with her readers.

Clearly, Anna believed that American nationality was no barrier to being a "true lover" of Austen. This conviction Eliza Susan elaborated at length in the rest of her own reply to Francis. She declared that her family has "long regarded" Austen "as having 'entered on that existence in which all the gifted writers of all ages and nations are associated in a world of their own.—The individual will gradually disappear as the author is more distinctly seen.'"[46] In her own words, she then developed an idea of how readers too become part of a transnational community, thanks to shared language and appreciation of literary works.

The sun, it is said, never sets on the dominions of the British Queen,—but the classics of English literature exercise a yet more permanent & extensive sway, recognised even by those sturdy republicans, who disown allegiance to any sovereign,—except the sovereign people.—

The aristocracy of the realm of intellect, which no Revolution can undermine, will rule the hearts and imaginations of all who claim the English language, as their mother tongue, when the glories of the reign of Victoria, are the theme of the historian of past ages.[47]

Unlike Anna's self-selecting coterie of devotees, the "aristocracy of the realm of intellect" imagined by Eliza Susan represents a social order apparently headed by the literary works themselves, which compel admiration and appreciation. Or, perhaps, such an "aristocracy" is headed by those members of distinguished families who properly esteem literary "classics": for instance, the Quincys. As an assertion of her own family's transcendence of national boundaries, Eliza Susan concluded her letter by celebrating the success of her patriot grandfather Josiah Quincy, Jr. in defending the British officers charged with murder after a violent 1770 riot, an incident commonly known in the US as the "Boston massacre."

These outpourings from Eliza Susan and Anna, together with the Quincy family's pedigree, impressed both Francis and the family members and close acquaintances with whom he shared these letters. He declared to Eliza Susan "the high gratification the perusal of it [her letter] afforded me, and the members of my family and some intimate friends to whom it has been shewn. They were all delighted at the enthusiasm displayed by yourself and friends . . . and are satisfied that the autograph of my late Sister could not have been placed in any hands where it would have been more highly appreciated."[48] Francis did not comment directly on either Anna's vision of a coterie of Austen devotees or Eliza Susan's philosophical musings about an international aristocracy of literary greatness. However, by conveying his own circle's hearty approval of the Boston enthusiasts, Francis indicated his sense of the commonality enjoyed by all these lovers of Austen's writings: those related to the author by blood or connected to her by friendship, as well as those linked solely through reading.[49]

In the chief currency of such devotees—enthusiasm and appreciation—Francis contributed two further tidbits to the curious

Bostonians. He remarked that his "vanity . . . could not but be gratified" by Anna's comparison of him to Captain Wentworth of *Persuasion*. "Perhaps" his sister might have been inspired by him, he ventured, but "I rather think parts of Capt. Harville's were drawn from myself; at least the description of his domestic habits, tastes and occupations bear a considerable resemblance to mine." And he offered an anecdote about Lord Morpeth, whose 1835 verses in praise of Austen Eliza Susan had quoted:[50] "a report has been circulated that on one occasion while absorbed in the perusal of Pride & Prejudice his Lordship was summoned to attend a Cabinet Council, but unable or unwilling to lay down the book, he did not reach the Council-chamber in time to escape a severe rebuke from the Minister for his tardiness." This evidence of readerly absorption was well calculated to appeal to the Quincys.

The correspondence between Eliza Susan and Francis continued through the summer of 1852, though with few further references to literature in general or Austen in particular. She offered him, and he accepted, gifts of a panoramic depiction of Boston and a copy of the book she had written (for publication under her father's name) about her patriot grandfather, *Memoir of the Life of Josiah Quincy, Jun.* In return, he shared his views on Anglo-American relations before and after the Revolutionary War, including his judgment that "the conduct of the British Ministry, in all that regarded the transatlantic Colonies, was most besotted, as well as unjust and oppressive." He expressed a hope that "there is now such a friendly feeling on both sides, as will secure a good understanding between them, such as ought to subsist between Nations sprung from the same origin, speaking the same language, governed in a great degree by similar laws, and above all acknowledging the same God and Saviour!"[51] Francis repeated the phrase "friendly feeling" when thanking Eliza Susan for her gifts and assuring her that he would always be glad "to receive any letter you may have leisure or inclination to send me."

Two families meet during Anna's literary pilgrimage

In April 1856, Eliza Susan took Francis up on his offer of a renewed correspondence, this time on behalf of Anna, who, with her husband

Robert Waterston and their daughter Helen, was about to embark on a tour of Europe. One of Anna's "chief objects" in visiting England, Eliza Susan explained, was "to perform a pilgrimage to the places once the abode of Jane Austen."[52] As an Austen devotee, Anna was once again in the vanguard. Austen-inspired travel was just beginning in the 1850s, according to Deirdre Le Faye, with Austen's grave in Winchester Cathedral the most commonly visited site.[53] Widespread Austen pilgrimage lay decades in the future, spurred by the publication of Austen-Leigh's *Memoir* and assisted by turn-of-the-century guides written for literary tourists.[54] Such later travelers, of course, did not have the opportunity, as Anna did, to meet a member of Austen's family from the author's own generation. As Eliza Susan phrased the request, for Anna "to see and to converse, with so near a relative of that gifted authoress as yourself, would be so high a gratification, that I cannot hesitate to claim a few moments of your time & attention."

In the same letter, Eliza Susan shared a new and very striking image for the transnational connections possible between lovers of literature. "Thus you perceive," she wrote, "the Electric Telegraph of Genius,—annihilates the barriers of time & space, & brings into friendly communication, those who are strangers to each other, & who dwell in distant regions.—" It is intriguing to wonder whether, in Eliza Susan's view, this almost terrifying-sounding power of literary genius could also annihilate barriers of social class, race, or religion. She certainly considered gender irrelevant, both to the possession of genius by an author and to the appreciation of it by readers. (Incidentally, her metaphor anticipated by two years the first successful transatlantic telegraph.[55])

Rather than mailing this letter directly, Eliza Susan gave it to Anna to send, with a cover letter of her own, when she had reached England. Anna first wrote to Francis's son Henry E. Austen in London. (Francis had supplied Henry's address in 1852 for the receipt of Eliza Susan's gift of the book and picture.) "Will you excuse the stranger who addresses you, when she makes the enquiry whether yr father Admiral Austen is still living?" Anna's letter began. "She is a member of a family in America, whose ardent admiration for the genius of Jane Austen, led to a correspondence with the Admiral several years since. . . . if the Admiral is yet with you in this world, and you think it will be proper for me to call upon him for an hour while visiting Portsmouth, with my husband

and daughter will you be kind enough to say so[.]"[56] Francis himself responded to apprise her that Henry had died, but he himself was alive and would welcome her to his home, Portsdown Lodge, located outside Portsmouth.[57] Anna's emotions are evident in the punctuation of her reply:

> I cannot tell you with how much interest I look forward to my visit to you—the brother of Jane Austen! whose genius I have so long prized, and whose works are associated with voices now silent, and Spirits, which like her own, have passed into another world.—Fit company were they to meet in that land, where death cannot enter.—To day we leave London, and go to Winchester a pilgrimage to her resting place which has given more interest to me in the old Cathedral, than all its buried Kings.[58]

Anna's phrasing in her final sentence is strikingly similar to that of another 1850s Austen pilgrim, the Englishwoman Lady Richardson, who recorded that she and her mother "visited the shrine of Jane Austen, with even more interest than that of William of Wickham."[59] Characteristically, Anna's thoughts on her own devotion to Austen developed in an explicitly religious direction. In her reference to departed "voices" and "Spirits," Anna was presumably thinking chiefly of her own mother, who had died in 1850. Though the mood of her remarks here is somber, her vision of Christian fellowship with Austen in the afterlife accords with her earlier expression of a desire to "glimpse" the author in heaven.

The much-anticipated visit took place on 18 June 1856: almost forty years after Austen's death, when Francis was over eighty and Anna Waterston in her mid-forties. Multiple accounts of the day survive: in Anna's travel journal, in her letters to Francis Austen, in his letters to her, and in his letters to Eliza Susan. I will begin with Anna's travel journal, the fullest and most intimate source, which I rediscovered at the Massachusetts Historical Society.

According to one headnote in Anna's handwriting, this volume contains "[s]elections from letters and journals" written during her time away. In a second note, Anna recorded that these "letters were copied, after our return in 1859—I regret now that I did not arrange them better."[60] Aside from these two notes, and occasional marginal comments evidently added later by Anna, the copperplate handwriting of this volume indicates a hired copyist.

Anna's excitement mounted in anticipation of her encounter with Admiral Austen. Her feeling of inhabiting the very world of Austen's novels was, understandably, more potent than ever as she visited for the first time the places that Austen knew and depicted. "I am actually in Portsmouth," she wrote the night before seeing the admiral,

> and like Mr Crawford at "the best Inn the Town affords," at the very one perhaps where he staid when he came down to see Fanny Price. . . . I can hardly believe I am actually here, so often I have said, "if I ever go to England I will go to Portsmouth and see Admiral Austen," and here I actually am, seated in the Portsmouth of Fanny Price's experiences. I rather think it looks very much the same as in Fanny's day, and I do not wonder she pined for Mansfield Park: such hosts of soldiers and sailors must bring a bad population, no wonder the young ladies did not like to walk out even in High Street. I saw I am sure Mr Price's house, and plenty of Mr Prices, and "Sams" & "Toms" racing about__ but no Fanny; we have been walking on the Ramparts where Mrs. Price took her Sunday walk, and wound up her spirits; where Fanny and Mr Crawford also walked around the Town.

Vertically in the right-hand margin of this page reads Anna's self-aware note, "All these allusions to the characters in Miss Austens novels, are interesting only to Austen-lovers & readers." That the ever-imaginative Anna felt she recognized the characters of *Mansfield Park* in the actual people of Portsmouth is not surprising. What is significant is that she registered her increased understanding of the motives and reactions of the novel's characters. Only upon seeing Portsmouth in person could she fully apprehend why Fanny Price "pined for Mansfield Park" and why "the young ladies did not like to walk out." Literary tourism, in other words, deepened Anna's appreciation of Austen's writing as no mere reading of criticism could.

So, too, did her hours-long conversation with the admiral and his family the next day. "The Austen illusion is not broken by our visit to the dear Old Admiral," she recorded with evident relief at the conclusion of the day. She, her husband Robert, and their daughter Helen were welcomed warmly both by the inhabitants of Portsdown

Lodge and also by other relatives of the admiral's who dropped in to meet them. Each one Anna sketched verbally for the benefit of her family at home. (In the following transcription, I have added further details and explanations in footnotes.) The conversation ranged from memories—direct and secondhand—of Jane Austen to conversation about the author's sources of inspiration, her family's pride in her achievement, and her comparative popularity in England and America. Throughout her account, Anna praised the admiral and the devotion of his family, which she repeatedly declared reminded her very much of her own family circle, likewise headed by an energetic, beloved octogenarian man.

We drove out this morning at 11 o'clk to Portsdown Hill famed for its view, which is one of the most extensive and beautiful I have ever seen. Portsdown Lodge is about half a mile after rising the hill, the sweep gates admitted us into a very pretty approach, and we were soon at the door of a handsome mansion; the servant immediately appeared, and ushered us into a pleasant sitting room where the Admiral received us with most affectionate kindness, and all the grace of the old school. He is of a very slight figure not tall, but has very fine features, and is still at 82, a very handsome man looking about ten years younger than he really is; with him was his daughter Miss Austen, and immediately after came in another daughter a Mrs. Hubbuck who resides at home with her children. I presume she is a widow.[61] They all received us with most hospitable expressions of pleasure at our visit, and expressed their gratification, that interest in Miss Jane Austen's writings had led to the acquaintance, we of course talked of her, there is no portrait of her in existence,[62] the ladies do not remember their Aunt, but said every one who had seen her, represented her as having been a very charming person, very pretty with a round face, and particularly sweet expression, when I said that I had always thought she must have been like Anne Eliot [sic] they replied, that those who knew her thought that in the extreme sweetness of her temper as well as beauty she was like Jane Bennett [sic]. She lived a very retired life, principally in the country, or at Bath, where she resided for several years; the perfect good taste and propriety of the family evidently led them to avoid anything like egotism, and altho' they are entirely aware of all Miss Austen's powers, & fully appreciate the works, they are not too ready to appear so, indeed the ladies said they had endeavored to avoid quoting from their Aunts words which was extremely difficult, as they like ourselves knew them by heart, and were daily reminded of them.[63] The Admiral said that Emma was a favorite of Janes, that when she wrote it she said that now she was going to make a character full of faults, but she liked her nevertheless;[64] she [he?] said he thought Capt. Wentworth described her favorite brother Charles, between whom and Jane Austen there existed the same devoted attachment as between Fanny and Wm. Price,[65] but that his sister never intended to draw any portraits from actual persons tho' several people took offence from imagining that they or their friends were the originals; one lady in particular insisted upon it, that old Mr Woodhouse was her father, and was excessively affronted in spite of all Miss Austen could say to the contrary.[66] One of the ladies said that as I was so strong an admirer, she must tell me a circumstance which had gratified them much, that a friend had told them that in staying at some Country Seat with a party of distinguished literary men, including Hallam[,] Macauley &c;[67] they were talking of different authors, and agreed to write down what work of fiction had given them most pleasure, and that seven wrote "Mansfield Park" on their seperate [sic] slips of paper, and were all highly amused at the coincidence, when the papers were read aloud. They asked me whether Miss Austen was generally popular in America, for in England her works were only appreciated by the minority, tho' they must say it was always the cleverest people who enjoyed them. I told them it was pretty much the same at home, and whenever we wished to give the most favorable impression of a new acquaintance we would say, why they are real Austen admirers, which at once established their cleverness with us, but as a cheap edition was now in circulation of several of her novels,[68] we hoped cleverness was on the increase. The Admiral is a charming man, and has much of his Sisters sweetness of manner, notwithstanding he has been a sailor all his life, up to 48 when he came ashore.

He was made Admiral in consequence of his success in the
French War, when like Capt. Wentworth he took several
prizes. There is a fine portrait of him,[69] in full uniform with
several orders &c, but he is the most unpretending of men, a
dear, dear old gentleman. The place is a very pretty one,
something as Hartfield[70] might have been, simple and yet
wearing the aspect of a Gentlemans Seat: a Captain and
Mrs Charles Austen next came in (a Nephew of the Admirals
also in the Navy) they were on a visit at the Lodge: their
little daughter 'Jane Austen' was brought in to see us on
account of her name, also Mrs. Hubbucks "two fine little
boys" were uprooted from the grounds where they were
playing evidently in the ground, to show us their fine
healthy blooming faces.[71] Luncheon was soon after
announced, and the Admiral escorted me into the dining
room, a very pleasant apartment looking out upon the lawn,
with its clumps of laurel and evergreens, and its distant view
of wooded hills. Here we were seated at a table, with the
usual cold meat &c, &c, English luncheon; while we were
partaking of sundry good things, another gentleman entered,
who seemed rather surprised at the collection of people
before him; this was Mr. George Austen, a Son of the
Admiral's who has a living about 8⁰ miles off.[72] They all
seemed much pleased to see him, he declared himself very
hot, tired, dusty, and hungry, and soon drew up to the table;
Helen said it was just like Uncle Edmund[73] coming over to
Quincy, indeed I had been strongly reminded of Quincy and
ourselves. The Old gentleman surrounded by children and
grand-children, all so fond of him and of each other, and
of the place, made us feel quite at home. After luncheon, we
all walked out in the grounds which are pretty and rural,
fine trees and grass, and a pretty flower garden &c, &c,
every thing looked lovely in the bright sun, and all so tranquil
and happy that we enjoyed ourselves much. I took out with
me Papa's Cameo likeness to show to the Admiral; they were
all very much pleased with it, thought it looked like 'the
Duke,'[74] only much handsomer than he was, and were also
much struck with the beauty of the Cameo. They showed us
some very beautiful sketches by another son and brother
Herbert Austen[75] now stationed in Ireland, his is certainly a

Masters hand. Mrs. Hubbuck gave me a little unfinished sketch of her own of the Lodge, and Robert also took one __ from a different and I think far prettier position. They very cordially invited us to remain and dine with them at six o'clk, but we thought a visit of four hours was enough from strangers like ourselves, strangers however no longer. "To meet and part is a Mortals lot"[76] __ but if we met as strangers, we certainly parted as friends, and we shall ever retain a most pleasing remembrance of our visit to Portsdown Lodge. There was a perfect simplicity and naturalness about the whole family, that made them particularly pleasing, and as to the Old Admiral, he is just such a character as Jane Austen's delicate powers of description would delight in. He apologized for not having written to Susan, but said he should now do so; I am sure we feel very much indebted to her for the great pleasure of the introduction. We all parted with mutual regret, and drove off amid the kind adieus of the group assembled on the Veranda, with roses in our hands and tears in our eyes.

Most striking about Anna's account is the sense of mutual interest and understanding shared by all the readers present, regardless of their different relationships to Jane. Francis, the only one to have known Jane personally, claimed no particular intimacy with her, yet still called up fresh memories of her sources of inspiration. The younger generation, none of whom could recall Jane directly, had gathered further anecdotes from older family members and acquaintances, in addition to developing such familiarity with the actual novels as to have practically memorized them—a trait, as Anna noted, that she and her family shared.

While we might expect this encounter to have been gratifying chiefly to the Waterstons, both Anna's and Francis's account of the day emphasize how important it was to the Austens, too. For them, the presence of ardent American readers evidently brought home, more than mere correspondence alone could do, how much Jane's writings meant to audiences beyond fellow English people. Such awareness may well have contributed, more than has been previously recognized, to the various efforts among Austen's nieces and nephews to record and publish memories of her; a later letter of the admiral's, which I will discuss in the next section, further corroborates this likelihood. After all, the more extensive the interest known to exist among readers, the more justified the Austen family would be in making public details of Austen's life and private writings of hers, thereby increasing her fame and renown.

Furthermore, the Americans, free of what Anna identified as English "good taste and propriety" regarding family pride, could express their regard for Jane's novels much more freely than the Austens themselves. For family members to proclaim Austen's greatness risked being seen (in Anna's word again) as "egotism." Readers unrelated to the family, in contrast, could—and, in the case of the Waterstons, did—wax as enthusiastic as they liked.[77]

For his part, Francis conveyed to Eliza Susan how touched he was by the encounter with her sister's family. "I cannot easily describe to you the degree of enjoyment I derived from thus becoming acquainted with your Relations, and from the various details I had to enter into with your Sister, relative to my late Sister: and indeed I may say others of my deceased family, respecting whom both M^r and Mrs Waterston seemed desirous of obtaining all possible information."[78] The admiral's perspective on the conversation is interestingly different from Anna's: while she emphasized how ready the Austens were to tell her things, he stressed the Waterstons' eagerness to learn as much as possible about Jane Austen and her family. That he did not take offense is evident from his invitation to them to stay longer and to return during their time in England.

Two final perspectives on the visit emerge from letters written to the admiral by Eliza Susan and by Anna, later in her trip. After Anna's detailed report on the afternoon reached Boston and, as she put it, was "enjoyed almost as much" as the Waterstons did the occasion itself, Eliza Susan wrote to thank Francis for his kindness to her sister.[79] She assured him that the Waterstons "enjoyed their visit to you and your family most highly,—and think you all worthy to be relatives of Jane Austen. My enthusiastic Sister could not pay a higher compliment."[80] Indeed she could not: such approbation, from Anna, represented profound admiration.

For Anna, the visit took on a deeper meaning as she reflected on it while continuing to travel. "I almost felt as if I were leaving a home, when we drove away from yr hospitable door," she wrote to Francis, "so kindly were we, strangers, taken into your home— The influence which brought us together, seemed to throw an almost sacred interest over our meeting—foreshadowing perhaps that, which we may hope for in a world where there are no farewells."[81] Nowhere in Anna's writings did she integrate religious devotion and author-love as seamlessly as here. Welcoming strangers as members of a larger family, a central tenet of Christian fellowship, carries over perfectly to the quasi-worship of a beloved author.[82]

Americans contribute to Austen's international fame

The impulse to evangelize, too, was clearly present in Anna's literary enthusiasm, especially in her remark during her visit to Portsdown Lodge that "as a cheap edition was now in circulation of several of her novels, we hoped cleverness was on the increase."[83] Half a dozen years later, in the middle of the American Civil War, Anna made her own effort to increase such "cleverness," by writing a substantial appreciation for an up-and-coming American periodical.

With her article "Jane Austen" for the February 1863 *Atlantic Monthly*, Anna took a public role promoting Austen's novels for the first time. This publication also represented Anna's debut as a writer. Later in 1863, she published a book titled *Verses*, and the *Atlantic* printed four more of her articles from 1864 to 1866.[84]

A combination of biography, digested criticism, and personal response, Anna's five-and-a-half-page article on Austen represented the culmination of the Quincy sisters' decades-long endeavor to collect information about their beloved author. Apparently drawing on the expanded "Memoir of Miss Austen" prefaced to the 1833 Bentley edition of *Sense and Sensibility*, Anna described Austen's father as "a man of great taste in all literary matters; from him his daughter inherited many of her gifts. He probably guided her early education and influenced the direction of her genius."[85] The subject of a father's encouragement of a daughter was doubtless very personally resonant for Anna. She also worked in several of the insights that the admiral and his children had shared with her, including the comment that in writing *Emma* Austen said she was "going to make a character full of faults"; the observation that some contemporary readers were offended by apparent portraits from life; and the anecdote about Macaulay, Hallam, and *Mansfield Park*.[86] And she incorporated numerous quotations earlier aired in her own and Eliza Susan's letters—including appraisals by Scott, Macaulay, Whately, Morpeth, and Lewes—augmented by others not previously mentioned by the Quincys, including Egerton Brydges and Robert Southey.

Valuably for reception history, Anna integrated throughout her own personal reminiscences, responses, and critical judgments. She began the essay with a description of the "pilgrimage" she took to England, evoking "the old Cathedral at Winchester" and Austen's grave, using the first-person plural then typical of such magazine pieces: "Many-colored as the light which streams through painted windows, came the memories which floated in our soul as we read the simple inscription: happy hours, gladdened by her genius, weary hours, soothed by her touch; the honored and the wise who first placed her volumes in our hand; the beloved ones who had lingered over her pages, the voices of our distant home, associated with every familiar story" (235). Compared with Anna's expressions of similar ideas in her private correspondence, this representation of Austen as a source of comfort and connection to "home" and family is sentimentalized, almost generic. So too is the article's conclusion, in which Anna recalled as follows her visit to the admiral: "There we spent a summer day, and the passing hours seemed like the pages over which we had often lingered, written by her hand whose influence had guided us to those she loved. That day, with all its associations, has become a sacred memory, and links us to the sphere where dwells that soul whose gift of genius has rendered immortal the name of Jane Austen" (240).

Beneath these conventional-sounding platitudes lay a deep and private pain. Anna's daughter Helen, who was present at the June 1856 visit to Portsdown Lodge, died in 1859 in Naples. (The Waterstons' only other child, a son, had died in 1846 at one year of age.[87]) As Anna wrote on the front page of her travel journal, "These volumes close with the end of our Roman winter__ The great trial that awaited us in Naples, and the loss of our beloved daughter need not be written.__"[88]

In her magazine essay, Anna channeled her intensity of feeling into passionate advocacy for the lasting importance of Austen's writings. Writing close to fifty years after Austen's death, Anna stressed much as fans and critics do today the capacity of Austen's novels to appeal to readers beyond the author's own time. She did so, however, with reference points appropriate to her own century:[89]

Those were days of post-chaises and sedan-chairs, when the rush of the locomotive was unknown. Steam, that genie of the vapor, was yet a little household elf, singing pleasant tunes by the evening fire, at quiet hearthstones; it has since expanded into a mighty giant, whose influences are no longer domestic. The circles of fashion are changed also. Those were the days of country-dances and India muslins; the beaux and belles of "the upper rooms" at Bath knew not the whirl of the waltz, nor the ceaseless involvements of "the German." Yet the measures of love and jealousy, of hope and fear, to which their hearts beat time, would be recognized to-night in every ballroom. Infinite sameness, infinite variety, are not more apparent in the outward than in the inward world, and the work of that writer will alone be lasting who recognizes and embodies this eternal law of the great Author.

Jane Austen possessed in a remarkable degree this rare intuition. (235)

Only after stating this judgment in her own words (and with characteristic religiosity) did Anna quote similar sentiments from Scott's journals.

Likewise, on Austen's sources of inspiration and the realism of her characters, Anna shared her own thoughts first before quoting Brydges and Southey. "Jane Austen's life-world presented such a limited experience," she declared, "that it is marvellous where she could have found the models from which she studied such a variety of forms. It is only another proof that the secret lies in the genius which seizes, not in the material which is seized" (236). The recognition of oneself in Austen's characters Anna expressed as "a feeling which we have frequently shared . . . we have been startled to recognize our own portrait come gradually out on the canvas" (236). Which depictions struck home to her, however, she did not reveal.

Anna was more forthcoming about her favorite Austen novel and character. Having retold the admiral's anecdote about the

illustrious men who identified *Mansfield Park* as their preferred
work, she confessed, "[h]ad we been of that party at the English
country-house, we should have written, 'The *last* novel by Miss
Austen which we have read'; yet, forced to a selection, we should
have named 'Persuasion.' But we withdraw our private preference,
and, yielding to the decision of seven wise men, place 'Mansfield
Park' at the head of the list, and leave it there without further
comment" (236). After bowing there to masculine critical judgment,
Anna proceeded to praise the "matured and perfected" style of
Persuasion in terms first critical and then very personal:

> Concise and clear, simple and vigorous, no word can be omitted
> that she puts down, and none can be added to heighten the effect
> of her sentences. In "Persuasion" there are passages whose depth
> and tenderness, welling up from deep fountains of feeling,
> impress us with the conviction that the angel of sorrow or
> suffering had troubled the waters, yet had left in them a healing
> influence, which is felt rather than revealed. (237)

Anna also proclaimed that Anne Elliot was her favorite heroine not
only in Austen but in all of fiction:

> Of all the heroines we have known through a long and somewhat
> varied experience, there is not one whose life-companionship we
> should so desire to secure as that of Anne Elliot. Ah! could she
> also forgive our faults and bear with our weaknesses, while we
> were animated by her sweet and noble example, existence would
> be, under any aspect, a blessing. This felicity was reserved for
> Captain Wentworth. Happy man! (237)

Either Anna viewed marriage as but one form of "life-
companionship," or she had forgotten (or not realized) that her
readers would know her own gender from her byline. The issue's
table of contents, though not the article itself, identified the author
as "Mrs. R. C. Waterston."

Austen's craft as a novelist Anna extolled most highly in
commentary on *Pride and Prejudice*. Describing that novel as
"piquant in style and masterly in portraiture," Anna singled out for
admiration Austen's handling of Mr. Darcy. "It is no small tribute to
the power of the author to concede that she has so managed the

workings of his real nature as to make it possible, and even probable, that a high-born, high-bred Englishman of Mr. Darcy's stamp could become the son-in-law of Mrs. Bennet." As an experienced reader of English fiction, Anna evidently considered herself well qualified, in spite of her American nationality, to evaluate the realism of Austen's depiction of an English landowner. Anna also held up Darcy's first proposal to Elizabeth Bennet as both "one of the most remarkable passages in Miss Austen's writings" and as having no equal as a depiction of the "culminating point of human destiny" (237).

On literary tourism as a way to feel closer to Austen and her world, Anna offered a mixed perspective. In some cases, she admitted, actual places fell short of their evocations by Austen. Referring to an episode from *Emma*, she remarked that "[o]nce we found ourselves actually on 'Box Hill,' but it did not seem half so real as when we 'explored' there with the party from Highbury" (237). While visiting the White Hart Inn in Bath, however, *Persuasion* was fully present to her, as she imagined "the conversation of Anne Elliot and Captain Harville, as they stood by the window, while Captain Wentworth listened and wrote" (238). In the presence of the admiral, too, Anna stated that she felt very near Austen herself: "[i]n the finely-cut features of the brother, who retained at eighty years of age much of the early beauty of his youth, we fancied we must see a resemblance to his sister, of whom there exists no portrait" (240).

With respect to the breadth of readership for Austen's novels, Anna returned to a version of the idea of a coterie that she had expressed in 1852. "[W]e are aware that to a class of readers Miss Austen's novels must ever remain sealed books. So be it. While the English language is read, the world will always be provided with souls who can enjoy the rare excellence of that rich legacy left to them by her genius" (239). Which non-appreciators of Austen Anna had in mind cannot be identified with certainty. The now-famous disparaging remarks about Austen made by Longfellow, Emerson, and Twain—or, for that matter, by Charlotte Brontë—were all recorded in private writings that, in 1863, had yet to be published.[90] Perhaps Anna was thinking more generally of her discussion with the admiral's family about the "minority" who appreciated Austen's novels.[91]

After Anna's article was published, Eliza Susan sent a copy of it to the admiral. He received it appreciatively as "further proof of the high estimation in which my late sister's works are held by yourself and near connections."[92] For the first time in their correspondence, too, he looked ahead to the possibility of Austen's future, and global, fame. He expressed his gratification at being "further assured that her talent as an authoress was duely appreciated on the other side of the Great Atlantic; such testimony affords reasonable expectation that her name will be well known long after the present generation has passed away, wherever the English language is spoken or understood." Francis, as a naval officer who had served abroad in North America, and whose brother Charles served and died in India, was very well aware of the potential for English authors to reach audiences throughout the British Empire. He also referred, as Anna's article did not, to the ongoing American Civil War, commiserating with Eliza Susan on the "dreadful loss of life" and the "horrors which have been enacted."

This letter of the admiral's reveals, too, another dimension to the literary exchanges between his family and the Quincys and to the latter's role in the development of Austen-Leigh's *Memoir*. "I was glad also to be assured," he wrote,

> that the Books I took the liberty of requesting you to accept the produce of my Daughter's pen, had been received and that the perusal of them had afforded you some pleasure. She has as you probably know, published several other works of imagination; not all in my opinion of equal merit, but the last she has given to the world, called "The Mistakes of a Life," is I think equal, if not superior in delineation of character, as well as beauty of language, to any of its predecessors.[93]

The daughter in question was Catherine Anne Hubback (1818–1877): the "Mrs. Hubbuck" whom Anna had met at Portsdown Lodge and had presumed to be a widow.[94] (In fact, Catherine had returned with her children to her father's house in 1850 after her husband entered a mental asylum; in 1870, she emigrated to California with one of her sons.[95]) Which of Catherine's novels her father sent to the Quincys is not known. Catherine's first novel, *The Younger Sister* (1850), took as its unacknowledged basis the unfinished fragment of Austen's now known as *The Watsons*. Catherine left her own readers in no doubt about her lineage: she dedicated *The Younger Sister* "To the memory of her Aunt, the Late Jane Austen" and identified herself on later title pages as "Mrs. Hubback, niece of Miss Austen."[96]

Though born after Austen's death, Catherine had grown up hearing about her aunt both from her father and from her aunt Cassandra, who often stayed at Portsdown Lodge (and who, indeed, died in 1845 while on a visit there).[97] Catherine's eagerness to claim relationship with Austen and her own status as the family's next published writer led other descendants to fear that she might, in Sutherland's words, "break the family silence" about Jane.[98] To forestall this possibility, nephews and nieces who did have firsthand, though distant, recollections of their aunt began to write them down following Francis's death in 1865. James Edward Austen-Leigh, the son of Jane's eldest brother James, gathered these together and issued them as the *Memoir of Jane Austen* in December 1869 (with 1870 printed on the title page), which was published by Bentley in London and by Scribner, Welford, & Co. in New York.[99]

An additional impetus for publishing biographical material on Austen was, as Le Faye has put it, "the gradually rising tide of interest in Jane and her works, not only on the part of elderly contemporary readers but also enquiries from those who had been born since she died."[100] Le Faye omits to credit the significant role of American readers in general, and of the Quincys in particular, in that "rising tide."

Austen-Leigh, however, was well aware of the Quincys' interest in his aunt's writings, thanks to an appreciative letter about the first edition of his *Memoir* that Eliza Susan wrote him early in 1870.[101] He chose to highlight this evidence of Austen's transatlantic renown in the second, expanded edition of his *Memoir* (1871). Chapter nine of that book featured, according to its headnote, *"Opinions expressed by eminent persons—Opinions of others of less eminence—Opinion of American readers."* That final "opinion" consisted of Eliza Susan's first letter to the admiral, printed in full, introduced by Austen-Leigh as "a voice of praise from across the Atlantic."[102] Austen-Leigh's taxonomy may amuse us now—did he consider Americans to be even *less* eminent, or to be another species entirely? But, nevertheless, his inclusion of Eliza Susan's letter made all his readers aware that, in 1852, an illustrious Boston family was reading and appreciating his aunt's novels.

Austen-Leigh neither asked Eliza Susan's permission to print her letter nor notified her in advance of his plans to do so. He did, however, ask her to hand-copy the Jane Austen letter in his possession, for extraction in the expanded *Memoir*. She swiftly complied, offering too to make copies of the admiral's letters. Austen-Leigh thanked her but declined, writing "I have no occasion to give you that trouble; I have already given you enough."[103] Whether Eliza Susan mentioned that Francis's letters contained some personal reminiscences of Austen we do not know. In any case, Austen-Leigh's decision not to see copies of Francis's letters meant that these recollections did not enter the published record.[104]

Austen-Leigh's exchange of letters with Eliza Susan in 1870 brings to light, furthermore, a hitherto overlooked American publication about Austen: an unsigned review of the first edition of the *Memoir* in the 24 February 1870 issue of the periodical *The Nation*. Austen-Leigh stated to Eliza Susan that he was "much obliged by the notice of Jane Austen which you sent. Few if any of the notices which my memoir elicited in England have pleased me so well. There is a beauty and delicacy of touch about it which is delightful to my taste."[105] It is not known whether Eliza Susan sent him the *Nation* review or another that has yet to be rediscovered. However, the very favorable tone of the *Nation* piece makes it a likely candidate.

In addition to summary of Austen-Leigh's *Memoir*, the *Nation* review includes observations on Austen's artistry and readership, as well as some criticism of individual works. Austen is "worthy of a memoir," this article's author declared, because her readership, while not broad, is dedicated: "if you ask at the libraries you will find that her works are still taken out; so that there must still be a faithful few who, like ourselves, will have welcomed the announcement of a Memoir of the authoress of 'Pride and Prejudice,' 'Mansfield Park,' and 'Emma.'"[106] The omission of *Persuasion* on this list is telling. Unlike Anna, who preferred *Persuasion* above all, this reviewer pronounced that Austen's final novel "betrays an enfeeblement of her faculties and tells of approaching death."[107]

Overall, too, the *Nation* author made much more limited claims about Austen's literary importance than had Anna. Having compared Austen at some length to Shakespeare in terms of characterization, and having contrasted her fiction's content favorably with that of sensation novels, this reviewer concluded that Austen was more "good"—in every sense of that word—than great. "She possessed a real and rare gift, and she rendered a good account of it. If the censer which she held among the priests of art was not of the costliest, the incense was of the purest. If she cannot be ranked with the greatest masters of fiction, she has at least delighted many, and none can draw from her any but innocent delight."[108] The moralizing tone harks directly back to the Philadelphia *National Gazette*'s 1832 praise of Austen's writings as "entertaining and ingenious, but free from all poison."[109]

Austen-Leigh developed the idea of purity in a quite different direction when thanking Eliza Susan for sending the American review of his *Memoir*. Complimenting his transatlantic correspondent, he observed that "[s]urely no language was ever so widely spread as the English, which not to mention our innumerable Colonies, is written & spoken in equal purity on both sides of the Atlantic."[110] As had the admiral in 1863, Austen-Leigh was clearly thinking about how the worldwide reach of the English language created a potential readership for Austen's novels.

In the coming decades, as Austen's international popularity rapidly grew, her family members continued to recognize her American readers. "[L]ikely to interest a public which, both in Great Britain and America, has learned to appreciate Jane Austen," read the introduction to the 1884 edition of her letters prepared by her great-nephew Edward, Lord Brabourne.[111] Likewise, in 1913, William and Richard Arthur Austen-Leigh (James Edward Austen-Leigh's son and grandson, respectively) stated in their new biography, *Jane Austen: Her Life and Letters: A Family Record*, that interest in Austen "has shown no signs of diminishing, either in England or in America."[112]

Two world wars later, in 1942, Richard Arthur devoted the final chapter of his privately printed *Austen Papers, 1704–1856* to the Quincy/Austen letters then in his possession. These he described in his preface as "concerning an incident showing the extent to which Jane's novels were appreciated in the United States in the middle of the nineteenth century."[113] Yet these documents are an odd fit in a volume otherwise dedicated to correspondence among branches of the Austen family. And Richard Arthur found nothing particular in the letters themselves on which to comment: "There seems nothing in this pleasant exchange of letters that needs elucidation," he remarked in a headnote. Only the admiral's generosity in giving the Quincys an entire Austen letter earned an editorial remark calling attention to the recent sale price of another such: "It may perhaps be worthy of mention—though the fact, could he have foreseen it, would hardly have affected the Admiral's action—that in 1930 a single letter of Jane Austen's was sold at Sotheby's for the sum of £1000."[114]

Indeed, in the eighty years since Eliza Susan first wrote to the admiral, Austen's letters had utterly changed in value. From family-owned materials passed down to descendants and shared, judiciously, with admirers, these manuscripts had become highly collectible. In one sense, this demand meant that Austen had achieved parity with nineteenth-century male authors whose private writings also commanded great prices. In 1920, the American mega-collector J. P. Morgan paid $3,000 for a set of forty-one Austen letters; evidently, he was persuaded by his dealer's statement that "it would be safe to say that no such collection of her letters will ever come into the market again."[115] Morgan had hoped to acquire a full manuscript of an Austen novel—a much greater prize than mere letters to Cassandra—but was informed, correctly, by the dealer that "no such manuscript exists, either in a library, museum, or among members of the family."[116]

From a novelist whose works were cherished and reread by a relatively small group of ardent admirers, Austen had become a major author whose name could sell biographies, whose manuscripts fetched high prices at auction, and whose novels—thanks in great part to R. W. Chapman's 1923 Clarendon Press edition, which ushered Austen definitively into the literary canon—offered prime material for the new academic discipline of literary criticism. In the course of the twentieth century, Austen scholarship and what we now call Austen fandom developed in almost completely separate directions.

Through collecting, however, a few exceptional readers continued to combine strong personal appreciation for Austen's writings with self-taught expertise in her publishing history. My final chapter presents the seemingly unlikely friendship between the foremost American Austen collector of the twentieth century, Alberta H. Burke, and David Gilson, the Englishman whose work on Austen bibliography she warmly supported.

Notes

1   David Kaser, ed., *The Cost Book of Carey & Lea, 1825–1838* (Philadelphia: University of Pennsylvania Press, 1963), 118–29. The

Carey & Lea Cost Book records the production costs for each Austen title and wholesale prices for some. The book does not record retail prices for the Austen novels, which have yet to be traced; unlike in the late 1810s, booksellers' advertisements did not include retail prices. The alternate title chosen for *Pride and Prejudice* is a mystery. Mary Elliott's novel *The Two Edwards; or, Pride and Prejudice unmasked* (London: William Darton, 1823) was available in the United States as an imported book, but seems not to have been well known enough to warrant the retitling of Austen's novel. I am grateful to Bruce Connolly, director of public services at the Union College Library, for first bringing Elliott's novel and other contemporary sources to my attention. On the role of the 1832–1833 Carey & Lea edition in promoting Austen's fame in the US and Britain, see Emily Schultheis, "Philadelphia and the Making of Jane Austen, 1816–1838," *Women's Writing*, special issue on "Bicentennial Essays on Jane Austen's Afterlives," ed. Annika Bautz and Sarah Wooton (forthcoming 2017). Schultheis's argument also addresses the two-volume *Novels of Jane Austen* published in 1838 by Carey, Lea & Blanchard, in a print run of 1,500.

2   For facsimiles of title pages and spine labels, plus extensive discussions of textual variants, see David Gilson, *A Bibliography of Jane Austen*, new edn (New Castle, DE: Oak Knoll Press, 1997), 99–132; and "Jane Austen's 'Emma' in America: Notes on the Text of the First and Second American Editions," *The Review of English Studies* n.s. 53: 212 (2002): 517–25.

3   In addition to reviews, newspapers' promotion took the form of reprinting selected quotations, a common publishing practice at the time. For instance, a series of five quotations from *Emma*, prefaced with the statement "We subjoin a few ways of Miss Austen's entertaining way of treating commonplace subjects," was published in the *New Bedford Mercury* [Massachusetts] 23 August 1833: [4], *AHN*. The last of those quotations, ending with the sentence "A mind lively and at ease can do with seeing nothing, and can see nothing that does not answer," also appeared under the headline "Aspect of a County Town" in *The Portsmouth Journal of Literature & Politics* [New Hampshire] 5 October 1833: [1], *AHN*. The extent and nature of reprinted quotations from Austen's novels in American newspapers of this time deserves fuller investigation.

4   [Untitled publication notice of *Elizabeth Bennet*], *Evening Post* [New York] 7 September 1832: [1], *AHN*. Amusingly, this notice continued: "This *a priori* judgment receives confirmation from the style and spirit of the few pages we have perused."

5   [Untitled publication notice of *Elizabeth Bennet*], *National Gazette*
    [Philadelphia] 6 September 1832: [1], *AHN*; cited in Gilson,
    Bibliography, 104. The *National Gazette* also subsequently spread
    information about Austen's life by reprinting the "Biographical Notice"
    in its entirety in February 1833, just after the Carey & Lea edition of
    Northanger Abbey was released: "Biographical Notice of Miss Austen,"
    National Gazette [Philadelphia] 9 February 1833: [1], *AHN*.

6   [Untitled publication notice of *Elizabeth Bennet*], *National Gazette*
    [Philadelphia] 6 September 1832: [1], *AHN*.

7   J. E. Austen-Leigh, *A Memoir of Jane Austen and Other Family
    Recollections*, ed. Kathryn Sutherland (Oxford: Oxford University Press,
    2002), 224. Sutherland repeats this description in *Jane Austen's Textual
    Lives: From Aeschylus to Bollywood* (Oxford: Oxford University Press,
    2005), although she does acknowledge there that the Quincy/Austen
    correspondence "suggests a receptive circle of devotees as far away as
    Boston" (71). No impact on Austen scholarship has been made by
    Beverly Wilson Palmer's edition of one of Anna's youthful diaries, *A
    Woman's Wit and Whimsy: The 1833 Diary of Anna Cabot Lowell
    Quincy* (Boston: Massachusetts Historical Society/Northeastern
    University Press, 2003). Palmer prints in appendices one of Anna's letters
    and the 1863 article on Austen she published in the *Atlantic Monthly*;
    Palmer also acknowledges, in passing, Anna's 1856 visit to Admiral
    Austen. The original Quincy/Austen documents are now divided
    between archives at the Massachusetts Historical Society in Boston and
    the Hampshire Record Office in Winchester, England. In "A Jane Austen
    Letter, with other 'Janeana' from an old book of autographs," *The Yale
    Review* 15 (Jan. 1926): 319–35, M. A. deWolfe Howe printed the side of
    the correspondence then owned by his wife, a Quincy descendant: i.e.,
    documents received by the Quincys, including the Jane Austen letter sent
    to them, plus Eliza Susan's initial letter, reprinted from J. E. Austen-
    Leigh's *Memoir*. (A transcript of Howe's article is publicly available at
    http://www.mollands.net/etexts/other/hvrdltrs.html.) Howe subsequently
    mentioned the Quincy women's "addiction to Austen" in his edited
    volume *The Articulate Sisters: Passages from Journals and Letters of
    the Daughters of President Josiah Quincy of Harvard University*
    (Cambridge, MA: Harvard University Press, 1946), 46; none of Howe's
    selections from the sisters' diaries, however, include direct references to
    Austen's work. R. A. Austen-Leigh printed the documents then in his
    own possession—i.e., letters received from the Quincys, plus two drafts
    of letters written by Francis Austen—in his edited volume *Austen Papers,
    1704–1856* ([Colchester, England]: privately printed by Spottiswood,
    Ballantyne, 1942), which had very limited circulation. Brief mentions of
    the Quincy/Austen acquaintance and of the 1856 Portsmouth visit are

made by David Hopkinson in "The Austens in North America, 1809–1875," *Persuasions* 20 (2000): 53–60. Brian Southam examines the correspondence from the point of view of the aging Francis Austen in *Jane Austen and the Navy* (London: Hambledon and London, 2000), 307–8, 313. Overviews of the Quincy/Austen correspondence and of the Quincy family's connections with Justice Story appear in two brief articles by Farnell Parsons: "The Quincys and the Austens: A Cordial Connection," *Jane Austen Society Report* (2000): 49–51 and "A Note on a Jane Austen Connection with the Massachusetts Historical Society: Justice Story, Admiral Wormeley, and Admiral Francis Austen," *Persuasions On-Line* 23.1 (2002). A few mentions of the Quincys appear in Claire Harman, *Jane's Fame: How Jane Austen Conquered the World* (Edinburgh: Canongate, 2009), 124, 134, 148.

8   The indefatigable Austen historian Deirdre Le Faye has noted only four instances of contact before 1870 between devotees and members of the Austen family. *Jane Austen: A Family Record*, 2nd edn (Cambridge: Cambridge University Press, 2004), 274.

9   In Kathryn Sutherland's words, the *Memoir* "has long been recognized as altering [Austen's] fortunes for ever—from a relatively select coterie writer, a critic's and a novelist's novelist, to a widely esteemed cultural asset, everybody's quintessential English novelist." *Austen's Textual Lives*, 1.

10   Palmer, ed., *Woman's Wit*, 41 (20 March 1833). On the Quincys' social and economic status, see Palmer's introduction, 3–24. Palmer makes an unconvincing argument that Anna's writing style and subject matter demonstrate Austen's influence. The crucial fact that Carey & Lea had very recently reprinted Austen's novels is not mentioned by Palmer.

11   Palmer, ed., *Woman's Wit*, 61–2, 82, 85.

12   Carey & Lea's cost book does not specify months of publication for the Austen titles released between March and May 1833. Advertisements for *Sense and Sensibility* suggest a publication date of early March. "Sense and Sensibility," *Southern Patriot* [Charleston, South Carolina] 12 March 1833: [3], *AHN*.

13   One of Eliza Susan's artworks, a drawing of Quincy House, is reproduced in Howe, *Articulate Sisters*, 4; another, an etching of Wadsworth House at Harvard, is reproduced in Palmer, ed., *Woman's Wit*, 46. See also Eliza Susan Quincy, *A Portfolio of Nine Watercolor Views, Relating to Certain Members of the Adams and Quincy Families and Their Quincy Houses and Environment Done in the Year 1822* (Boston: Massachusetts Historical Society, 1975). Quincy House is now a museum operated by Historic New England, which

interprets it in terms both of the property's Revolutionary War origins and of Eliza Susan's efforts to save it a century later: http://www.historicnewengland.org/historic-properties/homes/quincy-house. A likeness of Anna in later life is printed in Howe, *Articulate Sisters* and reprinted in Palmer, ed., *Woman's Wit*, 145.

14 Quoted in Howe, *Articulate Sisters*, 46.

15 In his memoirs, Josiah Quincy recalled as follows his discussions of British women writers with Justice Story: "Judge Story spoke of Mrs. Radcliffe in terms of great admiration, and wished she could have had some of the weird legends of Marblehead upon which to display her wealth of lurid imagery. Miss Burney's 'Evelina' he thought very bright and fascinating, while the conversations of Maria Edgeworth were Nature itself, and yet full of point—the duller speeches of her characters being simply omitted, as was proper in a work of art. On a subsequent occasion, I heard him place Jane Austen much above these writers, and compliment her with a panegyric quite equal to those bestowed by Scott and Macaulay." Josiah Quincy, *Figures of the Past*, 6th edn (Boston: Roberts Brothers, 1883), 195.

16 William Wetmore Story, *Life and Letters of Joseph Story*, vol. 1 (Boston: Charles C. Little and James Brown, 1851), 506–7, *GoogleBooks*. Wetmore Story does not comment on the remarkable conjunction of creating his father's portrait while a novel containing a memorable portrait-painting episode was read aloud.

17 Palmer, ed., *Woman's Wit*, 62.

18 ACLW, Journal, 3 – 15 August 1834, *Quincy, Wendell, Holmes, and Upham Family Papers*, microfilm edition, 67 reels (Boston: Massachusetts Historical Society, 1977), reel 10. In his commentary on this journal, Howe singles out Anna's first mention of "a real Mr. Knightley" as a way in which she "showed herself the thorough Janeite." *Articulate Sisters*, 242.

19 ACLW, Journal, 3 – 15 August 1834, *Quincy Papers*, reel 10.

20 W. J. Rorabaugh, "Edward C. Delavan," *American National Biography*, ed. John A. Garraty and Mark C. Carnes (Oxford: Oxford University Press, 1999), 6:384–5.

21 ACLW, Travel Journal, vol. 1, 7 May – 6 November 1856, *Quincy Papers*, reel 10.

22 *Quincy Papers*, reels 6, 47, 55, 61, 62, 63.

23 *Quincy Papers*, reels 45, 46, 49.

24 The nineteenth-century mania for collecting authors' signatures is well documented, though not explained, by A. N. L. Munby in *The Cult of the Autograph Letter in England* (London: Athlone Press, 1962).

25 Margaret Smith, "The Brontë Correspondence," in *The Brontës in Context*, ed. Marianne Thormählen (Cambridge: Cambridge University Press, 2012), 120. On the impulse to collect Austen's handwriting as a method of feeling closer to the author, see Juliette Wells, *Everybody's Jane: Austen in the Popular Imagination* (New York: Bloomsbury Academic, 2011), chapter two.

26 Le Faye, *Family Record*, 273. Building on a comment in one of Hutton's letters, Cheryl A. Wilson considers Hutton in relation to Austen in "'Something like mine': Catherine Hutton, Jane Austen, and Feminist Recovery Work," *The Eighteenth Century* 56.2 (2015): 151–64. Hutton's collection of an Austen autograph, which Wilson does not mention, adds a further dimension to her argument.

27 Quoted in Le Faye, *Family Record*, 273.

28 Le Faye, *Family Record*, 273. I observed the original Hutton manuscript on 11 June 2016, by kind permission of its owner, Mrs. Edith Lank.

29 ESQ to FWA, 6 January 1852, Austen-Leigh family papers, Hampshire Record Office (hereafter HRO), Winchester, 23M93/63/1/3. Prior publications of this letter transcribe the punctuation differently and incorrectly render "incidentally" as "accidentally."

30 In fact, by 1852, several critics had compared Austen to Shakespeare. First was Whately's unsigned 1821 *Quarterly Review* essay, from which Jeremiah Smith took notes in his copy of *Emma* (see Chapter 2). The comparison was subsequently taken up and elaborated by Thomas Babington Macaulay in 1843, in the *Edinburgh Review*, and by George Henry Lewes in 1847, in an influential assessment of Austen's novels for *Fraser's Magazine*. For Whately's review and excerpts from those of Macaulay and Lewes, see B. C. Southam, ed., *Jane Austen: The Critical Heritage* (London: Routledge & Kegan Paul, 1968), 87–105, 122–3, and 124–5. Anna quoted all three of these sources in her own 1863 article on Austen for the *Atlantic Monthly*. Mrs. R. C. Waterston, "Jane Austen," *Atlantic Monthly* vol. xi (February 1863): 238–9, EBSCO*host*.

31 Parsons, "A Note." Parsons records that Wormeley shared a stagecoach with Justice Story from New York to Boston in 1820: several years before Marshall recommended Austen's novels to the latter. Eliza Susan announced Wormeley's death to Francis in her letter of 16 August 1852; on his last visit to the Quincys, she recalled, he was "highly delighted" to see "your first letter to me, and your sister's autograph." ESQ to FWA, 16 August 1852, Austen-Leigh family papers, HRO, 23M93/63/1/7.

32 Gilson, *Bibliography*, 121.

33 In a poignant historical connection between the Austen and Dalhousie families, Rear-Admiral Charles Austen served as commander-in-chief of the East India station of the Navy while Lady Dalhousie's youngest son, James—by then Lord Dalhousie—was governor-general of India. For an account of Charles's illness and death, and of Lord Dalhousie's kindness to him during this period, see J. H. Hubback and Edith C. Hubback, *Jane Austen's Sailor Brothers: Being the Adventures of Sir Francis Austen, G.C.B., Admiral of the Fleet and Rear-Admiral Charles Austen* (London: John Lane, 1896), 278–81.

34 Hubback and Hubback, *Jane Austen's Sailor Brothers*, 282.

35 FWA to ESQ, 31 January 1852, *Quincy Papers*, reel 52. All quotations in this paragraph are from this source.

36 This passage appears in Le Faye, *Family Record*, 273–4, as transcribed from the draft letter in the HRO, which bears some minor differences from the version sent to Eliza Susan.

37 See in particular the recollections of Caroline Austen (1805–1880), which her brother James Edward Austen-Leigh quoted in his *Memoir*: "*Everything* she could make amusing to a child . . . she would tell us the most delightful stories chiefly of Fairyland." Caroline Austen, "My Aunt Jane Austen," in Austen-Leigh, *Memoir*, ed. Sutherland, 169.

38 Hopkinson, "Austens in North America," 55. Hopkinson points out the "generous courtesy" with which Francis Austen treated the Quincy family.

39 FWA to ESQ, 31 January 1852, *Quincy Papers*, reel 52.

40 FWA to ESQ, 26 March 1852, *Quincy Papers*, reel 52.

41 Jane Austen to Martha Lloyd, [12 Nov. 1800], *Quincy Papers*, reel 35. This letter is #26 in *Jane Austen's Letters*, ed. Deirdre Le Faye, 4th edn (Oxford: Oxford University Press, 2015), 60–2.

42 ESQ to FWA, 2 March 1852, Austen-Leigh family papers, HRO, 23M93/63/1/4. All quotations in this paragraph are from this source.

43 ACLW to ESQ, [undated], Austen-Leigh family papers, HRO, 23M93/63/1/1.

44 ACLW to ESQ, [undated], Austen-Leigh family papers, HRO, 23M93/63/1/1.

45 On Kipling, and on the founding of the Jane Austen Society, see Claudia L. Johnson, *Jane Austen's Cults and Cultures* (Chicago: University of Chicago Press, 2012), 100–4, 138–40. On the American Austen devotee Alberta H. Burke's 1935 call for likeminded readers to join in celebrating the author's birthday, see Wells, *Everybody's Jane*, 52.

46 The quotation, which Eliza Susan left unattributed, is from Lord
    Byron's historical notes to Canto IV of *Childe Harold's Pilgrimage*
    and concerns the works of Madame de Staël. *The Works of the Right
    Honourable Lord Byron, in Seven Volumes*, vol. 7 (Brussels: Demanet,
    1819), 110, *GoogleBooks*.

47 ESQ to FWA, 2 March 1852, Austen-Leigh family papers, HRO,
    23M93/63/1/4.

48 FWA to ESQ, 29 March 1852, *Quincy Papers*, reel 52. All quotations
    in this and the next two paragraphs are from this source. In a
    postscript to this letter, Francis corrected Eliza Susan's mistaken
    address to him: "my second name is William, and I am a full not Vice
    Admiral." A separate copy of this letter is in the HRO, 23M93/63/1/5,
    with the later annotation (evidently by R. A. Austen-Leigh): "must be
    a draft See letter itself in Yale Review Jan 1926."

49 Francis gratified Eliza Susan's family pride by expressing interest in
    reading a "published account," if available, about the trial in which
    her grandfather was involved. He also paid the Quincys the
    compliment of inquiring whether their two families might have a
    prior acquaintance: "I was in London last week and shewed your
    letter to a very intimate female friend who had known my Sister. She
    mentioned that some years ago she met at the house of a Mrs Coxe a
    young lady of the name of Anna Quincy a native of the U. S. If your
    Sister was ever in England perhaps she was the person. My friend's
    maiden name was Curling, but she married first a Capt. Hore of the
    Navy and secondly a M^r. Bedford, whose widow she now is." FWA to
    ESQ, 29 March 1852, *Quincy Papers*, reel 52. Eliza Susan replied that
    her sister had never previously visited England.

50 Sutherland describes these verses, which J. E. Austen-Leigh quoted in
    his *Memoir*, as "one of the earliest expressions of the sentimental
    enthusiasm that became known as 'Janeism'" and identifies their
    author as George Howard, sixth Earl of Carlisle (1773–1848). J. E.
    Austen-Leigh, *Memoir*, ed. Sutherland, 249.

51 FWA to ESQ, 24 June 1852, *Quincy Papers*, reel 52. All quotations in
    this paragraph are from this source. As with Francis's 29 March letter,
    a complete version (dated 23 June 1852) is in the HRO,
    23M93/63/1/8, with R. A. Austen-Leigh's annotation "Draft." The
    piety Francis expressed here is in keeping with family traditions about
    his religiosity: see the description of him as "*the* officer who kneeled
    at church" in J. E. Austen-Leigh, *Memoir*, ed. Sutherland, 17.

52 ESQ to FWA, 22 April 1856, *Quincy Papers*, reel 54. Both quotations
    in this paragraph and the first in the next paragraph are from this
    source.

53 Le Faye, *Family Record*, 275.

54 On the history of Austen-inspired literary tourism, see Wells, *Everybody's Jane*, chapter four. See too Nicola J. Watson's discussion of literary tourism, American identity, and gender in the American girls' novel *What Katy Did Next* (1886), in "Rambles in Literary London," in *Literary Tourism and Nineteenth-Century Culture*, ed. Nicola J. Watson (Houndmills, Basingstoke: Palgrave Macmillan, 2009), 146–8.

55 See Simone M. Müller, *Wiring the World: The Social and Cultural Creation of Global Telegraph Networks* (New York: Columbia University Press, 2016), 1.

56 ACLW to Henry E. Austen, 4 June 1856, Austen-Leigh family papers, HRO, 23M93/63/1/11. This letter and the others under this reference number are present in the HRO only in the typescript transcriptions prepared by R. A. Austen-Leigh for his *Austen Papers*; the current whereabouts of the manuscripts is unknown.

57 The current location of this letter is unknown; its contents can be deduced from Anna's reply to it and from Francis' statement, in a later letter to Eliza Susan, that his son Henry "was taken from this world in May 1854 after a short illness." FWA to ESQ, 19 June 1856, *Quincy Papers*, reel 54.

58 ACLW to FWA, 9 June 1856, Austen-Leigh family papers, HRO, 23M93/63/1/11.

59 Quoted in Le Faye, *Family Record*, 275.

60 ACLW, Travel Journal, vol. 1, 7 May – 6 Nov. 1856, *Quincy Papers*, reel 10. Until noted, all subsequent quotations are from this source.

61 Catherine Anne Hubback (1818–1877) was the eighth of Francis's eleven children. Le Faye, ed., *Letters*, 492.

62 Apparently unbeknownst to this branch of the family, two portraits of Austen were made during her lifetime, both drawn by her elder sister Cassandra (1773–1845). See Wells, *Everybody's Jane*, 146.

63 These comments accord with the recollections of John Hubback, Catherine's son, in the book he co-wrote, *Jane Austen's Sailor Brothers*: "How often I call to mind some question or answer, expressed quite naturally in terms of the novels; sometimes even a conversation would be carried on entirely appropriate to the matter under discussion, but the actual phrases were 'Aunt Jane's'" (viii). (This practice recalls the virtuoso performances of Shakespeare quotation in which Lady Dalhousie engaged; see Chapter 3.) Sutherland points out that the frequent visits of Cassandra Austen, Jane's devoted sister, to Portsdown Lodge would have encouraged such play and reminiscence. *Austen's Textual Lives*, 243.

64 This recollected sentiment is similar but not identical to James
     Edward Austen-Leigh's by now well-known report, in his *Memoir*,
     that Austen "was very fond of Emma, but did not reckon on her being
     a general favourite; for, when commencing that work, she said, 'I am
     going to take a heroine whom no one but myself will much like.'"
     Austen-Leigh, *Memoir*, ed. Sutherland, 119.

65 On Charles Austen, the other "sailor brother" of Jane's, see endnote
     33.

66 This comment does not accord with any of the responses to *Emma*
     collected by Austen. See Jane Austen, "Opinions of *Emma*," in *Later
     Manuscripts*, ed. Janet Todd and Linda Bree (Cambridge: Cambridge
     University Press, 2008), 235–9.

67 Henry Hallam (1777–1859) was a noted English historian and the
     father of Arthur Henry Hallam, to whom Tennyson dedicated his
     poem *In Memoriam*. For the published remarks of Thomas Babington
     Macaulay (1800–1859) on Austen, see Southam, ed., *Critical
     Heritage*, 122–3. See also Katie Halsey's discussion of the views on
     Austen held by Arthur Henry Hallam and by Macaulay in *Jane
     Austen and Her Readers, 1786–1945* (London: Anthem, 2012),
     146–51.

68 Most likely, Anna was referring to the publication by Bunce &
     Brother of New York of *Pride and Prejudice* (1855) and *Sense and
     Sensibility* (1856). George W. Briggs of Boston reissued *Pride and
     Prejudice* in 1849; Carey & Lea reprinted all six of Austen's novels in
     1845. Gilson, *Bibliography*, 240–56. On the reach of later
     inexpensive, and even free, American editions of Austen, see Janine
     Barchas, "Sense, Sensibility, and Soap: An Unexpected Case Study in
     Digital Resources in Book History," *Book History* 16 (2013):
     185–214.

69 Presumably the same portrait of Francis appears as the frontispiece to
     Jane Austen's Sailor Brothers.

70 Hartfield is the Woodhouse family's residence in Austen's novel
     Emma.

71 Charles-John Austen II (1821–1867) was the fifth child of Jane's
     brother Charles; his eldest daughter was Jane (1849–1928). Catherine
     Hubback's eldest son was John-Henry Hubback (1844–1939), who
     co-wrote *Jane Austen's Sailor Brothers* with his daughter Edith.
     Le Faye, ed., *Letters*, 491–2.

72 George Austen (1812–1903) was Francis's fourth child; at this time,
     he was rector of St. John's Church in Havant, Hampshire. Le Faye,
     ed., *Letters*, 491.

73 Edmund Quincy VII (1808–1877), the younger of Anna's two
    brothers, was an attorney and journalist in Boston. *A Woman's Wit*,
    ed. Palmer, 21.

74 Presumably, given the military orientation of Francis and his family,
    this reference is to Arthur Wellesley (1769–1852), Duke of
    Wellington, under whom—to draw another Dalhousie connection—
    Lord Dalhousie had served in the Battle of Waterloo.

75 Herbert-Grey Austen (1815–1888), Francis's sixth child and another
    naval officer.

76 This phrase was attributed to Walter Scott by several nineteenth-
    century writers. See for instance J. McVickar, *Tribute to the Memory
    of Sir Walter Scott, Baronet* (New York: George P. Scott, 1832), 40.

77 The Austen family's appreciation of, rather than repulsion by, readers'
    fervent enthusiasm is evident, too, in the responses of Jane's nieces
    Louisa and Fanny Knight to the great curiosity of one Lady
    Campbell. See Le Faye, *Family Record*, 274–5.

78 FWA to ESQ, 19 June 1856, *Quincy Papers*, reel 54.

79 ACLW to FWA, 13 August 1856, Austen-Leigh family papers, HRO,
    23M93/63/1/11.

80 ESQ to FWA, 6 August 1856, Austen-Leigh family papers, HRO,
    23M93/63/1/11.

81 ACLW to FWA, 9 July 1856, Austen-Leigh family papers, HRO,
    23M93/63/1/11. Anna referred in this letter to her family's receipt of
    her "letter describing my visit to Portsdown Lodge"—the text of
    which was evidently recopied into her travel journal.

82 The etymological origins of the word "enthusiast" lie in religious
    frenzy: see "enthusiast, n.," *OED Online*, December 2016, Oxford
    University Press.

83 ACLW, Travel Journal, vol. 1, 7 May – 6 Nov. 1856, *Quincy Papers*,
    reel 10.

84 Palmer, ed., *Woman's Wit*, 11.

85 Waterston, "Jane Austen," 237. Subsequent quotations from this
    article are cited parenthetically in text. The 1833 "Memoir of Miss
    Austen"—which, like the 1818 "Biographical Notice," was written by
    but not credited to Henry Austen—described Rev. Austen and his
    influence as follows: "Being not only a profound scholar, but
    possessing a most exquisite taste in every species of literature, it is not
    wonderful that his daughter Jane should, at a very early age, have
    become sensible to the charms of style, and enthusiastic in the
    cultivation of her own language." Reprinted in David Gilson, "Henry

Austen's Memoir of Miss Austen," *Persuasions* 20 (1998): 12 and in Austen-Leigh, *Memoir*, ed. Sutherland, 147.

86 ACLW, Travel Journal, vol. 1, 7 May – 6 November 1856, *Quincy Papers*, reel 10. This *Emma* comment is rendered in Anna's *Atlantic Monthly* article as a direct quotation: "'Emma' we know to have been a favorite with the author. 'I have drawn a character full of faults,' said she, 'nevertheless I like her.'" Waterston, "Jane Austen," 237. On the status of *Mansfield Park* in turn-of-the-twentieth-century approbation, see Linda Troost and Sayre Greenfield, "A History of the Fanny Wars," *Persuasions* 36 (2014): 15–33.

87 Palmer, ed., *Woman's Wit*, 10.

88 ACLW, Travel Journal, vol. 1, 7 May – 6 November 1856, *Quincy Papers*, reel 10.

89 For an insightful recent treatment of Austen's enduring appeal, see Maggie Lane, Introduction to *The Joy of Jane: Thoughts on the First 200 Years of Austen's Legacy*, ed. Tim Bullamore (Edinburgh: Lansdown Media, 2016), 4–10.

90 For the comments of Longfellow, Emerson, and Brontë, see Southam, ed., *Critical Heritage*, 117, 28, 126–8. On Twain, see Halsey, *Austen and Her Readers*, 184–7.

91 ACLW, Travel Journal, vol. 1, 7 May – 6 November 1856, *Quincy Papers*, reel 10.

92 FWA to ESQ, 19 May 1863, *Quincy Papers*, reel 57; all quotations in this paragraph are from this source. Legacies were much on Francis's mind in this letter. As he informed Eliza Susan, with characteristic modesty, he had recently received his final promotion, "to the highest grade in the Naval Service, that of Admiral of the Fleet. . . . It is gratifying to have attained this last step; but it would be bad for England if all her Admirals were such poor enfeebled objects as he who is now addressing you."

93 FWA to ESQ, 19 May 1863, *Quincy Papers*, reel 57.

94 ACLW, Travel Journal, vol. 1, 7 May – 6 November 1856, *Quincy Papers*, reel 10.

95 Sutherland, *Austen's Textual Lives*, 260, 264.

96 Sutherland, *Austen's Textual Lives*, 264.

97 Le Faye, *Family Record*, 271.

98 Sutherland, *Austen's Textual Lives*, 72.

99 The US publisher is listed at the end of the review titled "Austen-Leigh's Memoir of Jane Austen," *The Nation* 243 (24 February 1870), 124, *American Literary Periodicals, 1859–1891.*

100 Le Faye, *Family Record*, 275.

101 This letter apparently has not survived; Austen-Leigh refers to it, in his reply, as "a very kind & acceptable letter on the subject of my memoir of my Aunt Jane Austen." JEAL to ESQ, 28 November 1870, *Quincy Papers*, reel 60. Whether Austen-Leigh had earlier been informed about the Quincys' correspondence with Francis is not known.

102 Austen-Leigh, *Memoir*, ed. Sutherland, 110, 114.

103 JEAL to ESQ, 30 December 1870, *Quincy Papers*, reel 60.

104 As Howe pointed out in 1926, had Austen-Leigh "accepted Miss Quincy's offer of copies of the Admiral's letters, the fragments of information and of sidelight upon Miss Austen and her brother which have waited all these years for publication might have become accessible to her host of lovers more than half a century ago." "A Jane Austen Letter," 335.

105 JEAL to ESQ, 30 December 1870, *Quincy Papers*, reel 60.

106 "Austen-Leigh's Memoir," 124.

107 "Austen-Leigh's Memoir," 125.

108 "Austen-Leigh's Memoir," 126.

109 [Untitled publication notice of *Elizabeth Bennet*], *National Gazette* [Philadelphia] 6 September 1832: [1], *AHN*.

110 JEAL to ESQ, 30 December 1870, *Quincy Papers*, reel 60. In his commentary in *Austen Papers*, R. A. Austen-Leigh mentions two further letters from ESQ to JEAL: "The publication of the Second Edition of the Memoir of Jane Austen brought a letter dated Dec. 13 1870, to the Author from Miss Eliza Quincy, followed by one dated July 15, 1871, thanking him for a gift of a copy of the second edition. In the former letter Miss Quincy says that her brother Edmund Quincy, Mrs. Waterston, and she herself had each bought a copy from Messrs. Little & Brown of Boston at £1 each" (320). These two letters are not in the HRO archives.

111 Edward, Lord Brabourne, ed., *Letters of Jane Austen*, 2 vols. (London: Richard Bentley & Son, 1884), 1:xiii. Brabourne's *Letters* represented the first publication of Austen's correspondence following the excerpts included in Austen-Leigh's *Memoir*.

112 William Austen-Leigh and Richard Arthur Austen-Leigh, *Jane Austen: Her Life and Letters: A Family Record*, 2nd edn (London: Smith, Elder & Co., 1913), vi.

113 *Austen Papers*, ed. Austen-Leigh, vii.

114 *Austen Papers*, ed. Austen-Leigh, 296.

115 Ernest Dressel North to J. P. Morgan, 26 April 1919, Morgan
Collections Correspondence, 1887–1948, Morgan Library and
Museum, New York, ARC 1310. Unlike North's practice when
referring to male authors, he gave Austen's full name and a detailed
sketch of her authorial career, evidently from the expectation that
Morgan would need such hints.

116 Ernest Dressel North to J. P. Morgan, 17 April 1920, Morgan
Collections Correspondence, ARC 1310. Dressel's correspondence
with Morgan makes it possible to compare his asking prices for
Austen letters with those for other authors. In 1909, for example,
Dressel offered Morgan thirty-three letters written by Arthur H.
Hallam to Emily Tennyson for the total price of $1,975. Ernest
Dressel North to J. P. Morgan, 9 December 1909, Morgan
Collections Correspondence, ARC 1310.

5

Collectors and Bibliographers:

Alberta H. Burke of Baltimore and David J. Gilson of Oxford

"It is such a pleasure to meet a fellow collector," Alberta H. Burke wrote on 11 July 1972, after she and her husband spent an afternoon with David J. Gilson at his home in Oxford.[1] By "meet" she meant "spend time with": Mrs. Burke and Gilson had by then been corresponding for five years and had met on several previous occasions during the Burkes' travels to England. The two continued to exchange letters regularly until Mrs. Burke's death in 1975, very shortly after Gilson's only visit to her home in Baltimore.

On the surface, these two dedicated Austen collectors could hardly have been more different. Born 26 December 1906 in La Crosse, Wisconsin, Alberta Hirshheimer grew up as the privileged granddaughter of Albert Hirshheimer, a German Jewish émigré and successful businessman. (Artifacts from the first business he founded, the La Crosse Plow Works, are still to be seen in that town on the site of the company's factory.[2]) Following in the footsteps of a neighbor, Alberta traveled east to Goucher, then an all-women's institution, for college; she graduated in 1928. After completing an M.A. in English literature at the University of Wisconsin, she

married Henry Gershon Burke and settled in his home city of
Baltimore.[3] Henry, known as Harry to his family and friends, was a
lawyer and accountant who also earned a Ph.D. in political science
from Johns Hopkins University. His parents—the family name was
originally Berkowitz—had emigrated from eastern Europe, making
his match with Alberta a "mixed marriage" according to the mores
of the Baltimore Jewish community of the time.[4]

Living modestly and having no children, the Burkes were able to
devote themselves fully to their cultural interests, which included
theater, ballet, domestic and international travel, and—for Alberta,
most of all—Jane Austen. As I established in *Everybody's Jane*, Mrs.
Burke had no interest in publishing on Austen or receiving publicity
for her incomparable Austen collection, which she began in the 1930s
and which ranged from first and rare editions to ephemera. Upon her
death, the dozen Austen manuscripts she had acquired went to the
Pierpont Morgan Library in New York; her books, scrapbooks,
correspondence files, and all other materials went to Goucher.[5]

David Gilson was three decades Mrs. Burke's junior, having been
born in 1938, the son of a clergyman in Hampshire, Austen's native
county. He attended Peter Symonds' School in Winchester before
earning an Oxford degree in modern languages; he then remained at
the university as a librarian in that subject area, at the Taylor
Institution Library, until his retirement in 1995.[6] Beyond Austen,
Gilson's interests spanned, to quote one of his letters to Mrs. Burke,
"furniture, especially French Royal furniture, country houses, and
châteaux, especially Versailles, and Russia before the Revolution—
besides much else."[7] He pursued these topics both through book
collecting and through travel to the Continent. In addition to many
articles on Austen publishing history, Gilson authored the landmark
A Bibliography of Jane Austen in 1982, with a revised edition in 1997.

Gilson's retired parents lived with him during much of the time
of his acquaintance with Mrs. Burke.[8] At his death in 2014, he
was survived by his longtime partner Chris Viveash, who shared
his scholarly interests in Austen. To King's College, University of
Cambridge, Gilson bequeathed his Austen collection, which by
then contained a copy of the 1816 Philadelphia *Emma* (the fourth
to be discovered). To Goucher he gave the hundred and twenty-six
letters he had received from Mrs. Burke, to join those of his that
she had carefully saved: a rare example of a complete, two-sided
correspondence.

The importance of the Burke/Gilson letters has recently been recognized with the inclusion of several in exhibits on Austen's legacy in Chawton and Winchester.[9] Yet the correspondence as a whole has never been fully examined.

Not surprisingly, the Burke/Gilson letters differ considerably from the Quincy/Austen correspondence in subject matter and tone. While references to Austen's novels are certainly present, discussions of the fiction were not of concern to Mrs. Burke and Gilson. Many of their letters are almost exclusively technical in content, since both of them were keenly concerned with what might seem to others to be minutiae concerning historic editions and translations of Austen's novels. Without easy access to photocopying, they relied on hand-copied transcriptions of title pages and detailed descriptions of the physical condition of books. (Regarding a request from an author for one of the Jane Austen letters in her possession, Mrs. Burke remarked, "I'm waiting till Harry comes home to see if it will reproduce satisfactorily on the office Xerox, or if I'll have to have a professional Photostat made of it."[10]) They exchanged information about newly published books and gave each other gifts of publications unavailable in their respective countries. On several occasions, Mrs. Burke invited Gilson to choose duplicate copies from her collection to be sent or brought to him.

Over time, the letters grew more personal, especially on Mrs. Burke's side. In her exuberantly scrawling handwriting, she warmly applauded Gilson's article publications and indulged herself in criticizing academics whose work she disdained. Candid about her failing health, she regularly stated the hope that she would live to see Gilson's bibliography published. In contrast, Gilson's letter-writing style—like his meticulous penmanship—remained more stiffly formal, although he allowed himself to wax enthusiastic about new discoveries and to share his aspiration of creating a truly comprehensive, scholarly guide to Austen bibliography. The physical contrast between Mrs. Burke's crammed missives, which ranged from postcards to aerograms, and Gilson's beautifully inked letters is striking. (Quotations will show, too, how casual Mrs. Burke's spelling could be, even of Austen's characters' names.)

Despite these surface differences, Mrs. Burke and Gilson shared a fundamental approach to Austen. Both cared deeply about building an account of Austen's publishing history that was as complete and accurate as possible. Towards that end, both considered to be crucial—and collected whenever available—material that most academics thought unimportant, including American editions, popular titles, translations, and ephemera.

In *Everybody's Jane*, I attended to the rare occasions in Mrs. Burke's personal papers on which she articulated her goals as an Austen collector.[11] Her letters to Gilson offer new insight into how and why she built her Austen archives, as she thought of her collection, as well as into the challenges of doing so as a person of relatively moderate means. Gilson's letters show that he experienced this difficulty even more sharply, as an impecunious librarian who missed out on the glory days of 1930s and 1940s collecting. The two bonded further over their respective outsider status vis-à-vis the academic establishment.[12] As uncredentialed, self-taught experts in Austen book history who were also enthusiasts (Mrs. Burke strongly so), they felt that they represented a type of reader in danger of becoming extinct.

Unusual approaches to collecting Austen

"I'm not a real collector!" Mrs. Burke exclaimed to Gilson at one point.[13] What she meant by that remark is not clear, either in its immediate context (a discussion of a visit by aspiring scholars) or in general. She possessed items of undisputable historical value, principally first English editions of Austen's novels, manuscript letters, and exceptionally rare publications from Austen's period. She had taken care, too, to purchase first editions in physical states considered most desirable by book historians, though unprepossessing to the viewer: volumes in boards (see Chapter 1) and in contemporary bindings, rather than the elaborately rebound books popular among prestige collectors at the turn of the twentieth century.

Perhaps Mrs. Burke was comparing herself to high-profile American collectors of earlier generations such as A. S. W. Rosenbach (1876–1952) of Philadelphia, a rare-book dealer and collector who commissioned staggeringly impressive leather bindings for his extensive holdings in British and American literature, Austen among them.[14] Or perhaps she had in mind J. P. Morgan (1867–1943), who, as I noted at the end of Chapter 4, owned the largest group of Austen letters in America, one of innumerable literary and artistic rarities in his possession. Or she may have been thinking of Henry Folger (1857–1930) and Emily Folger (1858–1936), whose obsession with

Shakespeare closely paralleled her own focus on Austen. Certainly Mrs. Burke was no match for such titans either in purchasing power or in the capacity to leave to the public an institution with her name on it, full of her treasures, comparable to the Rosenbach Library, the Morgan Library and Museum, or the Folger Shakespeare Library.

In other ways, however, Mrs. Burke had much in common with the Folgers. Their Shakespeare collection ran the gamut from First Folios to playbills to souvenir figurines to Emily's scrapbooks recording impressions of performances attended: in other words, from materials of acknowledged scholarly importance—and financial value—to those of less obvious worth.[15] "[I]n a collection completeness outweighs merit," Henry Folger once wrote.[16] Mrs. Burke certainly operated according to that principle. (In *Everybody's Jane*, I called her an "Austen omnivore.") Anything at all that bore any association, however tenuous, with Austen she captured for her scrapbooks or shelves. As she remarked to Gilson, "[i]f a pill box or a patent medicine came out with some reference to J.A. I'd feel the need to cut out the ad and, probably, to buy a sample of the medicine as well!"[17] She was not joking: advertisements with Austen references, as well as crossword puzzles with Austen clues, appear throughout the ten volumes of her scrapbooks.

Esoteric books that mentioned Austen delighted Mrs. Burke too. She described as one of her "prizes" *From Pioneer to Poet, or the Twelve Great Gates* (1930), "which includes J.A.'s horoscope on pp. 94, 240. I suppose one might class that item as 'Curiosa' in a non-technical sense."[18] Her interest extended further to mass-market editions of Austen's novels that shed light on the growth of the author's popularity. A "Literary Classics Club" edition of *Pride and Prejudice* she saw as "an amusing specimen of rising interest in J.A. (c 1945-55) with the general public!"[19]

In her letters to Gilson, Mrs. Burke twice referred to her collection as "archives," a term that is very helpful for understanding how she thought of it: a repository of historical materials that might, in the future, be seen to have significance unknown to or unimagined by its compiler. On both such occasions, she was referring to material she had sought out even though she could not personally make use of it.

I do have, however, the recording of the extracts from J.A.'s novels made at the National Portrait Gallery. Last summer I saw it listed there on a poster, but the shop at the gallery did not have it and wouldn't take an order for it. A kind gentleman at the place where I had checked my umbrella overheard my pleas and told me where to go on Oxford Street to purchase it. As I have no record player, I've never heard the recording—it's simply a part of the "archives", together with the recording of selections from the musical "First Impressions" of some years ago. So I can't tell you what is on the recording.[20]

Likewise, she mentioned that a friend "tells me that there's a long play record about J.A. I shall try to get it just as an item for the archives."[21] Charmingly, Gilson later offered, when she was visiting London, to play one of those records for her if she had not yet heard it.[22]

Contextual materials too were crucial to Mrs. Burke's archives. "Of course I believe nothing in the 1st 20 years of the 19th C. in England is alien to an understanding of Jane Austen (except politics!)," she explained, so she sought out "fashion magazines (Heideloff's, Ackerman's Repository, etc.) [and] color plate books— (Repton, Rowlandson, Microcosm, etc.)."[23] Some of the latter titles, she noted, had appreciated in value as much as the English first editions.[24] A set of so-called "Northanger Novels" (Gothic works mentioned in Northanger Abbey) also seemed to her to be important to own, if not to read herself. "They look very handsome, but I doubt very much that I shall read them (or at most one or two of them). They are [the] sort of curiousa [sic] which I felt that I MUST have as background material."[25]

In contrast to Mrs. Burke's wide-ranging reach for her archives, Gilson concentrated on acquiring items that, in his view, deserved to be included in a bibliography, that is, a reference work on Austen publishing history. In a rare moment of levity, he reported to her that his "younger nephew recently sent me a cigarette card depicting JA—issued by Carreras at some date unknown, in a series called 'Celebrities of British History'. I don't think I can include this in the bibliography!"[26] In two respects, however, Gilson drew more capacious boundaries than had his predecessors in Austen bibliography, Geoffrey Keynes and R. W. Chapman.[27] The table of contents for Gilson's typewritten catalogue of his personal collection, which he shared with Mrs. Burke in 1968, included the categories "Continuations, dramatisations, and miscellanea" and "Translations."[28] Of the former, he ventured to Mrs. Burke, "I don't know how you feel about these completions and continuations, but

I think they have a place in a JA collection, if only as curiosities."[29]
She heartily agreed: "the dramatizations and continuations I find of
real interest."[30] Characteristically, she did not explain why.

Mrs. Burke's greatest influence on Gilson's eventual *Bibliography*
resulted from her encouragement of his interest in translations. For
her, editions in languages unfamiliar to her fell into the "archives"
category: of importance, but not of personal utility. "Of course I
can not read all the languages in which I have J.A. translations! I
can stab at a few, but the Finnish, Modern Greek, Hebrew and
Japanese and Chinese, most of which were gifts from kind friends,
are possessions, not useful tools."[31] Following her offer—the first of
many—to send him duplicate copies of translated novels in her
possession, Gilson commented in February 1968,

> I have never really gone into the question of translations—those I
> have were largely chance acquisitions; but I feel I would like to
> have at least one in each of as many languages as possible, together
> with as many French ones as come my way. Your kind offer will
> go a long way towards the achievement of this aim. I intend one
> day to go through the Unesco lists of translations—a job I once
> started in the Bodleian.[32]

He described himself as "amazed" at Mrs. Burke's possession of
seventy translations, declaring, "I hope to have a representative
selection in time, but am unlikely to approach this figure!"[33]

Gilson did his best, however, and happily apprised his appreciative
audience of his progress. In April 1968, he wrote, "I have one minor
triumph to report—I now own a copy of the Russian translation of
'Pride and Prejudice' . . . the Taylorian's Slavonic expert found this
copy for me during a recent visit to Russia. The binding is a little
damaged, so it may have been withdrawn from sale, but it is perfect
internally. You may imagine how I shall value this rarity!"[34] Mrs.
Burke loved nothing more than to trade stories about discovering
and tracking down rare or surprising translations. "Did you know
that the Danes are the only ones of whom I know, who have ever
translated Lady Susan?" she wrote, referring to the epistolary
novella that was first published after Austen's death. "They must
really like J.A.! I remember in 1953 walking almost all over
Copenhagen to try to find a copy, ending up at the publisher's office,
where a kindly, handsome, tall, blond Danish gentlemen took us to

the firm's warehouse where he gave me their last copy. They had nothing left but an imperfect one (which was indeed a grand gesture) so I've always treasured my copy with especial regard."[35]

As Gilson's expertise in translations developed, Mrs. Burke wholeheartedly cheered his discoveries and proclaimed her eager anticipation of his finished work. "Congratulations on your find!" she wrote exuberantly in 1973, following his establishment of the first date of publication of a Dutch translation of *Sense and Sensibility*. "You're now the ultimate authority on translations as well as on so much else in J.A.! I do hope that I live to see your bibliography in print!"[36] Gilson and Mrs. Burke were more aware than anyone else in the world of how dismissively earlier Austen bibliographers had treated translations. As Mrs. Burke remarked to Gilson in 1972, "though Sir Geoffrey tried in 1929 to be inclusive, Dr. Chapman in 1952 clearly stated that he was only listing the things which were of interest to him—translations were not— articles in magazines only if they tied in with his own work or were in themselves outstanding."[37]

Mrs. Burke and Gilson were distinctive, too, in sharing the conviction that first American editions of Austen's novels were as worthy of investigation as the more conventionally valued first English editions. Indeed, their correspondence began when Mrs. Burke answered an advertisement Gilson placed seeking information about copies of the 1816 Philadelphia *Emma*. "I wish to inform you," she wrote, "that I have the Frank J. Hogan copy of the 1816 Philadelphia Emma, which formerly belonged to Siegfried Sassoon, and earlier to the Dalhousie family." Of the 1832–1833 Philadelphia editions, she explained, she owned just two: "Miss Elizabeth Bennet [*sic*] and Persuasion." She mentioned that she had heard of a "reprint of the 1832-3 edition, 2 volumes in one" but had never seen a copy.[38]

For Mrs. Burke, who was well aware of her own status as an American devotee of Austen, interest in first American editions came naturally.[39] It is worth stressing, however, how exceptional Gilson's interest was for an English researcher. In his first letter to Mrs. Burke, he declared, referring to the 1816 Philadelphia *Emma*, "I feel that sufficient emphasis has not been laid on the fact that an American edition of this novel was published, not only in the author's lifetime but also in the same year as that in which the first English edition appeared." He stated, "I fear there is not sufficient material for a book on the American editions of Jane Austen, but I hope to write a short article giving what facts I can discover, and also if possible a census of copies known to me."[40] Of course, such an endeavor was a way for Gilson to make an original scholarly contribution in Austen bibliography, as he longed to do. But he seems to have been driven less by ambition than by curiosity and a sense that others had overlooked an important aspect of publishing history.

Unfortunately for Gilson, such research was difficult to conduct in Britain, given how few libraries there owned copies of first American editions of Austen's novels. Jane Austen's House in Chawton had a complete set of the 1832–1833 Carey & Lea editions, which he explained had been "presented by an American lady in 1952."[41] While studying them, he saw too what he called "the real gem: Elizabeth Bennet, Philadelphia, Carey and Hart 1845, 100 pp., 2 columns, original price 25 cents. (containing also MP from the same source but bound in without titlepage)." Only Gilson—and Mrs. Burke—would have considered a cheap, tightly formatted American reprint to be a "real gem"! "You may imagine," he wrote, "how much I coveted some of these items."[42] He reported that the American collector Charles Beecher Hogan planned to bequeath to Jane Austen's House his own "rich and extensive" collection, so that "England will thus at last have one copy of the 1816 Philadelphia Emma, plus the French translation of the same year & much else."[43] (Hogan's Emma eventually went to the Beinecke Rare Book and Manuscript Library at Yale: see Appendix.)

Gilson took advantage too of the kindness of friends, who shared their own holdings and research. "My New York friend Jack Grey has a copy of the 1832 Philadelphia Mansfield Park which he brought, with his card indexes, for me to check," he told Mrs. Burke following the 1974 annual meeting of the Jane Austen Society in Chawton.[44] (With Henry Burke and Joan Austen-Leigh, J. David Grey co-founded the Jane Austen Society of North America in 1979, as I discussed in chapter seven of Everybody's Jane.) Mrs. Burke, in contrast, politely but firmly refused to travel with her copy of the 1816 Philadelphia Emma. "No I am sorry that I do not want to take my American 1816 E to England, even though it is a slip case," she declared. "Please come to the U.S.A. and see all the J.A. material here."[45]

On his librarian's salary, Gilson began to acquire his own copies of first and early American editions of Austen's novels, which sold for much lower prices than English firsts. "I have also made an expensive purchase from America," he announced proudly in September 1972,

> nothing less than the 1ˢᵗ American collected edition, 2 vols. in 1, Philadelphia 1838! I owe this to Mr. Sidney Ives of Harvard, who found a 2ⁿᵈ copy recently & allowed me to buy his original copy (mentioned in my article). The one I now have is in a contemporary leather binding (possibly a publisher's binding); both covers are almost off, so it will need repair, but I felt I had to have it. I know of no other copy in this country.[46]

His description of his urge to purchase directly echoed a statement Mrs. Burke made earlier that year in a letter to him: "I never bought books for investment, but because I <u>had</u> to have them."[47]

Both Gilson and Mrs. Burke lamented what they saw as the exorbitant prices at which English first editions of Austen were advertised and sold, even those in less than desirable physical condition. "£500 for a rebound <u>S&S</u> seems in the realms of fantasy, not the real world of books!" exclaimed Mrs. Burke in April 1973. "My 1st <u>S&S</u> in a contemporary binding using the original pink boards and having the half titles cost me about $100.00 about 35 years ago."[48] Such comparisons are important reminders that Mrs. Burke acquired the majority of her valuable books and manuscripts when prices for Austen's novels, and for titles by her contemporaries, were relatively affordable. Mrs. Burke's single-minded focus on Austen to the exclusion of other rarities is well captured by this recollection: "When, about 1935 Dr. W. O. Hassall offered to show me anything in the B. M. [British Museum] or Bodley which I might want to see, I think that he was a little disgusted that what I asked for was Jane Austen—not some precious 10th C. illuminated ms!"[49]

Even when prices were lower, Mrs. Burke did not purchase everything she wanted. Still on her mind decades later was her decision not to buy a presentation copy of *Emma* that John Murray had sent to Augusta Leigh, Byron's half-sister. "That," she told Gilson, "is an association item which I'll always regret passing up, but it seemed over priced for a rebound copy in poor condition 25 years ago."[50]

Mrs. Burke blamed one buyer in particular for driving up prices of Austen editions and manuscripts: T. Edward Carpenter, who had bought the Chawton house in which Austen lived and wrote in order to convert it into a museum, and who was keen to obtain all possible authentic items. As I recounted in *Everybody's Jane*, Carpenter's declaration at a meeting of the Jane Austen Society in 1949 that important Austen relics were being lost to American buyers outraged Mrs. Burke, who defiantly proclaimed—in the sole public speech of her lifetime related to her collecting—that she would donate to the museum the lock of Austen's hair that she had recently acquired.[51] Her bitterness towards Carpenter did not abate over time. "He ran me out of the market when he started buying with no regard to price in the late 40's!" she told Gilson.[52] When Austen items fetched more than Mrs. Burke thought they should, Carpenter remained her first suspicion: "That nasty little fragment of a letter which was sold at Sotheby's for £65 is certainly preposterous! It was sold previously Nov. 1964 for much less! I hope the present buyer (Mr. Carpenter?) keeps it a while!"[53]

In spite of Mrs. Burke's frequent proclamations that she could no longer afford to buy historic editions, she did indulge in one last significant purchase at the end of 1973: the 1833 Carey & Lea first American edition of *Northanger Abbey*. She described her acquisition as "a copy in boards with labels of the Phila. 1833 N.A. The price was $175^{00} which seems outrageous, but I suppose I'm paying $50^{00} for the Morocco slip case. They have a copy of P ditto, from $150^{00} also with slipcase. I think I paid about $20^{00} for my Phila. P. and $10^{00} for Elizabeth Bennet! But I haven't bought anything in ages & will be very happy to have the N.A."[54] For his part, Gilson mused, "I sometimes think I ought to collect Scott instead"—and then began to do so, with happy results. "I have just bought my second Scott first edition: Peveril of the Peak, 4 vols., 1822, original paper boards uncut, labels entirely present, all half titles, errata slip etc.— all for £10! Would that JA could be bought so cheaply!"[55] Of course, Scott first editions were inexpensive because so many copies of them had been printed, and because, as I discussed in Part One, Scott's popularity decreased as Austen's precipitately rose.

Balancing erudition with enthusiasm

In addition to their intense interest in Austen bibliography, Mrs. Burke and Gilson shared a further purpose: countering what they saw as the dual threat of uncritical Austen admirers on the one hand and bloodless academics on the other. Both of them were far too knowledgeable and concerned with accuracy to tolerate the uninformed interpretations and poor research of many popular writers on Austen. And, as self-taught experts who were outsiders to the academic literary establishment, both strongly resisted being condescended to by those with credentials, whose work often lacked the rigor of their own.

Complaints about mistakes in new publications about Austen are frequent in the Burke/Gilson correspondence, especially on Mrs. Burke's end. Sometimes she was light-hearted, as when she thanked Gilson for one of his many gifts of ephemera, a pamphlet: "I enjoyed it and had fun correcting the small errors of fact. The author was evidently not some-one who knows the novels & letters well."[56] Likewise, on receipt of the Jane Austen Society's *Annual Report* for 1968, she "spent a happy half hour copiously annotating the article on translations, which is full of errors—such as assigning to Buenos Aires the print of translations which were first published in Spain in the 90's, Danish having nothing but P&P, nothing in Norwegian, etc."[57] On other occasions, mistakes depressed her. "I just finished reading the Craik J.A. In Her Time," she reported, "which is largely a re-hash of Chapman's appendices and crawling with errors of fact and inference. I made bad-tempered corrections on almost every page."[58] On occasion, she took the trouble to inform perpetrators of their mistakes, as when she complained to the British Travel Association in 1972 that its advertisement in the *New York Times* for a tour to Bath misidentified the architect whose work could be seen in that Georgian city, where Austen lived in the very early 1800s and where she set portions of *Northanger Abbey* and *Persuasion*. Knowing Gilson would share her sense of outrage, she grumbled, "I'm sure it will do no good, and the error will be repeated, but someone who uses Nash architecture as an appeal ought to do a bit of home work!"[59]

Equally disturbing to both Gilson and Mrs. Burke were popular publications that, in their view, perpetuated old-fashioned, unscholarly attitudes about Austen. "On sale at the JA [Jane Austen Society] meeting was the new book by Constance Pilgrim," Gilson wrote in 1971. "I felt I had to buy it, but it is a very bad book, merely a string of farfetched hypotheses, strung together with lengthy quotations from the novels (all taken as autobiographical!)."[60] Not deterred, Mrs. Burke obtained her own copy, only to agree that the book was "a bit sickening & in the worst style of 'Janeolatry' and 'St. Jane' traditions."[61] At least they had each other for company. As Gilson put it, "like you, I feel impelled to buy every new book on JA."[62]

They bonded, too, over the lack of concern for historic editions that, they felt, was shown by influential members of the Jane Austen Society and the Jane Austen Memorial Trust, which administered Jane Austen's House. Gilson declared himself "surprised to find how many rarities are preserved there, in no proper order, with no visible catalogue, some bundled away in a potentially damp cupboard— with no bookplate or any mark of ownership; theft would be all too easy."[63] He recommended to a member of the Society and the Trust that "a nicely printed catalogue of the books at Chawton would be an admirable publication for the bicentenary year," 1975, and offered to undertake that work. His idea, however, was not approved, "partly for security reasons. (The 1st ed. of SS in boards is in a case secured only by an ordinary household screw, so loose at the time of my visit that it could be undone with the fingers!)."[64] "You're quite right about the J.A. Soc. having small feeling for books," Mrs. Burke reassured Gilson. "They are more in the lunatic fringe of 'Janeites' than book lovers."[65]

"Janeites" Mrs. Burke and Gilson agreed that they themselves certainly were not. She sought out his feelings about the term early in their acquaintance: "I am always very eager to hear from a fellow 'Janeite' (Do you hate Kipling's word too?)"[66] "I do indeed hate Kipling's word 'Janeite,'" he replied, "and think that his story, and his vulgar verses, do Jane Austen great disservice."[67] Neither suggested a replacement. Indeed, both steered clear throughout their correspondence of describing with any specificity the nature of their respective, or mutual, attachment to Jane Austen. "I am very interested in Jane Austen and collect material by and about her in a mild sort [of] way," Mrs. Burke wrote in her first letter to Gilson; he replied that one of his "chief private interests is the work of Jane Austen."[68] Having recognized each other as kindred spirits, they evidently felt no need to label themselves.

Mrs. Burke's resistance to the term "Janeite" might seem especially surprising, since along with her great expertise in Austen matters, she manifested many of the behaviors typical of enthusiasts. For example, she frequently dropped references and quotations from Austen into her letters. Departing from Oxford with a parcel of gifts from Gilson, she thought of a gluttonous character from *Mansfield*

Park: she declared that she "felt like Mrs. Norris with the pheasant eggs and rare heath and other loot from Sotherton, but my envelop, full of marvelous acquisitions—especially the new Spanish <u>Emma</u>— was much more precious and exciting!"[69] A hard-to-read letter she described as "worthy of Jane Fairfax!"—who, in *Emma*, often wrote vertically as well as horizontally to save paper.[70] When Gilson was upset at the criticism of one of his articles, she advised, "You can soothe yourself with Mr. Bennet's consolation to Lizzy"— presumably, the reassurance that wherever Elizabeth Bennet and her sister are personally known, they will be valued.[71] Gilson occasionally tried to reciprocate, but could produce only such unfelicitous observations as "I fancy (or 'I dare say—', in Jane Austen's language) we shall need some more shelving."[72]

Mrs. Burke also had somewhat more tolerance than did Gilson for the kinds of observances in which members of author societies engaged (and, indeed, still do). A longtime member of the Jane Austen Society, she encouraged him to attend its meetings, which he had not previously done.[73] He remained resistant, however, to what he saw as more frivolous activities. "I was sent a leaflet recently advertising 'A Jane Austen weekend in Bath', taking place at this moment under the auspices of the Friends of Bath Festival Society— you may have had one too," he wrote in 1971. "I fear that the programme (including a lecture on 'The Navy in Jane Austen's day', a dinner at the Assembly Rooms with an 18th cent. menu, followed by the playing of games such as whist and speculation, and a communal walk up Milsom Street) filled me with horror!"[74] For her part, Mrs. Burke especially disliked the vogue for adding more commemorative objects and statues to Austen sites. As she colorfully explained, she felt "that the simple grave slab and the awful Austen-Leigh tablet and window in Winchester Cathedral are memorial enough to one whose monument lies in her works and letters and not in (to use the expression of another friend) the idolatrous devotion of 'old trouts.'"[75]

In their own ways, however, both Mrs. Burke and Gilson were dedicated literary tourists, much as Anna Waterston was in her time. Gilson, having grown up in Hampshire, was familiar with many sites associated with Austen's life, especially her burial site in Winchester Cathedral. He assured Mrs. Burke, "I often revisit the Cathedral now when on holiday in Hampshire with my parents— never failing to walk down the north nave aisle and stop at a certain point!"[76] Of a trip to Bath, he complained that on his last day he was "forced to visit the Roman baths which I find very tedious. I had previously of course looked at all houses & streets in which JA or her characters lived or stayed!"[77]

Having taken her own literary pilgrimages beginning in the 1930s, Mrs. Burke could recall first experiencing such sites when they were still relatively well preserved. "I do envy you a few days in Bath," she responded,

> though I fear that with the almost wholesale destruction which has taken place there in the last years, there is not too much of the Jane Austen Atmosphere left. The first time I went there in the early 30's I could still feel the footsteps of Catherine Morland & Anne Eliot [sic] on the cobblestones under my feet, but that had gone in war-time destruction & post-war improvements the last time I was there about 6 years ago.[78]

The Burkes also visited Jane Austen's birthplace in the village of Steventon and her final home at Chawton before the latter was a museum, resulting in the following valuable recollections. "Nearly 40 years ago," she wrote in 1973, "we made a journey to see the pump, the church, the outside of Steventon manor, and to talk our way into a glimpse of the Chawton Cottage, then divided into workman's tenements. A very ancient dame showed us her two rooms (which included J.A.'s bedroom) and a young mother her rooms which included the present sitting room with the bricked up window to the road."[79]

Mrs. Burke's lifelong dedication to Austen equipped her, moreover, with a historical perspective on scholarly approaches to her favorite author. "I am sorry to hear that Miss Lascelles is going blind," she responded to Gilson in 1969. "It was her excellent 1939 book [*Jane Austen and Her Art*] which really opened the floodgates to serious J.A. criticism, not of the 'Dear Dear Jane' variety."[80] Having lived through, and carefully tracked, the evolution of "serious J.A. criticism," Mrs. Burke was very impatient with academic newcomers whose knowledge did not hold a candle to her own.

How much Mrs. Burke bristled when condescended to by scholars comes across most clearly in her interactions with two young American academics, Barry Roth and Joel Weinsheimer, who sought her out while working on what they called a critical bibliography of

Austen studies. (Roth and Weinsheimer eventually co-edited several
such reference works.) After initial correspondence with them, Mrs.
Burke reassured Gilson that the men were no competitors to him.
"You'll be amused and amazed to know that I finally heard from
Roth and Weinsheimer," she reported in December 1972. "Their
sheer ignorance even to such an unscholarly and untrained person
as I is quite appalling! I had out of the kindness of my heart sent
them a list of quite a few less obvious items from my own shelves—
things which I knew to exist because I own them."[81]

Her poor impression was reinforced when the two men visited
to consult her copies of books of which they had no other record.
"The Roth-Weinsheimer visitation has come and gone," she reported
with relief in March 1973. "They are both quite young—Roth has
his Ph.D., Weinsheimer expects to receive his in June. I was really
shocked at some of their shortcomings, though Harry says that I
ought not to have been, for they were taught not by scholars but by
people only slightly more knowledgeable than they."[82] She was
especially dismayed by their insistence that "real" Jane Austen
scholarship began in 1952. "[T]hey justify their use of the 1952 cut
off date as that of the year of publication of the Mudrick book and
the beginning of 'serious' J.A. study and criticism. I challenged them
with the Lascelles and Leavis works far earlier as well as several
other publications but they felt that those did not lead on to 'serious'
academic study of the works!"[83]

Mrs. Burke's sense that the young scholars, while happy to take
advantage of her collection, did not really respect her expertise was
confirmed by their failure to follow up about the publication of their
book. "No, I never heard from either Roth or Weinsheimer about
any of their J.A. work," she wrote to Gilson in November 1974, a
year and a half after the two men's visit. "You see I am not going to
publish anything on J.A. so keeping up with me is not worthwhile!"[84]

Mrs. Burke's treatment at the hands of these young members of
the academic establishment rankled in particular because she
remembered an earlier, more inclusive era, when her interest,
knowledge, and connections to respected Austen scholars had
opened doors to her. She had decided, she explained to Gilson, to
bequeath her Austen manuscripts "to the Morgan Library where, 30
or more years ago, a kindly curator let me examine all their J.A. mss.,
although I walked in from the street bearing no proper credentials
(but I was wearing a mink coat!) I've never forgotten the gracious

kindness."[85] She had a similar experience, albeit with a bit more gatekeeping, at the New York Public Library, when she asked in 1951 to view items from the Austen-rich Berg Collection:

> I had half agreed, then changed my mind, to make a census of J.A. mss. in the U.S. for Dr. Chapman. I have never forgotten my conversation with the curator when I, an unknown, walked in off the street and said that R.W.C. wanted me to look at their J.A. mss. To establish my bona fides the gentleman asked me, "Does he write you on the back of old laundry lists?" "No" said I, "on the back of proofs for his book on Johnson." And the place was then opened for me![86]

Having paid forward to Roth and Weinsheimer the generosity once shown to her, Mrs. Burke was understandably miffed by feeling taken advantage of. Reflecting on the men's visit a year later, she indulged herself what she knew were catty remarks, knowing that Gilson would be a sympathetic audience: "I really don't think that they know very much about what they are doing, & I'm rather sorry that the spirit of J.A. fellowship moved me to help. I am a nasty so-&-so. Meow, meow!"[87]

As Mrs. Burke expected, Gilson soothed her with full agreement regarding both her visitors' scholarly methods and their arrogant attitude. Like her, he was well aware of how much important and influential writing on Austen had been produced in earlier eras, before academic credentials existed for literary study. "The new justification for starting the bibliography at 1952 sounds just as ridiculous as the original one," he responded, adding that "the idea of serious academic study is something of a straitjacket. Do they then discount all 19th century criticism? Criticism or proper appreciation have not always been the province of the humourless Ph.D. student!"[88] In a later letter, he expressed his further anxiety that "JA seems in danger of becoming the sole property of the academics: a sad & soul-destroying fate."[89]

Mrs. Burke and Gilson mutually supported each other during a time of change for Austen devotees, when collecting on a moderate income was becoming more and more difficult and when professional academics threatened the "private" scholarly work they cherished. Exchanging information about new publications and uncovering solutions to bibliographical mysteries kept their spirits up during

Gilson's seemingly endless labor on his bibliography and while Mrs. Burke coped with increasing ill health. To her many expressions of hope that she would live to see Gilson's bibliography published, she added in August 1974 the more modest hope that she would "live to see some of the 1975 celebrations" of the Austen bicentennial.[90]

In the last weeks of Mrs. Burke's life, in March 1975, she and her husband welcomed Gilson to their apartment for his long-awaited trip to see her collection. At last, he was able to study her copy of the 1816 Philadelphia *Emma*! Evidently, their time together brought down remaining barriers of formality. After eight years of writing to each other as "Mr. Gilson" and "Mrs. Burke," her next—and last—correspondence with him, a postcard, began "Dear David." His last letter to her opened, "Dear Alberta (if I may indeed so address you!)" and was signed simply "David."[91]

Both Austen scholarship and what we now call Austen fandom owe great debts to the work of Alberta Burke and David Gilson. Her dedication to seeking out everything from rare editions to ephemera resulted in an incomparable collection that rewards the explorations of researchers and enthusiastic readers alike. His enormous curiosity about Austen's publication history fueled the creation of one of the most important reference works for Austen scholars and collectors—who continue, despite ever-rising prices, to build personally meaningful and historically significant sets of Austen material.

Mrs. Burke explained to Gilson at one point that her most treasured item was not the 1816 Philadelphia *Emma* but the Jane and Cassandra Austen manuscripts in her possession: "the 8 J.A. letters and page accounts plus the two of CEA & her 'Notes on the composition of the novels'. They are what I'd save first from a fire!"[92] Like the Quincys before her, Mrs. Burke cherished items in Austen's handwriting more than copies of her novels, however rare.

Like the Quincys, too, Mrs. Burke found common ground with an English counterpart, distant from her in geography and age, who nevertheless shared her sensibilities about Austen. While the Quincys delighted in discussing Austen's novels with members of the author's own family, however, what brought Mrs. Burke and Gilson together was the thrill of discovering more about the actual books through which Austen's readers, over time and around the world, have encountered her: above all, the mysterious 1816 Philadelphia *Emma*.

The unknowns that fascinated Mrs. Burke and Gilson about Carey's *Emma*—its print run and exact date of publication, Carey's reasons for choosing this Austen novel to reprint, the circumstances of Lady Dalhousie's ownership—prompted my initial research for *Reading Austen in America*. As I studied the surviving copies of the 1816 Philadelphia *Emma* and explored the papers of its original owners, I realized that this apparently minor moment in Austen publishing history revealed a great deal about her earliest transatlantic readers. Similarly, my investigation of the Quincys' enthusiasm, which Austen reception history has treated as a footnote, uncovered a significant episode in the development of Austen appreciation in the United States.

I hope that the stories I have brought to light in *Reading Austen in America* inspire others to seek out further traces of Austen's historical readers, both in the US and around the world. Clues to these readers' experiences await discovery in the margins of books, as well as in personal letters and journals. Publishing records, library records, and long-forgotten treatments of Austen in print merit study, too, as evidence of how Austen's novels have circulated and how they have been publicly discussed. Through such investigations, we can continue to develop a richer understanding of Austen's widespread influence and remarkable legacy.

Notes

1 AHB to DJG, 11 July 1972, Alberta H. and Henry G. Burke papers and Jane Austen research collection, MS 0020/1/7, Special Collections and Archives, Goucher College, Baltimore, Maryland. All quotations from the Burke/Gilson correspondence are from items in this collection. In their letters, the correspondents addressed each other formally as "Mrs. Burke" and "Mr. Gilson." Although I called Alberta Burke "Alberta" in *Everybody's Jane*, I have decided to refer to her here by the name by which Gilson addressed her.

2 Observed on 1 July 2014. I am grateful to Peggy Derrick, Curator of the La Crosse County Historical Society, for her assistance in tracing Hirshheimer history in La Crosse.

3 Goucher lore has it that Alberta chose to write her master's thesis on the novels of Maria Edgeworth rather than those of her idol, Austen. However, no thesis title appears in the 1929 University of Wisconsin commencement program under Alberta Hirshheimer's name, and the university graduate bulletin at the time specified that seminar papers "generally constitute the equivalent of a master's thesis." For this information, I am grateful to David Null, Director of the University

Archives and Records Management at UW-Madison (email to author, 11 February 2014). Alberta's graduate school application has also allowed me to correct her year of birth, which, in *Everybody's Jane*, I gave as 1907, following information in the Goucher College archives.

4 For insight into Baltimore Jewry and the Burkes' marriage, I am appreciative of conversations with Betty Sweren, Goucher class of 1952, and Margie Warres, Goucher class of 1940.

5 In *Jane's Fame: How Jane Austen Conquered the World* (Edinburgh: Canongate, 2009), Claire Harman accurately describes Alberta Burke's collection as including "first editions of all the novels, manuscript letters, memorabilia, rare editions (Siegfried Sassoon's first edition of *Emma* among them) and over 1,000 books by and about Austen" but erroneously reports that "her eventual bequest of much of this material to the Morgan Library in New York has made that the most valuable Austen archive in the world" (223).

6 DJG to AHB, 10 August 1967, 28 March 1968, MS 0020/10/20; "David John Gilson," *Oxford Times*, 21 May 2014.

7 DJG to AHB, 16 December 1967, MS 0020/10/20.

8 DJG to AHB, 5 July 1970, MS 0020/10/20; "David John Gilson."

9 Gilson's letters were featured in a summer 2016 Chawton House Library exhibit commemorating the bicentenary of *Emma*, curated by Gillian Dow. See Gillian Dow, "*Emma* at 200: From English Village to Global Appeal," *Persuasions On-Line* 37.1 (Winter 2016). The exhibit "Jane Austen 200—The Mysterious Miss Austen" ran in summer 2017 in Winchester.

10 AHB to DJG, 24 March 1972, MS 0020/1/7.

11 Juliette Wells, *Everybody's Jane: Austen in the Popular Imagination* (New York: Bloomsbury Academic, 2011), 36–47.

12 Harman points out Gilson's lack of literary-historian credentials—as well as those of the equally respected Austen scholars Deirdre Le Faye and Brian Southam—in *Jane's Fame*, 238.

13 AHB to DJG, 22 March 1973, MS 0020/1/7.

14 Observed on 7 October 2016 at the Rosenbach Library.

15 In *Collecting Shakespeare: The Story of Henry and Emily Folger* (Baltimore: Johns Hopkins University Press, 2014), Stephen H. Grant vividly sums up the Folgers' collection as "a dazzling array of objects: books, manuscripts, essays, pamphlets, magazines, newspapers, playbills, prompt books, autograph letters, autographs, letters, diaries, journals, memoirs, commonplace books, scrapbooks, sheet music, phonograph records, maps, charts, public documents, prints, drawings, engravings, woodcuts, oil paintings, watercolors, mezzotints; furniture,

building models, coins, weapons, armor, heraldic documents, tapestries, musical instruments, globes, costumes, scenic designs, stage properties, statues, busts, carvings, miniatures, medallions, figurines, relics, curios, works in stained glass, bronze, ivory, wood, china, ceramics, and marble" (75). The Folger/Burke comparison was highlighted by curators Janine Barchas and Kristina Straub in the 2016 Folger Library exhibition "Will & Jane: Shakespeare, Austen, and the Cult of Celebrity." See Janine Barchas and Kristina Straub, "Curating *Will & Jane*," *Eighteenth-Century Life* 40.2 (April 2016): 1–35.

16 Grant, *Collecting Shakespeare*, 80.

17 AHB to DJG, 14 January 1974, MS 0020/1/7.

18 AHB to DJG, 10 August 1971, MS 0020/1/6.

19 AHB to DJG, 1 December 1970, MS 0020/1/6.

20 AHB to DJG, 1 December 1970, MS 0020/1/6.

21 AHB to DJG, 31 January 1970, MS 0020/1/6.

22 DJG to AHB, 28 May 1972, MS 0020/10/20.

23 AHB to DJG, 9 April 1968, MS 0020/1/6.

24 AHB to DJG, 19 May 1972, MS 0020/1/7.

25 AHB to DJG, 15 May 1968, MS 0020/1/6.

26 DJG to AHB, 1 October 1974, MS 0020/11/22.

27 Geoffrey Keynes, *Jane Austen: A Bibliography* (London: Nonesuch Press, 1929); R. W. Chapman, *Jane Austen: A Critical Bibliography* (Oxford: Clarendon Press, 1953).

28 DJG to AHB, 21 January 1968, MS 0020/10/20.

29 DJG to AHB, 27 March 1968, MS 0020/10/20.

30 AHB to DJG, 9 April 1968, MS 0020/1/6.

31 AHB to DJG, 9 April 1968, MS 0020/1/6.

32 DJG to AHB, 10 February 1968, MS 0020/10/20.

33 DJG to AHB, 27 March 1968, MS 0020/10/20.

34 DJG to AHB, 25 May 1968, MS 0020/10/20.

35 AHB to DJG, 26 February 1969, MS 0020/1/6.

36 AHB to DJG, 27 February 1973, MS 0020/1/7.

37 AHB to DJG, 5 December 1972, MS 0020/1/7.

38 AHB to DJG, 5 August 1967, MS 0020/1/6.

39 On the attitudes of English members of the Jane Austen Society towards the Burkes, and Mrs. Burke's towards them, see Wells, *Everybody's Jane*, 51–8.

40 DJG to AHB, 10 August 1967, MS 0020/10/20.

41 DJG to AHB, 10 August 1967, MS 0020/10/20.

42 DJG to AHB, 22 September 1972, MS 0020/10/20.

43 DJG to AHB, 28 July 1974, MS 0020/11/22. On Hogan's gift to Jane Austen's House of the topaz crosses once owned by Jane and Cassandra Austen, see Harman, *Jane's Fame*, 208–9.

44 DJG to AHB, 28 July 1974, MS 0020/11/22.

45 AHB to DJG, 18 February 1970, MS 0020/1/6.

46 DJG to AHB, 22 September 1972, MS 0020/10/20.

47 AHB to DJG, 19 May 1972, MS 0020/1/7. She had expressed a similar sentiment to Percy Muir, one of the dealers through whom she purchased, in 1948: see Wells, *Everybody's Jane*, 46.

48 AHB to DJG, 1 April 1973, MS 0020/1/7.

49 AHB to DJG, 5 August 1974, MS 0020/1/7.

50 AHB to DJG, 10 June 1969, MS 0020/1/6.

51 Wells, *Everybody's Jane*, 55–7.

52 AHB to DJG, 28 May 1969, MS 0020/1/6.

53 AHB to DJG, 16 December 1968, MS 0020/1/6.

54 AHB to DJG, 24 November 1973, MS 0020/1/7.

55 DJG to AHB, 24 March 1973, 10 November 1973, MS 0020/11/22.

56 AHB to DJG, 5 April 1969, MS 0020/1/6.

57 AHB to DJG, 28 May 1969, MS 0020/1/6.

58 AHB to DJG, 31 January 1970, MS 0020/1/6.

59 AHB to DJG, 5 December 1972, MS 0020/1/7.

60 DJG to AHB, 27 July 1971, MS 0020/10/20.

61 AHB to DJG, 6 November 1971, MS 0020/1/6.

62 DJG to AHB, 13 September 1971, MS 0020/10/20.

63 DJG to AHB, 22 September 1972, MS 0020/10/20.

64 DJG to AHB, 11 November 1972, MS 0020/10/20.

65 AHB to DJG, 15 October 1974, MS 0020/1/7.

66 AHB to DJG, 1 December 1967, MS 0020/1/6.

67 DJG to AHB, 18 December 1967, MS 0020/10/20.

68 AHB to DJG, 5 August 1967, MS 0020/1/6; DJG to AHB, 10 August 1967, MS 0020/10/20.

69 AHB to DJG, 11 July 1972, MS 0020/1/7.

70 AHB to DJG, 26 November 1974, MS 0020/1/7.

71 AHB to DJG, 18 February 1970, MS 0020/1/6.

72 DJG to AHB, 5 July 1970, MS 0020/10/20.

73 AHB to DJG, 11 July 1968, MS 0020/1/6.

74 DJG to AHB, 4 April 1971, MS 0020/10/20.

75 AHB to DJG, 12 January 1968, MS 0020/1/6.

76 DJG to AHB, 28 March 1968, MS 0020/10/20.

77 DJG to AHB, 13 September 1971, MS 0020/10/20.

78 AHB to DJG, 10 August 1971, MS 0020/1/6.

79 AHB to DJG, 9 October 1973, MS 0020/1/7. On tourism to Chawton Cottage before its museum conversion, see Claudia L. Johnson, *Jane Austen's Cults and Cultures* (Chicago: University of Chicago Press, 2012), 173–5.

80 AHB to DJG, 10 June 1969, MS 0020/1/6.

81 AHB to DJG, 5 December 1972, MS 0020/1/7.

82 AHB to DJG, 22 March 1973, MS 0020/1/7.

83 AHB to DJG, 22 March 1973, MS 0020/1/7.

84 AHB to DJG, 26 November 1974, MS 0020/1/7.

85 AHB to DJG, 5 August 1974, MS 0020/1/7.

86 AHB to DJG, 15 October 1974, MS 0020/1/7.

87 AHB to DJG, 26 December 1976, MS 0020/1/7.

88 DJG to AHB, 22 April 1973, MS 0020/11/22.

89 DJG to AHB, 28 December 1973, MS 0020/11/22.

90 AHB to DJG, 5 August 1974, MS 0020/1/7.

91 AHB to DJG, undated [April 1975], MS 0020/1/7; DJG to AHB, 2 May 1975. Gilson continued to correspond with Henry Burke until the latter's death in 1989.

92 AHB to DJG, 16 March 1973, MS 0020/1/7.

APPENDIX:

CENSUS OF SURVIVING COPIES OF THE 1816 PHILADELPHIA *EMMA*[1]

Catalogue number in Gilson, *Bibliography*	Current location and accession date (if known)	Owner's/owners' names and life dates (*marks original owner, if known)	Distinctive attributes of copy and ownership	Availability of family papers for contextual study	Availability of digital images of the copy
B1.1	Goucher College, Baltimore, Maryland, USA; 1975	*Christian Broun Ramsay, Countess of Dalhousie (1786–1839); Siegfried Sassoon (1886–1967); Frank J. Hogan (1877–1944); Alberta H. Burke (1906–1975)	Bears the bookplate and signature of Lady Dalhousie; the bookplate of Frank Hogan; the bookplate of Alberta Burke; and pencil notes about Lady Dalhousie in Sassoon's handwriting	Lady Dalhousie's papers are currently held in Scotland at Colstoun House, with plans to transfer them to the John Gray Centre in Haddington, East Lothian	Full digital facsimile available at http://www.emmainamerica.org
B1.2	Beinecke Rare Book and Manuscript Library, Yale University, New Haven, Connecticut, USA; 1998	Charles Beecher Hogan (1906–1983)	Bears the signature of M. J. Eaton		

B1.3	New York Society Library, New York City, USA; 1868	*James Hammond's Circulating Library, Newport, Rhode Island, USA	Bears a label stating the circulating library's policies. Annotated in pencil by pre-1868 readers, with a combination of doodled marginalia and comments on the novel	Madeline McMahon, "Jane Austen's *Emma* in Early America," The New York Society Library *Library Blog*, 4 May 2015
No catalogue number; described in Gilson, "*Emma* in America"	King's College Library, University of Cambridge, England	David Gilson (1935–2014)	Bears the signatures of Virginia Arnold and Louisa Bruorton	
No catalogue number	Winterthur Library, Winterthur, Delaware, USA	*E. I. (Éleuthère Irénée) du Pont (1771–1834)	Extensive du Pont family papers held at the Hagley Museum and Library in Wilmington, Delaware	

(Continued)

(Continued)

Catalogue number in Gilson, *Bibliography*	Current location and accession date (if known)	Owner's/owners' names and life dates (*marks original owner, if known)	Distinctive attributes of copy and ownership	Availability of family papers for contextual study	Availability of digital images of the copy
No catalogue number	Rauner Special Collections Library, Dartmouth College, Hanover, New Hampshire, USA; 1972	*Jeremiah Smith (1759–1842)	Purchase price and bookseller's name noted; printers' errors corrected in ink; annotations about Austen's life	Part of Smith's intact 601-item collection of books and pamphlets, which includes several other novels by Austen	Juliette Wells, "A Rare Edition," web log post, Rauner Special Collections Library, Dartmouth College, 19 August 2015

1 For complete descriptions of the first three copies, including style of binding and pages damaged or missing, see David Gilson, *A Bibliography of Jane Austen*, new edn (New Castle, DE: Oak Knoll Press, 1997), 100–101. Gilson mentions his acquisition of a fourth copy in "Jane Austen's 'Emma' in America: Notes on the Text of the First and Second American Editions," *The Review of English Studies* n.s. 53: 212 (2002): 518. The name "Louisa Bruorton" in that copy, now at King's College, represents my own effort at deciphering.

BIBLIOGRAPHY

Archival Sources

Alberta H. and Henry G. Burke papers and Jane Austen research
collection: Goucher College Special Collections and Archives,
Baltimore, Maryland.

Austen-Leigh family papers: Hampshire Record Office, Winchester,
England.

Broun-Lindsay papers: via National Register of Archives for Scotland.

Edward Carey Gardiner collection: Historical Society of Pennsylvania,
Philadelphia, Pennsylvania.

Henry Carey Letter Book, 1815–1835: Manuscripts Division, William L.
Clements Library, University of Michigan, Ann Arbor, Michigan.

Lea & Febiger records, 1785–1982: Historical Society of Pennsylvania,
Philadelphia, Pennsylvania.

Longwood MSS: Hagley Museum and Library, Wilmington, Delaware.

Mathew Carey papers, 1785–1859: American Antiquarian Society,
Worcester, Massachusetts.

Morgan Collections correspondence, 1887–1948: Morgan Library and
Museum, New York.

Winterthur MSS: Hagley Museum and Library, Wilmington, Delaware.

Published Sources

Ard, Patricia M. "Betrayal: Jane Austen's Imaginative Use of America."
Persuasions On-Line 33.1 (Winter 2012).

Ardizzone, Heidi. *An Illuminated Life: Belle da Costa Greene's Journey
from Prejudice to Privilege.* New York: W. W. Norton, 2007.

Austen, Jane. *Emma.* Ed. Richard Cronin and Dorothy McMillan.
Cambridge: Cambridge University Press, 2005.

———. *Jane Austen's Fiction Manuscripts: A Digital Edition.* Ed. Kathryn
Sutherland. 2010.

———. *Jane Austen's Letters.* 4th edn. Ed. Deirdre Le Faye. Oxford:
Oxford University Press, 2015.

————. *Later Manuscripts.* Ed. Janet Todd and Linda Bree. Cambridge: Cambridge University Press, 2008.

————. *Mansfield Park.* Ed. John Wiltshire. Cambridge: Cambridge University Press, 2005.

————. *Northanger Abbey.* Ed. Barbara Benedict and Deirdre Le Faye. Cambridge: Cambridge University Press, 2006.

————. *Persuasion.* Ed. Janet Todd and Antje Blank. Cambridge: Cambridge University Press, 2006.

————. *Pride and Prejudice.* Ed. Pat Rogers. Cambridge: Cambridge University Press, 2006.

Austen-Leigh, J. E. *A Memoir of Jane Austen.* London: R. Bentley, 1870.

————. *A Memoir of Jane Austen, to which is added Lady Susan and fragments of two other tales by Miss Austen.* London: Richard Bentley & Son, 1871.

————. *A Memoir of Jane Austen and Other Family Recollections.* Ed. Kathryn Sutherland. Oxford: Oxford University Press, 2002.

Austen-Leigh, R. A., ed. *Austen Papers, 1704–1856.* [Colchester, England]: privately printed by Spottiswood, Ballantyne, 1942.

Austen-Leigh, William, and Richard Arthur Austen-Leigh. *Jane Austen: Her Life and Letters: A Family Record.* 2nd edn. London: Smith, Elder & Co., 1913.

"Austen-Leigh's Memoir of Jane Austen." *The Nation* 243 (24 February 1870): 124–6. *American Literary Periodicals, 1859–1891.*

"Author of 'Emma,' &c." *The Atheneum; Or, Spirit of the English Magazines,* vol. II (October 1817 to April 1818): 488.

Barchas, Janine. *Matters of Fact in Jane Austen: History, Location, and Celebrity.* Baltimore: Johns Hopkins University Press, 2012.

————. "Sense, Sensibility, and Soap: An Unexpected Case Study in Digital Resources in Book History." *Book History* 16 (2013): 185–214.

Barchas, Janine, and Kristina Straub. "Curating *Will & Jane.*" *Eighteenth-Century Life* 40.2 (April 2016): 1–35.

Barnes, Elizabeth. "Novels." In *A History of the Book in America Vol. 2: An Extensive Republic: Print, Culture, and Society in the New Nation, 1790–1840,* ed. Robert A. Gross and Mary Kelley, 440–9. Chapel Hill: American Antiquarian Society/University of North Carolina Press, 2010.

Bautz, Annika. *The Reception of Jane Austen and Walter Scott: A Comparative Longitudinal Study.* London: Continuum, 2007.

Baym, Nina. *Novels, Readers, and Reviewers: Responses to Fiction in Antebellum America.* Ithaca: Cornell University Press, 1984.

Black, Fiona A. "Book Availability in Canada, 1752–1820, and the Scottish Contribution." PhD diss., Loughborough University, 1999.

————. "Importation and Book Availability." In *History of the Book in Canada Vol. 1: Beginnings to 1840*, ed. Patricia Lockhart Fleming, Gilles Gallichan, and Yvan Lamonde, 115–37. Toronto: University of Toronto Press, 2004.

Brabourne, Edward, Lord, ed. *Letters of Jane Austen*. 2 vols. London: Richard Bentley & Son, 1884.

Briggs, Asa. "The Longmans and the Book Trade, c1730–1830." In *The Cambridge History of the Book in Britain, vol. 5: 1695–1830*, ed. Michael F. Suarez, S. J., and Michael L. Turner, 397–412. Cambridge: Cambridge University Press, 2007.

Brodie, Laura Fairchild. "Jane Austen and the Common Reader: 'Opinions of Mansfield Park,' 'Opinions of Emma,' and the Janeite Phenomenon." *Texas Studies in Literature and Language* 37.1 (1995): 54–71.

Brownstein, Rachel M. *Why Jane Austen?*. New York: Columbia University Press, 2011.

Burroughs, Peter. "Ramsay, George, 9th Earl of Dalhousie." In *Dictionary of Canadian Biography*, vol. 7, 722–33. Toronto: University of Toronto Press, 2007.

Byrne, Paula. *The Real Jane Austen: A Life in Small Things*. New York: Harper, 2012.

Byron, Lord. *The Works of the Right Honourable Lord Byron, in Seven Volumes*, vol. 7. Brussels: Demanet, 1819. *GoogleBooks*.

Carey, Mathew. *Autobiography*. New York: Schwaab, 1942.

Carpenter, Kenneth E. "Libraries." In *A History of the Book in America Vol. 2: An Extensive Republic: Print, Culture, and Society in the New Nation, 1790–1840*, ed. Robert A. Gross and Mary Kelley, 273–85. Chapel Hill: American Antiquarian Society/University of North Carolina Press, 2010.

Carson, Susannah, ed. *A Truth Universally Acknowledged: 33 Great Writers on Why We Read Jane Austen*. New York: Random House, 2009.

Catalogue of an Extensive Collection of Books in Every Department of Ancient and Modern Literature, for Sale by M. Carey and Son. Philadelphia: Thomas H. Palmer, 1818. *GoogleBooks*.

A Catalogue of Books for 1818; Including Many Rare and Valuable Articles in Ancient and Modern Literature, Now on Sale by James Eastburn & Co. at the Literary Rooms, Broadway, Corner of Pine-Street, New-York, at the Prices Affixed. New York: Printed by Abraham Paul, May 1818. *GoogleBooks*.

Catalogue of Books in the Boston Library, June 1824. Boston: Munroe and Francis, 1824. *GoogleBooks*.

Catalogue of Novels and Romances, Being Part of an Extensive Collection for Sale by M. Carey and Son. N.p., n.d. *EAI*.

Catalogue of Recent Publications, for sale by W. B. Gilley. New York: J. [S]eymour, 1819. *EAI, Series 2.*

Catalogue of the Charlestown Circulating Library. Boston: True & Weston for T. M. Baker, 1819. *EAI, Series 2.*

Catalogue of the Washington Circulating Library. Boston: T. G. Bangs, 1817. *EAI, Series 2.*

Cavicki, Daniel. "Fandom before 'Fan': Shaping the History of Enthusiastic Audiences." *Reception: Texts, Readers, Audiences, History* 6 (2014): 52–72.

Chapman, R. W. *Jane Austen: A Critical Bibliography.* Oxford: Clarendon Press, 1953.

Clarke, Avis. "Printers' File." American Antiquarian Society, n.d. MS.

Cooper, Henry S. F., Jr., and Jenny Lawrence, eds. *The New York Society Library: 250 Years.* New York: The New York Society Library, 2004.

Copeland, Edward. *The Silver Fork Novel: Fashionable Fiction in the Age of Reform.* Cambridge: Cambridge University Press, 2012.

Crone, Rosalind, and Shafquat Towheed, eds. *The History of Reading, Volume 3: Methods, Strategies, Tactics.* New York: Palgrave Macmillan, 2011.

Davidson, Cathy N. "The Life and Times of *Charlotte Temple*: The Biography of a Book." In *Reading in America: Literature & Social History*, ed. Cathy N. Davidson, 157–79. Baltimore: Johns Hopkins University Press, 1989.

———. *Revolution and the Word: The Rise of the Novel in America.* Oxford: Oxford University Press, 1986.

Doody, Margaret. *Jane Austen's Names: Riddles, Persons, Places.* Chicago: University of Chicago Press, 2015.

Dow, Gillian. "*Emma* at 200: From English Village to Global Appeal." *Persuasions On-Line* 37.1 (Winter 2016).

———. "Reading at Godmersham: Edward Knight's Library and Marianne's Books." *Persuasions* 37 (2015): 152–62.

———. "Translations." In *The Cambridge Companion to* Emma, ed. Peter Sabor, 166–85. Cambridge: Cambridge University Press, 2015.

Dow, Gillian, and Clare Hanson, eds. *Uses of Austen: Jane's Afterlives.* Houndmills, Basingstoke: Palgrave Macmillan, 2012.

Dow, Gillian, and Katie Halsey. "Jane Austen's Reading: The Chawton Years." *Persuasions On-Line* 30.2 (Spring 2010).

Eaton, Rev. Arthur Wentworth Hamilton. *The Cochran-Inglis Family of Halifax.* Halifax: C. H. Ruggles & Co., 1899.

Elwood, Marie. "Studies in Documents: The Discovery and Repatriation of the Lord Dalhousie Collection." *Archivaria* 24 (Summer 1987): 108–16.

"*Emma:* a Novel." *Augustan Review* no. XIII vol. II (May 1816): 484–6. *GoogleBooks.*

Emsley, Sarah, and Sheila Kindred. "Among the Proto-Janeites: Reading *Mansfield Park* for Consolation in Halifax, Nova Scotia, in 1815." *Persuasions On-Line* 35.1 (Winter 2014).

Essex Circulating Library Catalogue of Books, for sale or circulation by Cushing & Appleton. Salem: Thomas C. Cushing, 1818. *EAI, Series 2.*

Favret, Mary A. "Free and Happy: Jane Austen in America." In *Janeites: Austen's Disciples and Devotees,* ed. Deidre Lynch, 166–87. Princeton: Princeton University Press, 2000.

Fergus, Jan. *Jane Austen: A Literary Life.* New York: St. Martin's, 1991.

Ferris, Ina. "Scott's Authorship and Book Culture." In *The Edinburgh Companion to Sir Walter Scott,* ed. Fiona Robertson, 9–21. Edinburgh: University of Edinburgh Press, 2012.

Fleming, Patricia Lockhart. "Bookbinding." In *History of the Book in Canada Vol. 1: Beginnings to 1840,* ed. Patricia Lockhart Fleming, Gilles Gallichan, and Yvan Lamonde, 109–12. Toronto: University of Toronto Press, 2004.

Ford, Susan Allen. "A Sweet Creature's Horrid Novels: Reading in *Northanger Abbey.*" *Persuasions On-Line* 33.1 (Winter 2012).

———. "Reading *Elegant Extracts* in *Emma*: Very Entertaining!" *Persuasions On-Line* 28.1 (Winter 2007).

Galarneau, Claude, and Gilles Gallichan. "Working in the Trades." In *History of the Book in Canada Vol. 1: Beginnings to 1840,* ed. Patricia Lockhart Fleming, Gilles Gallichan, and Yvan Lamonde, 80–6. Toronto: University of Toronto Press, 2004.

Gallagher, Catherine. *Nobody's Story: The Vanishing Acts of Women Writers in the Marketplace, 1670–1820.* Berkeley: University of California Press, 1994.

Gay, Penny. *Jane Austen and the Theatre.* Cambridge: Cambridge University Press, 2002.

Gilson, David. *A Bibliography of Jane Austen.* New edn. New Castle, DE: Oak Knoll Press, 1997.

———. "The Early American Editions of Jane Austen." *Book Collector* 18 (1969): 340–52. Reprinted in Gilson, *Jane Austen: Collected Articles and Introductions,* 23–37. Privately printed, 1998.

———. "Henry Austen's Memoir of Miss Austen." *Persuasions* 20 (1998): 12–19.

———. *Jane Austen: Collected Articles and Introductions.* Privately printed, 1998.

———. "Jane Austen and *Rhoda.*" *Persuasions* 20 (1998): 21–30.

———. "Jane Austen and *Rhoda*: A Further Postscript to *Persuasions* 20 (1998)." *Persuasions* 22 (2000): 109–11.

———. "Jane Austen and Sir Egerton Brydges." *Jane Austen Society Report for 1976* (1977): 9, 11.

———. "Jane Austen and the *Athenaeum* Again." *Persuasions* 19 (1997): 20–2.

———. "Jane Austen's Books." *Book Collector* 23 (1974): 547–50. Reprinted in Gilson, *Jane Austen: Collected Articles and Introductions*, 73–89. Privately printed, 1998.

———. "Jane Austen's 'Emma' in America: Notes on the Text of the First and Second American Editions." *The Review of English Studies* n.s. 53: 212 (2002): 517–25.

———. "Obituaries." In *The Jane Austen Companion*, ed. J. David Grey, 320–1. New York: Macmillan, 1986.

Gingerich, Owen. *The Book Nobody Read: Chasing the Revolutions of Nicolaus Copernicus*. New York: Walker, 2004.

Goldstein, Philip. *Modern American Reading Practices: Between Aesthetics and History*. New York: Palgrave Macmillan, 2009.

Goldstein, Philip, and James L. Machor, eds. *New Directions in American Reception Study*. Oxford: Oxford University Press, 2008.

Grant, Stephen H. *Collecting Shakespeare: The Story of Henry and Emily Folger*. Baltimore: Johns Hopkins University Press, 2014.

Green, James N. "Introduction to *Emma* Exhibit." Lecture. Jane Austen Society of North America, Eastern Pennsylvania Region at the Library Company of Philadelphia, 19 September 2015.

———. *Mathew Carey: Publisher and Patriot*. Philadelphia: The Library Company of Philadelphia, 1985.

———. "The Rise of Book Publishing." In *A History of the Book in America Vol. 2: An Extensive Republic: Print, Culture, and Society in the New Nation, 1790–1840*, ed. Robert A. Gross and Mary Kelley, 75–127. Chapel Hill: American Antiquarian Society/University of North Carolina Press, 2010.

Gross, Robert A., and Mary Kelley, eds. *A History of the Book in America Vol. 2: An Extensive Republic: Print, Culture, and Society in the New Nation, 1790–1840*. Chapel Hill: American Antiquarian Society/University of North Carolina Press, 2010.

Groves, David. "Jane Austen and Scotland." *Persuasions* 7 (1985): 66.

Halsey, Katie. *Jane Austen and Her Readers, 1786–1945*. London: Anthem, 2012.

Halsey, Katie, and W. R. Owens, eds. *The History of Reading, Volume 2: Evidence from the British Isles, c. 1750–1950*. New York: Palgrave Macmillan, 2011.

Harman, Claire. *Jane's Fame: How Jane Austen Conquered the World*. Edinburgh: Canongate, 2009.

Hart, Julia Catherine Beckwith. *St. Ursula's Convent, Or, The Nun of Canada*. 1824. Ed. Douglas G. Lochhead. Ottawa: Carleton University Press, 1991.

Higgonet, Anne. *A Museum of One's Own: Private Collecting, Public Gift*. Pittsburgh: Periscope, 2009.

Highfill, Philip H., Jr., Kalman A. Burnim, and Edward A. Langhans. *A Biographical Dictionary of Actors, Actresses, Musicians, Dancers, Managers, and Other Stage Personnel in London, 1660–1800*. Carbondale: Southern Illinois Press, 1982.

Hinsley, Jacqueline Ann. "The Reading Tastes of Educated Women of a Manufacturing Family in America, 1810–1835." MA diss., University of Delaware, 1976.

Hogan, Charles Beecher. "Jane Austen and Her Early Public." *The Review of English Studies* n.s. 1 (1950): 39–54.

Hopkinson, David. "The Austens in North America, 1809–1875." *Persuasions* 20 (2000): 53–60.

Horrocks, Hilary. *Newhailes*. Printed for the National Trust for Scotland, 2014.

Horwood, Catherine. *Gardening Women: Their Stories from 1600 to the Present*. London: Virago, 2010.

Howe, M. A. de Wolfe. *The Articulate Sisters: Passages from Journals and Letters of the Daughters of President Josiah Quincy of Harvard University*. Cambridge, MA: Harvard University Press, 1946.

———. "A Jane Austen Letter, with other 'Janeana' from an old book of autographs." *The Yale Review* 15 (Jan. 1926): 319–35.

Howlett, David J. "Ramsay, James Andrew Broun, first marquess of Dalhousie (1812–1860)." *Oxford Dictionary of National Biography*, online edn. 2011.

Hubback, J. H. and Edith C. Hubback. *Jane Austen's Sailor Brothers: Being the Adventures of Sir Francis Austen, G.C.B., Admiral of the Fleet and Rear-Admiral Charles Austen*. London: John Lane, 1896.

Jackson, H. J. *Marginalia: Readers Writing in Books*. New Haven: Yale University Press, 2001.

———. *Romantic Readers: The Evidence of Marginalia*. New Haven: Yale University Press, 2005.

———. *Those Who Write for Immortality: Romantic Reputations and the Dream of Lasting Fame*. New Haven: Yale University Press, 2015.

Jaffe, Deborah. *Among the Janeites: A Journey through the World of Jane Austen Fandom*. New York: Mariner, 2013.

Johnson, Claudia L. *Jane Austen's Cults and Cultures*. Chicago: University of Chicago Press, 2012.

Jones, Hazel. *Jane Austen's Journeys*. London: Robert Hale, 2015.

Kaser, David, ed. *The Cost Book of Carey & Lea, 1825–1838.* Philadelphia: University of Pennsylvania Press, 1963.

Keynes, Geoffrey. *Jane Austen: A Bibliography.* London: Nonesuch Press, 1929.

MacKenzie, Scott R. *Be It Ever So Humble: Poverty, Fiction, and the Invention of the Middle-Class Home.* Richmond: University of Virginia Press, 2013.

LaCroix, Alison L. "The Lawyer's Library in the Early American Republic." In *Subversion and Sympathy: Gender, Law, and the British Novel*, ed. Martha C. Nussbaum and Alison L. LaCroix, 251–73. Oxford: Oxford University Press, 2013.

Lajeunesse, Marcel. "Personal Libraries and Bibliophilia." In *History of the Book in Canada Vol. 1: Beginnings to 1840*, ed. Patricia Lockhart Fleming, Gilles Gallichan, and Yvan Lamonde, 202–6. Toronto: University of Toronto Press, 2004.

Lane, Maggie. Introduction to *The Joy of Jane: Thoughts on the First 200 Years of Austen's Legacy*, ed. Tim Bullamore, 4–10. Edinburgh: Lansdown Media, 2016.

Le Faye, Deirdre. *A Chronology of the Austen Family.* Oxford: Oxford University Press, 2006.

———. *Jane Austen: A Family Record.* 2nd edn. Cambridge: Cambridge University Press, 2004.

Looser, Devoney. *The Making of Jane Austen.* Baltimore: Johns Hopkins University Press, forthcoming 2017.

Lord, Ruth. *Henry F. du Pont and Winterthur: A Daughter's Portrait.* New Haven: Yale University Press, 1999.

Low, Betty-Bright, and Jacqueline Hinsley. *Sophie du Pont, A Young Lady in America: Sketches, Diaries, & Letters 1823–1833.* New York: Abrams, 1987.

Lynch, Deidre Shauna. *Loving Literature: A Cultural History.* Chicago: University of Chicago Press, 2015.

Lynch, Deidre, ed. *Janeites: Austen's Disciples and Devotees.* Princeton: Princeton University Press, 2000.

McClay, David, and Kirsty Archer-Thompson. *Rave Reviewer: Scott on Frankenstein, Emma, & Childe Harold.* Printed for National Library of Scotland and Abbotsford, 2016.

McGill, Meredith L. *American Literature and the Culture of Reprinting, 1834–1853.* Philadelphia: University of Pennsylvania Press, 2003.

McMahon, Madeline. "Jane Austen's *Emma* in Early America." The New York Society Library *Library Blog*, 4 May 2015.

Mandal, Anthony. *Jane Austen and the Popular Novel: The Determined Author.* Houndmills, Basingstoke: Palgrave Macmillan, 2007.

Mandal, Anthony, and Brian Southam, eds. *The Reception of Jane Austen in Europe.* London: Continuum, 2007.

Mann, Barbara Alice. *The Cooper Connection: The Influence of Jane Austen on James Fenimore Cooper*. New York: AMS Press, 2014.

Matson, Cathy, and James N. Green. "Ireland, America, and Mathew Carey: Special Issue Introduction." *Early American Studies* 11:3 (2013): 395–402.

The Monthly Literary Advertiser, no. 17. Philadelphia: January 1817. EBSCO*host*.

Montolieu, Isabelle de. *Caroline of Lichtfield*. Ed. Laura Kirkley. London: Routledge, 2016.

Morison, John H. *Life of the Hon. Jeremiah Smith, LL.D.* Boston: Charles C. Little and James Brown, 1845.

Morrison, Rodney J. "Henry C. Carey and American Economic Development." *Transactions of the American Philosophical Society* 76.3 (1986): 1–91.

Mosley, James. "The Technologies of Print." In *The Book: A Global History*, ed. Michael F. Suarez, S. J. and H. R. Wooudhuysen, 130–53. Oxford: Oxford University Press, 2014.

Munby, A. N. L. *The Cult of the Autograph Letter in England*. London: Athlone Press, 1962.

Murphy, Olivia. *Jane Austen the Reader: The Artist as Critic*. London: Palgrave Macmillan, 2013.

Murray, Heather. "Readers and Society." In *History of the Book in Canada Vol. 1: Beginnings to 1840*, ed. Patricia Lockhart Fleming, Gilles Gallichan, and Yvan Lamonde, 172–82. Toronto: University of Toronto Press, 2004.

Müller, Simone M. *Wiring the World: The Social and Cultural Creation of Global Telegraph Networks*. New York: Columbia University Press, 2016.

Nipps, Karen. *Lydia Bailey: A Checklist of Her Imprints*. Philadelphia: Pennsylvania State University Press, 2013.

Palmer, Beverly Wilson, ed. *A Woman's Wit and Whimsy: The 1833 Diary of Anna Cabot Lowell Quincy*. Boston: Massachusetts Historical Society/Northeastern University Press, 2003.

Parker, George. "Courting Local and International Markets." In *History of the Book in Canada Vol. 1: Beginnings to 1840*, ed. Patricia Lockhart Fleming, Gilles Gallichan, and Yvan Lamonde, 339–54. Toronto: University of Toronto Press, 2004.

Parsons, Farnell. "A Note on a Jane Austen Connection with the Massachusetts Historical Society: Justice Story, Admiral Wormely, and Admiral Francis Austen." *Persuasions On-Line* 23.1 (Winter 2002).

———. "The Quincys and the Austens: A Cordial Connection." *Jane Austen Society Report* (2000): 49–51.

Pearson, David. *Books as History*. Rev. edn. London and New Castle, DE: The British Library and Oak Knoll Press, 2012.

Pearson, Jacqueline. *Women's Reading in Britain, 1750–1835: A Dangerous Recreation.* Cambridge: Cambridge University Press, 2005.

Pringle, James S. "Canadian Botanical Specimens Collected 1826–1828 by the Countess of Dalhousie, Acquired by the Royal Botanical Gardens." *Canadian Horticultural History/Histoire de l'horticulture au Canada* 3.1 (1995): 1–21.

Quincy, Eliza Susan. *A Portfolio of Nine Watercolor Views, Relating to Certain Members of the Adams and Quincy Families and Their Quincy Houses and Environment Done in the Year 1822.* Boston: Massachusetts Historical Society, 1975.

Quincy, Josiah. *Figures of the Past.* 6th edn. Boston: Roberts Brothers, 1883.

Quincy, Wendell, Holmes, and Upham Family Papers. Microfilm edition, 67 reels. Boston: Massachusetts Historical Society, 1977.

Ramsay, Edward Bannerman. *Reminiscences of Scottish Life and Character.* 23rd edn. Introd. Cosmo Innes. Edinburgh: Edmonston & Douglas, 1874. *GoogleBooks.*

Ray, Joan Klingel, ed. *Jane Austen's Popular and Critical Reception: A Documentary Volume.* Detroit: Gale, 2012.

Reid, Deborah Anne. "Unsung Heroines of Horticulture: Scottish Gardening Women, 1800 to 1930." PhD diss., University of Edinburgh, 2015.

Rezek, Joseph. *London and the Making of Provincial Literature: Aesthetics and the Transatlantic Book Trade.* Philadelphia: University of Pennsylvania Press, 2015.

Riggs, John Beverley. *A Guide to the Manuscripts in the Eleutherian Mills Historical Library: Accessions through the Year 1965.* Greenville, DE: Eleutherian Mills Historical Library, 1970.

Rink, Ewald. "A Family Heritage: The Library of the Immigrant du Ponts." Unpublished MS., [1980s].

Rorabaugh, W. J. "Edward C. Delavan." In *American National Biography,* ed. John A. Garraty and Mark C. Carnes, 6:384–5. Oxford: Oxford University Press, 1999.

Scheil, Katherine West. *She Hath Been Reading: Women and Shakespeare Clubs in America.* Ithaca: Cornell University Press, 2012.

Schultheis, Emily. "Philadelphia and the Making of Jane Austen, 1816–1838." *Women's Writing.* Special issue on "Bicentennial Essays on Jane Austen's Afterlives," ed. Annika Bautz and Sarah Wooton: forthcoming 2017.

Scott Standard Postage Stamp Catalogue. 141st edn, volume 1. New York: Scott Publishing, 1985.

Scott, Walter. *The Journals of Sir Walter Scott.* Ed. W. E. K. Anderson. Edinburgh: Canongate, 2009. EBSCO*host.*

Seville, Catherine. *The Internationalisation of Copyright Law: Books, Buccaneers and the Black Flag in the Nineteenth Century*. Cambridge: Cambridge University Press, 2006.

Shapiro, James, ed. *Shakespeare in America: An Anthology from the Revolution till Now*. New York: Library of America, 2014.

Shteir, Ann B. *Cultivating Women, Cultivating Science: Flora's Daughters and Botany in England 1760–1860*. Baltimore: Johns Hopkins University Press, 1996.

Silverman, Gillian. *Bodies and Books: Reading and the Fantasy of Communion in Nineteenth-Century America*. Philadelphia: University of Pennsylvania Press, 2012.

Smith, Emma. *Shakespeare's First Folio: Four Centuries of an Iconic Book*. Oxford: Oxford University Press, 2016.

Smith, Karen. "Community Libraries." In *History of the Book in Canada Vol. 1: Beginnings to 1840*, ed. Patricia Lockhart Fleming, Gilles Gallichan, and Yvan Lamonde, 144–51. Toronto: University of Toronto Press, 2004.

Smith, Margaret. "The Brontë Correspondence." In *The Brontës in Context*, ed. Marianne Thormählen, 115–22. Cambridge: Cambridge University Press, 2012.

Southam, B. C., ed. *Jane Austen: The Critical Heritage*. London: Routledge & Kegan Paul, 1968.

Southam, Brian. "*Emma*: England, Peace, and Patriotism." 2000. Reprinted in *Jane Austen's Emma: A Casebook*, ed. Fiona J. Stafford, 269–91. Oxford: Oxford University Press, 2007.

———. *Jane Austen and the Navy*. London: Hambledon and London, 2000.

Story, William Wetmore. *Life and Letters of Joseph Story*, vol. 1. Boston: Charles C. Little and James Brown, 1851. *GoogleBooks*.

St Clair, William. *The Reading Nation in the Romantic Period*. Cambridge: Cambridge University Press, 2004.

Sutherland, Kathryn. *Jane Austen's Textual Lives: From Aeschylus to Bollywood*. Oxford: Oxford University Press, 2005.

Todd, William B., and Ann Bowden. *Sir Walter Scott: A Bibliographical History, 1796–1832*. New Castle, DE: Oak Knoll Press, 1998.

Towheed, Shafquat, and W. R. Owens, eds. *The History of Reading, Volume 1: International Perspectives, c. 1500–1900*. New York: Palgrave Macmillan, 2011.

Tremaine, Marie. *A Bibliography of Canadian Imprints, 1751–1800*. Toronto: University of Toronto Press, 1952.

Troost, Linda, and Sayre Greenfield. "A History of the Fanny Wars." *Persuasions* 36 (2014): 15–33.

Tucker, Andie. "Newspapers and Periodicals." In *A History of the Book in America Vol. 2: An Extensive Republic: Print, Culture, and Society in the New Nation, 1790–1840*, ed. Robert A. Gross and Mary Kelley,

389–408. Chapel Hill: American Antiquarian Society/University of North Carolina Press, 2010.

Tytler, Sarah. *Jane Austen and Her Works*. 1879. London: Bloomsbury Academic, 2014.

Vaughan, Alden T., and Virginia Mason Vaughan. *Shakespeare in America*. Oxford: Oxford University Press, 2012.

Villeneuve, René. *Lord Dalhousie: Patron and Collector*. Ottawa: National Gallery of Canada, 2008.

Viveash, Chris. "Jane Austen and Madame de Staël." *Persuasions* 13 (1991): 39–40.

Waterston, Mrs. R. C. "Jane Austen." *Atlantic Monthly* 11 (February 1863): 235–40. EBSCO*host*.

Watson, Nicola J. "Rambles in Literary London." In *Literary Tourism and Nineteenth-Century Culture*, ed. Nicola J. Watson, 139–49. Houndmills, Basingstoke: Palgrave Macmillan, 2009.

Wells, Juliette. *Everybody's Jane: Austen in the Popular Imagination*. New York: Bloomsbury Academic, 2011.

———. "A Harpist Arrives at Mansfield Park: Music and the Moral Ambiguity of Mary Crawford." *Persuasions* 28 (2006): 101–14.

———. "'In Music She Had Always Used to Feel Alone in the World': Jane Austen, Solitude, and the Artistic Woman." *Persuasions* 26 (2004): 98–110.

———. Introduction to *Emma*, by Jane Austen, xiii–xxix. New York: Penguin Classics, 2015.

———. "Reading *Pride and Prejudice* from Afar: Alberta H. Burke and American Reception of Austen." *Sensibilities* 47 (December 2013): 108–21.

———. "'Some of Your Accomplishments Are Not Ordinary': The Limits of Artistry in *Jane Eyre*." In *The Brontës in the World of the Arts*, ed. Sandra Hagan and Juliette Wells, 67–80. Houndmills, Basingstoke: Ashgate, 2008.

Whitelaw, Marjory, ed. *The Dalhousie Journals*. 3 vols. Ottawa: Oberon Press, 1978–1982.

Wilson, Cheryl A. "'Something like mine': Catherine Hutton, Jane Austen, and Feminist Recovery Work." *The Eighteenth Century* 56.2 (2015): 151–64.

INDEX

1816 Philadelphia edition of
    Emma
advertisements for 4
    Augustan Review quotation in
        31–2, 45–6 n. 75
    in catalogues of the Carey firm
        33
    by circulating libraries 34–5
    identification of Austen in 22
    in *Monthly Literary Advertiser*
        21, 31
    by partner booksellers 33–4
    Quarterly Review quotation in
        22, 32
bibliographers' interest in origins
    of 5, 192–3
binding of 14, 29
date of publication 26
errors in 27
format of 4, 16, 27–8
gaps in archival evidence relating
    to 21, 23, 35, 41 n. 33
identification of Austen on title
    page of 16, 22, 27
impetus for publishing 20–1, 22,
    42 n. 39
influence of *Quarterly Review*
    on 21–23
influence on Austen's American
    renown of 4, 36–7
omission of in bibliographies 13
only Austen edition in America
    published during author's
    lifetime 1, 13
paper used in 24, 28
previously unknown facts
    regarding 4, 13–14
print run of 26, 44 n. 60
printers of *see* Justice & Cox
process of printing 14, 23–5
reciprocal publishing of 30, 35
rediscovered copies of 14
relationship to Carey & Lea
    1833 edition 13, 38 n. 1
relationship to Murray's 1816
    London edition 4, 26–7
sale prices of 29, 31, 33
sales of 30–1, 35
surviving copies of 1, 4, 13,
    28–9, 49–50; *see also*
    Dalhousie, Christian
    Broun Ramsay, Countess
    of, copy of 1816
    Philadelphia *Emma* owned
    by; du Pont, E. I., copy
    of 1816 Philadelphia
    Emma owned by; James
    Hammond's Circulating
    Library, copy of 1816
    Philadelphia *Emma* owned
    by; Smith, Jeremiah, copy
    of 1816 Philadelphia
    Emma owned by
title page of 16
1832–1833 Carey & Lea editions
    of Austen's novels
advertising and promotion of 70,
    138–9, 172 n. 5

and Austen's fame 171 n. 1
collecting of 192, 193, 195
identification of Austen on the
    title pages of 137
print runs of 137
publication of 13, 19, 69, 137–8,
    173 n. 12
sale prices of 170–71 n. 1
sales of 35, 138, 170–1 n. 1
text of 27, 38 n. 1, 138, 146,
    171 n. 2

Abbotsford 104, 127 n. 76
accomplishments, feminine 92–3,
    112–13, 122 n. 26
Alexander, Francis 64
American Austen reception
Carey & Lea edition as turning
    point in 5
gaps in history of 1, 7 n. 1
in Halsey's *Jane Austen and Her
    Readers* 2
in Southam's *Critical Heritage*
    1–2, 7 n. 3
why neglected by scholars 2
see also Austen, Jane, fame
    of; James Hammond's
    Circulating Library, copy
    of 1816 Philadelphia
    Emma owned by; Smith,
    Jeremiah, copy of 1816
    Philadelphia *Emma* owned
    by
Anderson, Mrs. 111, 115,
    126 n. 67, 128 n. 83
annotations 66–70, 74–77,
    85 n. 67, 85 n. 68,
    134 n. 135
Ard, Patricia M. 17
Atlantic Monthly 140, 161–5,
    172 n. 7
Augustan Review 31, 32,
    45–6 n. 75

Austen, Anna 115
Austen, Caroline 176 n. 37
Austen, Cassandra
portraits of Jane Austen 103,
    127 n. 71
reminiscences about Jane Austen
    167, 178 n. 63
Austen, Charles 146, 179 n. 33
Austen, Charles-John II 158
Austen, Admiral Sir Francis W.
Anna Waterston's visit to 139,
    156–61
appearance 165
comments on promotion to
    Admiral of the Fleet
    181 n. 92
comparison of self to Captain
    Harville of *Persuasion* 152
correspondence with Anna
    Waterston 154
correspondence with Eliza Susan
    Quincy 5, 147–52, 160,
    165–6
description of Jane Austen
    147
gift of Jane Austen letter 144,
    148, 151
interest in Jane Austen's renown
    166
religious piety of 152, 171 n. 51
Austen, Rev. George 36, 47 n. 92,
    93, 180 n. 85
Austen, George 158, 179 n. 72
Austen, Henry
"Biographical Notice" 129 n. 93,
    146, 148
"Memoir of Miss Austen"
    180 n. 85
Austen, Herbert-Grey 158–9,
    180 n. 75
Austen, Jane
anonymity as author 15, 22, 31,
    35, 47 n. 90, 63

appearance 103
book ownership and reading
    39 n. 5, 55
fame of, in America
    compared to that of other
        writers of her era 37–8, 63
    contribution of 1816
        Philadelphia *Emma* to 4,
        36–7, 50
    contribution of obituaries to 4,
        14, 36–7, 47 n. 92
    contribution of periodicals to
        14
    contributions of the Quincy
        family to 5, 139, 161–9
    growth of 3
    H. J. Jackson's theory regarding
        131 n. 115
    lack of during lifetime 63
    role of Austen-Leigh's *Memoir*
        in relation to 3, 173 n. 9
    see also American Austen
        reception
historical scholarship on 9 n. 12
letters by, collecting of 144–50,
    170, 202
manuscripts
    Lady Susan 131, 191
    "Opinions of *Emma*" 17, 76,
        179 n. 77–9
    "Profits of my Novels" 17
novels
    American editions of *see* 1816
        Philadelphia *Emma*;
        1832–1833 Carey & Lea
        editions of Austen's novels
Emma
    Alberta Burke's comparison
        of her writing to that of
        Jane Fairfax from 198
    Anna Waterston's discussion
        of in *Atlantic* article 162,
        165, 181 n. 86

as favorite of Austen's,
    according to Francis
    Austen 157
as most English of Austen's
    novels 22
Augustan Review piece on
    45–6 n. 75
Austen's dedication of to the
    Prince Regent 15, 90
Joseph Story's reading of
    141–2
Lady Dalhousie in
    comparison to Emma
    Woodhouse of 93–4, 96,
    110–14
Lady Dalhousie's reading of
    109–10
Murray's 1816 London first
    edition of 15–16, 27,
    28
presentation copy of given to
    Augusta Leigh 194
Scott's *Quarterly Review*
    piece on 21–2
see also 1816 Philadelphia
    Emma
Mansfield Park
    Alberta Burke's comparison
        of herself to Mrs. Norris
        of 198
    Anna Waterston's discussion
        of in *Atlantic* article
        163–4
    and Anna Waterston's literary
        tourism to Portsmouth
        155
    Egerton's 1814 London first
        edition of 15
    Jeremiah Smith's ownership
        of second London edition
        of 68
    Lady Dalhousie's reading of
        108–9

Lady Sherbrooke's reading
  of with Mary Wodehouse
  107, 116, 128–9 n. 92
omission from *Quarterly
  Review* and *Augustan
  Review* notices and from
  Carey's advertising 31
preference for among
  "distinguished literary
  men" 157, 162
reception at turn of twentieth
  century 181 n. 86
Quincy family's reading of
  140
Victorine Bauduy's reading
  of 62–3
Northanger Abbey
Anna Waterston's similarity
  to Catherine Morland of
  145
Henry Tilney's comments
  about journal-writing in
  85
Lady Dalhousie's reading of
  105, 107, 118, 128 n. 81
Murray's 1818 London first
  edition of 15
narrator's defense of novels
  in 100
Quincy family's reading of 140
Whately's review of 68
Persuasion
Anna Waterston's favorite
  Austen novel 164
and Anna Waterston's literary
  tourism to Bath 165
comparison of Francis Austen
  to characters from 150,
  152
Lady Dalhousie's reading of
  104–8, 114–15
Murray's 1818 London first
  edition of 15

Nation reviewer's
  disparagement of 168
Quincy family's reading of
  140
relation to Cooper's
  Precaution 1
Whately's review of 68,
  138
Pride and Prejudice
Alberta Burke's allusion to in
  letter to Gilson 198
Anna Waterston's praise of
  164–5
Augustan Review's
  comparison of *Sense and
  Sensibility* to 45 n. 75
availability in US in 1810s as
  imported book 27
Bunce & Brother's 1855 New
  York edition of 179 n. 68
discussion of gentleman's
  library in 101
Egerton's 1813 London first
  edition of 15
feminine accomplishments in
  93
George W. Brigg's 1849
  Boston edition of
  179 n. 68
Jeremiah Smith's ownership
  of third London edition
  of 68
Lady Dalhousie's reading of
  108–9
Literary Classics Club edition
  of 189
Lord Morpeth's reading of
  152
Sense and Sensibility
Augustan Review's
  comparison of *Pride and
  Prejudice* to 45 n. 75
Bentley's 1833 edition of 161

Egerton's 1811 London first edition of 15
identification of Austen on title page of 15
Jeremiah Smith's ownership of 68–9
Quincy family's reading of 140
translations of 108, 129 n. 97, 187–8, 190–2, 196, 198
obituaries for 4, 15, 35–6, 38, 69, 148
personality 147
Austen-Leigh, J. E. (James Edward)
American review of *A Memoir of Jane Austen* 168–9, 181 n. 99
correspondence with Eliza Susan Quincy 167–9
A Memoir of Jane Austen 5, 139, 153, 166, 167, 176 n. 37, 177 n. 50, 177 n. 51, 179 n. 64
reception of *A Memoir of Jane Austen* 173, 182 n. 101, 182 n. 110
Austen-Leigh, R. A. (Richard Arthur)
Austen Papers 5, 172 n. 7, 178 n. 56, 182 n. 110
notes on Quincy/Austen correspondence 177 n. 48, 177 n. 51

Barchas, Janine 125 n. 54, 179 n. 68, 205 n. 15
Bauduy, Victorine (Mme Ferdinand) née Victorine Elizabeth du Pont
book ownership 53
book purchases 62

comments on Edgeworth 60–1
comments on *Glenarvon* 61
dislike of Shakespeare 58
likely response to *Mansfield Park* 63
marriage to Ferdinand Bauduy 53
opposition to sister Eleuthera's reading Scott 59–60
range of reading 57, 80 n. 26
reading lists kept by 62–3
mention of Austen's *Mansfield Park* 62
mentions of works by Charlotte Brontë
Jane Eyre 63
The Professor 63
mentions of works by Elizabeth Gaskell
Life of Charlotte Brontë 63
North and South 63
mentions of George Eliot's *Adam Bede* 63
recommendation of Byron to cousin Frank 58–9
Rembrandt Peale portrait of 54
role in educating siblings 53, 59–60, 81 n. 34
similarities to and differences from Austen's characters 61
visit to Mathew Carey's bookshop 62
Bautz, Annika 114
Bay Psalm Book 14, 38–9 n. 2
Beinecke Rare Book and Manuscript Library, Yale University 49, 193
Bentley edition of Austen's novels 69, 161
Black, Fiona A. 132 n. 125, 133 n. 132

bookbinding 14, 26, 62,
133 n. 132
book manufacturing in hand-
press period 17, 24, 26,
43 n. 45, 44 n. 66
book ownership 2
in early nineteenth-century
America 21
owners' role in making books
unique objects 77 n. 1
book purchasing and American
patriotism 17
book trade, history of 2–3
Boston Library 37, 85 n. 67
Boston massacre, 151
Brabourne, Edward, Lord 169,
182 n. 111
Brontë, Charlotte 63, 94, 143,
165
Broun, Charles 91–5
Broun, Christian see Dalhousie,
Christian Broun Ramsay,
Countess of
Brydges, Sir Egerton 69–70
Burke, Alberta H.
and American editions of Austen
192, 195
bequests of Austen collection
185, 200–1, 204 n. 5
collecting and "Austen archives"
186, 187, 189–91, 197,
201
comments on asking prices
for Austen editions
194
correspondence with David
Gilson 185–202
education 185–6, 203 n. 3
encouragement of Gilson's
Bibliography 187, 191–2,
202
family background 185
literary tourism 199

low opinion of academics
199–201
marriage 185
and Morgan Library 200
ownership of Carey & Lea
Elizabeth Bennet and
Persuasion 192
ownership of the Dalhousie copy
of the 1816 Philadelphia
Emma 192–3
purchase of Carey & Lea
Northanger Abbey
195
references to Austen's novels
197–8
and translations of Austen
187–8, 190–2, 196,
198
Burke, Henry G. "Harry" 186,
187, 200, 207 n. 91
Burney, Frances 38, 57, 71,
83 n. 53, 174 n. 15
Burns, Robert 97–8, 124 n. 48
Burroughs, Peter 199 n. 2
Byron, George Gordon, Lord
and Austen 115
poetry
advertisements for American
editions of 33
Childe Harold's Pilgrimage
115, 177 n. 46
The Corsair 58–9
Don Juan 115
English Bards and Scotch
Reviewers 118,
137 n. 134
popularity of in America 50,
58–9, 78 n. 8, 100, 114

Carey, Henry C.
involvement in printing Emma
23
partnership with father 22

possible authorship of
    encyclopedia article on
    Austen 70–1, 83–4 n. 58
professional difficulties
    40–1 n. 22
Carey, Mathew
achievements in publishing 17,
    18–21, 40 n. 16
biography 17–19
catalogues of firm 20, 31–2,
    83 n. 53
correspondence with printers
    and booksellers 23–6,
    30–31, 35
diaries 21, 41 n. 13
love of reading novels 20
Monthly Literary Advertiser, The
    21, 31, 32
role of reprinted English novels
    in publishing business 21
views on *Emma* 21–3
Carlisle, George Howard, 6th Earl
    of 177 n. 50
Carpenter, T. Edward 194–5
Cary, Thomas 117, 133 n. 132
Cervantes, Miguel de 99,
    126 n. 56
Chapman, R. W. 9 n. 13,
    122 n. 19, 170, 190, 192,
    196, 201
Chawton Cottage *see* Jane
    Austen's House Museum
circulating libraries 4, 20, 29,
    34, 35, 50, 57, 71, 73–5,
    84 n. 65
Civil War, American 161, 166
Clarke, James Stanier 15
Clavering *see* Brydges, Sir Egerton
Coalstoun *see* Colstoun House
Cochrane, Isabella 112, 127 n. 80,
    130 n. 109
collecting, literary 1, 3, 5,
    9 n. 13, 13, 29, 143–4,

202, 204–5 n. 15; *see
    also* Austen, Jane, letters
    by, collecting of; Burke,
    Alberta H., collecting
    and "Austen archives";
    1832–1833 Carey &
    Lea editions of Austen,
    collecting of; Morgan, J.
    P.; Quincy, Eliza Susan,
    collecting of literary letters
    by; Shakespeare, William,
    collecting of works by
Colstoun House 91, 93, 96,
    97, 99, 101, 118–19,
    121 n. 18, 122 n. 20,
    133 n. 134
Cooper, James Fenimore 1, 34,
    57, 116
Copernicus 49
copyright law 16–17
Cox, Horatio 23, 25, 27, 42 n. 42
Craik, W. A. 196

Dalhousie, Christian Broun
    Ramsay, Countess of, née
    Christian Broun
book of riddles 96, 123–4 n. 41
book ownership 109, 116,
    117–19
    American editions 118,
        133 n. 133
botanical collecting 88, 95
commonplace book 95–6
copy of 1816 Philadelphia
    Emma owned by
    acquisition by Goucher College
        118
    binding of 88, 117–19,
        120–21 n. 8
    later owners of 118
    on list of books owned 109
    probable date of reading of
        109–10

purchase of 88, 117
signature and bookplate in 16,
    88, 118, 120–1 n. 8
death 130 n. 109
described by contemporaries
    103–4
diaries 88, 102–3
drawings 94, 96, 110, 111, 113
education 92–5
friendship with Isabella
    Cochrane 114
library use 116, 132 n. 127
likely responses to *Persuasion*
    105–7
literary patronage 91
literary taste 98–9
mineral collecting 12
motherhood 107
portraits 88–9, 97, 103
reading
    of Byron's poetry 114–16
    of *Emma* 109–114
    of *Mansfield Park* 108–9
    of *Northanger Abbey* 105,
        107
    of *Persuasion* 104–5
    of *Pride and Prejudice* 108–9
    of Scott's novels 114–16
    range of 108, 116
recognition during lifetime as a
    botanist 87–8
relationship with father 91–5
religion 107, 115
similarities to and differences
    from Austen
    in ambition 90
    in appearance 103
    in life experiences 88–90, 93
    in social rank 88
similarities to and differences
    from Austen's characters
    in creation of book of riddles
        96

in discussion of "immoral"
    literature 115–16
in education 93–5, 112–14
in journal-keeping 95
in marriage 96, 98
in personality 110–14
in social rank 89, 110–11
travel 90
Dalhousie, George Ramsay, 9th
    Earl of
administrative positions 87, 90,
    103
book purchases 101, 116–17
Dalhousie Castle library
    100–101
education 96–7
founding of Dalhousie University
    87
founding of Garrison Library
    99–100
inventory of possessions 101–2
library use 116
literary tastes 98–100
military service 87, 97
reading 99
religion 107
views on novel-reading, in
    relation to *Northanger*
    Abbey 100
Dalhousie, James Andrew Broun
    Ramsay, first Marquess of
    87, 103, 117, 176 n. 33
Dalhousie Castle 97, 100–1, 105,
    126 n. 61
Dalhousie University 87
Dalrymple, Miss Christian 101,
    112, 122 n. 23
Dartmouth College Library 14,
    49, 63, 65–7
Delavan, Edward C. 142–3, 150
de Montolieu, Isabelle 108,
    129 n. 97
de Staël, Madame 36, 177 n. 46

Dickens, Charles 2, 17, 25
Discipline 53, 79 n. 10
Douglas, William 127 n. 70
Dow, Gillian 80 n. 25, 129 n. 97, 204 n. 9
du Pont, Alexis 79 n. 13, 79 n. 20
du Pont, E. I. (Éleuthère Irénée) 4
  acquaintance with Mathew Carey 55
  book ownership and family library 52, 56, 57, 78 n. 8
  book purchases 55, 62
  botanical interests 52
  copy of 1816 Philadelphia *Emma* owned by
    binding of 50–1, 78 n. 3
    Carey catalogue bound into 57
    displayed at Winterthur Museum 52
    purchase of 55–6
    signatures in 51
    US stamp in 52, 78 n. 5
  emigration from France 52
  encouragement of daughters' reading 56
  fluency in English 52
  founder of E. I. du Pont de Nemours and Company 52
  frugality 55
  home at Eleutherian Mills 52
du Pont, Eleuthera
  education 59–60, 62
du Pont, Evelina 55
  as poetess 80 n. 23
  range of reading 57, 80 n. 26
du Pont, Henry Francis 52, 54
du Pont, Pierre Samuel 52, 78 n. 8
du Pont, Samuel Francis "Frank" 53, 58–9
du Pont, Sophie Madeleine
  book dedications by 53

"carics" (caricature drawings) 56–7
  dislike of Shakespeare 58
  role in preserving family library 54–5
du Pont, Sophie Madeleine Dalmas 53
du Pont, Victor 52, 53
du Pont, Victorine Elizabeth *see* Bauduy, Victorine (Mme Ferdinand)

Edgeworth, Maria 38, 57, 60–1, 71, 129 n. 98, 143, 174 n. 15, 203 n. 3
Edinburgh Museum 128 n. 85
Egerton, Thomas 14–15, 68
Elegant Extracts 118
Eliot, George 63
Eleutherian Mills 52, 53, 55, 56, 78 n. 7; *see also* Hagley Museum and Library
Elliott, Mary 171 n. 1
Elwood, Marie 130 n. 102
Emerson, Ralph Waldo 7 n. 3, 139, 165, 181 n. 90
Emsley, Sarah 107, 128–9 n. 92
Encyclopædia Americana 70–1

fan culture 2, 3, 5, 202
Favret, Mary A. 2
Fergus, Jan 39 n. 4, 121 n. 10, 121 n. 15, 122 n. 24
Ferrier, Susan 81 n. 128
First Folio 14, 38 n. 2, 49, 189
Folger, Emily 188–9, 204–5 n. 15
Folger, Henry 188–9, 204–5 n. 15
Foster, John Welsh 65–6, 82 n. 52
Foster, Victorine E. 53
Franklin, Benjamin 18

Galbraith, David A. 119–20 n. 4
Garrick, David 96

Gaskell, Elizabeth 63
Gay, Penny 125 n. 55
George IV, king of England 15, 90
Gilley, W. B. 30, 33–5, 44 n. 66
Gilson, David
  and American editions of Austen
    1–2, 21, 27, 38 n. 1, 75,
    88, 120–1 n. 8, 171 n. 2,
    188, 192–4
  bequest of Austen collection
    to King's College 186
  collecting interests 186, 195
  correspondence with Alberta H.
    Burke 185–202
  education 186
  friendship with J. David Grey
    193
  literary tourism 198–9
  ownership of a copy of the 1816
    Philadelphia *Emma* 186
  profession as librarian 186
  purchase of Carey & Lea 1838
    collected edition of Austen
    194
  and translations of Austen
    187–8, 190–2
  work on *A Bibliography of Jane
    Austen* 186, 187, 190–1,
    193, 202
Glenarvon 61, 63
Gordon, Sir John Watson 88, 89,
  120 n. 7
Goucher College 1, 5, 42 n. 41,
  88, 118, 185–6, 203 n. 3
Granby 37–8, 48 n. 99
Grant, Stephen H. 204 n. 15
Green, James n. 22, 29, 42 n. 39,
  44 n. 60
Grey, J. David "Jack" 193

Hagley Museum and Library
  52, 79 n. 10, 80 n. 26,
  81 n. 31

Halifax, Nova Scotia 110, 116,
  117
Halifax Garrison Library 99, 116,
  126 n. 57, 128 n. 81
Hallam, Arthur Henry 179 n. 67,
  183 n. 116
Hallam, Henry 157, 163,
  179 n. 67
Halsey, Katie 2, 179 n. 67,
  181 n. 90
Harman, Claire 2, 204 n. 5,
  204 n. 12, 206 n. 43
Hart, Julia Catherine Beckwith 91,
  121 n. 17
Hassall, W. O. 194
Hinsley, Jacqueline Ann 56, 57,
  80 n. 26, 81 n. 34
Hirshheimer, Albert 185
Hirshheimer, Alberta *see* Burke,
  Alberta H.
Hogan, Charles Beecher 84 n. 59,
  193
Hogan, Frank J. 118, 192
Hooker, Sir William Jackson 90
Hopkinson, David 176 n. 38
Horrocks, Hilary 122 n. 23
Horwood, Catherine 120 n. 5
Houstoun, Isabella 117
Howe, Joseph 103
Howe, M. A. deWolfe 172 n. 7
Hubback, Catherine 166–7,
  178 n. 61
Hubback, Edith C. 179 n. 71
Hubback, J. H. (John-Henry)
  179 n. 71
Hutton, Catherine 144, 175 n. 26

Jacson, Frances Margaretta 108–9
Jackson, H. J. 131 n. 115
James Eastburn & Co. 33–4,
  46 n. 81, 133 n. 133
James Hammond's Circulating
  Library

book collection, range of 73,
  84 n. 65
copy of 1816 Philadelphia
  Emma
  acquisition by New York
    Society Library 73
  annotations in 73–4
    comments on dislike of novel
      75
    comments on Emma
      Woodhouse 75
    comments on Mrs. Elton 75
    descriptions of novel's
      characters 75–6
    compared to Austen's
      "Opinions of *Emma*"
      76–7, 84 n. 65–8
    doodles 85 n. 67
    two apparent creators of
      74
  binding of 73
  cataloguing of by Hammond
    Library 84 n. 65
  damage evident in 73
  description of by Gilson 73
  exhibited by New York Society
    Library 73–4
Jane Austen Society (UK)
  176 n. 45
Jane Austen Society of North
  America 1, 193, 195–8
Jane Austen's House Museum
  194–5, 199
"Janeites" 150, 197
John Murray Archives, National
  Library of Scotland
  122 n. 19
Johnson, Claudia L. 2, 176 n. 45,
  207 n. 79
Justice, Joseph 23–5, 42 n. 42,
  43 n. 44
Justice & Cox 23–7, 31, 42 n. 42,
  42 n. 43

Kemble, John Philip 99
Keynes, Geoffrey 13, 190
Kindred, Sheila 107, 128–9 n. 92
Kipling, Rudyard 150, 197
Kirk, Thomas 30–1, 45 n. 72
Knapp, Samuel 71, 84 n. 59
Knight, Ann Cuthbert 108

LaCroix, Alison L. 72
Lamb, Lady Caroline 61
Lane, Maggie 181 n. 89
Lascelles, Mary 199
Le Faye, Deirdre 153, 173 n. 8,
  204 n. 12
Lea, Isaac 19
Leigh, Augusta 194
Lewes, George Henry 162,
  175 n. 30
Library Company of Philadelphia
  18, 42 n. 39
literary tourism 127 n. 76, 152–4,
  165, 178 n. 54, 198–9;
  see also Abbotsford; Jane
  Austen's House Museum
Lloyd, Martha 148
Lochhead, Douglas G. 121 n. 17
Lodge, Charles 117, 133 n. 132
Longfellow, Henry Wadsworth
  7 n. 3, 139, 165
Longman & Co. 33, 42 n. 38
Low, Betty-Bright 56

Macaulay, Thomas Babington
  162, 174 n. 15, 175 n. 30,
  179 n. 67
McMahon, Madeline 74, 85 n. 67
marginalia 73–6, 85 n. 67
Marshall, John 1, 141, 144, 145,
  175 n. 31
More, Hannah 57
Morgan, J. P. 170, 188
Morgan Library and Museum
  186, 189, 200

Morison, John H. 71, 82 n. 47
Morpeth, Lord 152, 162
Murray, John
  editions of Austen 14–16, 17,
    23, 25–8, 35, 68, 90 n. 47,
    104, 105, 127 n. 76,
    194
  Quarterly Review 21, 104

Nation, The 168–9
Neagle, John 18
Neilson, John 117, 133 n. 132
New York Society Library 73–4
Newhailes 101, 122 n. 23
North, Ernest Dressel 183 n. 115,
    183 n. 116
Nova Scotia Museum 110–11

Opie, Amelia Alderson 20

Palmer, Beverly Wilson 172 n. 7,
    173 n. 10
paper, cost of 24
Parker, George 121 n. 17
Parsons, Farnell 175 n. 31
Peale, Rembrandt 53–4
Philadelphia, Pennsylvania 17, 55,
    56, 59, 62
Pilgrim, Constance 196–7
piracy *see* reprinting
Prince Regent *see* George IV

Quincy, Anna *see* Waterston, Anna
    Cabot Lowell (Mrs. R. C.)
Quincy, Edmund (VII) 158
Quincy, Eliza Susan
  and Austen reception history
    139
  collecting of literary letters by
    143–4, 145, 149
  correspondence with Francis W.
    Austen 144–6, 149–53,
    160, 165–6

correspondence with James
    Edward Austen-Leigh
    167–8
correspondence with living
    authors 143
published writings 141
reference to Austen's characters
    149
vision of transnational
    connections among
    devotees 151, 153
Quincy, Eliza Susan Morton
    141
Quincy, Josiah, Jr. 151, 152
Quincy, Josiah III 140, 141,
    174 n. 15

Radcliffe, Ann 58, 116,
    174 n. 15
Ramsay, Edward Bannerman 104,
    130 n. 109
reception studies 3, 8–9 n. 10
Reid, Deborah Anne 120 n. 5,
    131 n. 112
reprinting 16–18, 20–22, 25,
    26–7, 30, 35–7,
    47–8 n. 95, 171 n. 3
Rhoda 53, 55–6, 61, 79 n. 10,
    108–9, 133 n. 133
Richardson, Lady 154
Richardson, Samuel 57, 100
Rink, Ewald 52, 55, 78 n. 8
Rosenbach, A. S. W. 188
Roth, Barry 199–201
Rowson, Susanna 21
Roxburghe Club 70

Sassoon, Siegfried 118,
    134 n. 135, 192
Schultheis, Emily 171 n. 1
Scott, Sir Walter
  acquaintance with Dalhousies
    90, 104, 121 n. 12

novels
American reprinting of 26,
59–60
The Fortunes of Nigel 117
Ivanhoe 100, 118
Kenilworth 20, 59–60, 100
Old Mortality 115
Peveril of the Peak 116, 195
Rob Roy 59, 71, 100
St Ronan's Well 117
Waverley 20, 101, 115
reception of 38, 50, 59–60, 62,
63, 114, 115
poetry 95, 100
review of *Emma* 4, 21–2, 68, 71,
90, 107
views on Austen 138
Seville, Catherine 45 n. 72
Shakespeare, William
and Americans 2, 8 n. 7, 58
Beauties of Shakespeare 58
collecting of works by 14, 50,
188–9, 204 n. 15
compared to Austen 125 n. 54,
144, 168, 175 n. 30
discussed and quoted by Lord
and Lady Dalhousie 98–9,
125 n. 52
Sherbrooke, Lady 107, 116
Siddons, Sarah 99, 125 n. 55
Smith, Emma 77 n. 2
Smith, Jeremiah 4, 27
as first identifiable Austen
enthusiast in US 50, 73
biography of 63
book collection 63
ownership of Burney's
Geraldine Fauconberg 71,
83 n. 53
ownership of Edgeworth's
Castle Rackrent 71
ownership of Scott's *Rob Roy*
71

chief justice of New Hampshire
63, 82 n. 47
copies of Austen novels owned
by
Mansfield Park 68
Pride and Prejudice 68
Sense and Sensibility 68–9
copy of 1816 Philadelphia
Emma owned by
acquisition by Dartmouth
College 63, 82 n. 48
annotations in 37, 67–70
binding of 64–5, 82 n. 50
card tucked into 82–3 n. 51
corrections to text of 27, 65–7
damage evident in 65
purchase of 65–6
repairs to 64–5
signatures in 65–7
education 63
founder of social library in New
Hampshire 71
personality 72–3
portrait 64
private writings to first wife
72
reading practices 71–2
similarities to Austen's characters
72
Smith, Karen 126 n. 57
Southam, B. C. (Brian) 1, 7 n. 3,
31, 71, 173 n. 7, 204 n. 12
Southey, Robert 162–3
Spencer, Sir Robert Cavendish
107
Story, Joseph
comments on Austen at 1826 Phi
Beta Kappa meeting 2, 141
comments on Austen to Josiah
Quincy 174 n. 15
comments on Burney 174 n. 15
comments on Edgeworth
174 n. 15

comments on Radcliffe
    174 n. 15
recommendation of Austen to
    the Quincys 141
responses to *Emma* 141–2,
    174 n. 16
Story, William Wetmore 141–2,
    174 n. 15, 174 n. 16
Sutherland, Kathryn 9 n. 13,
    43 n. 45, 139, 167,
    172 n. 7, 173 n. 9,
    177 n. 50

Temple, Rev. Mr. J. 117
Trenton, New Jersey 24–6
Tucker, Andie 47–8 n. 95
Twain, Mark 2, 50, 165
Tytler, Sarah 122 n. 19

Villeneuve, René 103, 119 n. 2
Viveash, Chris 186

Wakefield, Priscilla 117,
    132 n. 129
Wakeling & Allen 26, 28, 30,
    44 n. 62, 55, 78 n. 3
War of 1812 19
Waterston, Anna Cabot Lowell
    (Mrs. R. C.), née Anna
    Cabot Lowell Quincy
  Atlantic Monthly article on
    Austen
    appreciation of by James
      Edward Austen-Leigh
      166
    comments on non-appreciators
      of Austen 165
    comments on timelessness of
      Austen's writings 163
    description of Francis Austen
      156–7, 159, 165
    description of own "literary
      pilgrimage" 162, 165

identification of *Persuasion* as
    favorite novel 164
inclusion of anecdotes from
    Francis Austen family 162,
    181 n. 86
inclusion of critical quotations
    162, 175 n. 30
praise for *Persuasion* 164
praise for *Pride and Prejudice*
    164–5
reprinting of 172 n. 7
treatment of Austen's sources
    of inspiration 163
and Austen reception history 139
comments on receipt of Jane
    Austen letter 149–50
and literary tourism 152–5, 165,
    198
on Quincy family reading of
    Austen in 1830s
  Northanger Abbey 140
  Persuasion 140
  Sense and Sensibility 140
rediscovered travel journal 139,
    143, 146, 155–9
references to Austen's characters
    150, 155
religious expressions 150, 154,
    161, 162
similarities to Austen's characters
    143
vision of "coterie" of admirers of
    Austen 150–1, 165
visit with a "real Mr. Knightley"
    142–3
visit with Francis W. Austen in
    1856 154–61
youthful diaries as inspired by
    Austen 173 n. 10
Waterston, Helen 153, 162
Waterston, Robert 153
Watson, Nicola J. 178 n. 54
Weinsheimer, Joel 199–201

Wells & Lilly 30, 34–6, 43 n. 46,
    44 n. 60, 79 n. 10
Wellington, Arthur Wellesley,
    Duke of 98, 180, n. 74
Whately, Richard 68, 71, 162,
    175 n. 30
Whitelaw, Marjory 119 n. 2
Wilde, Oscar 2
Wilson, Cheryl A. 175 n. 26

Winchester Cathedral 153,
    198
Winterthur Library 50–1, 78 n. 4,
    78 n. 6
Winterthur Museum 62
Wodehouse, Mary 107, 129 n. 92
Wollstonecraft, Mary 93
Wormeley, Admiral Ralph 145–6,
    175 n. 31

CPSIA information can be obtained
at www.ICGtesting.com
Printed in the USA
LVOW13*1947271017

554038LV00010B/128/P